DATING DOWN...

And Those of US Who Do It

CAROLE H. FIELD, M.A., M.F.T

S0-BCO-465

~ This book is dedicated to my parents ~

ACKNOWLEDGEMENTS

1. Karin Gable – my graphic artist and photographer.

2. David Beckmann – my informative, supportive, and accommodating publishing consultant.

3. Of course, Bonnie, P.J. and Abe.

4. Todd Rohrbacher

5. My friends and family who thought this was a great idea from the gate. Go figure.

6. My guardian angels, with whom I regularly dine.

TABLE OF CONTENTS

HOW TO READ THIS BOOK

For starters, simply read and enjoy the short stories in this book (chapters 1 though 8) as you would any short story or novelette. After that, go back and study the corresponding Red Flags, which are elaborated upon at the end of each chapter.

It also would be a good idea to start a notebook and take notes from the Red Flags section. This book is a different kind of learning manual. You will not see a chapter titled "Ten Surefire Ways to Stop Dating Down for the Rest of Your Entire Life." No. The learning from this book will occur differently. It will be more personal, subjective, and deeper than learning from a written outpouring of superficial how-tos.

If you have purchased the corresponding workbook, utilize it after you have read this entire book. It also might be a terrific notion, for further learning, to create a dating down support group with your friends, co-workers, dorm mates, church group, etc.

After all this, it is my hope that you will have the beginnings of a new consciousness; the beginnings of a new method of processing relationships.

Let us all join together to grow, to help ourselves and each other. And now for our journey.

DISCLAIMER

This is not a book about men who have found themselves in unfortunate circumstances. This is a book about men who insist upon staying in unfortunate circumstances, and because of this, bring everyone around them down.

Regrettably, women date men with these "down" orientations. This is a book about that phenomenon; about those of us who date men that bring us down.

I conducted more than fifty in-depth interviews of women from my patient population. The interviews chosen for these stories were the ones most clearly depicting the specific dysfunction.

The names of the interviewees have been altered for confidentiality.

INTRODUCTION

Welcome to the Turbulent World of Dating Down

It was your third date with Richard. The Italian restaurant, with its strolling violinists, checkered tablecloths, and soft candlelight romantically enveloped the two of you.

So...you revealed a little more about yourself, lowered yet one more tiny defense, and gazed into his big brown eyes for their response.

To your surprise, you immediately realized Richard wasn't "getting" it. He wasn't getting the point of your touching and emotion-packed story. He wasn't getting your vulnerable and brave attempt at being open. He was getting nothing about you.

You slowly retreated and took refuge in one of the flickering candles. Once more, the conversation abruptly reverted back to him.

You don't know why you went out with him a fourth time, or a fifth. Mostly, you don't quite understand why you are still seeing him—three years later.

But then again, Mom said your dad was the exact same way. And what about your best

1

friend and her fast-talking fiancé, who can't quite kick his cocaine habit? And what about your cousin with the guy who is still promising to leave his wife?

So maybe Richard's not that bad. Granted, he doesn't remember your middle name or what city you're from, but you sure learned a great deal about football in the last three years.

I am a licensed psychotherapist in private practice in Los Angeles. Throughout my years of practice, I have been constantly amazed at the number of women with "Richards" showing up on my couch.

I have sadly accepted the fact that this is not exclusive to my psychotherapy patients. I find friends, relatives, and acquaintances commonly finding themselves in love relationships whereby one person is holding the integrity while the other is only watching.

I have found myself to be progressively angered by this widespread emotional felony. I have observed that this interaction is never easily tolerated, or correctly minimized as "little personality differences."

On the contrary, I have observed it to be painful, wicked, and deeply injurious. Consequently, I have decided to speak out, for this emotional felony must be exposed.

Thanks to my professional background, I have gathered an understanding of its roots, germination process, and strangulating overgrowth. It is time to bring forth and define this up-to-now well-cloaked dynamic that I call "dating down." Too many of my beautiful and well-meaning patients, friends, and loved ones have been on the receiving end of this emotional felony.

With a clearer understanding of "dating down," it is my hope that you, I, and even "Richard" might be able to activate this long-needed change.

Let us start with a definition.

Some of you may feel you are immune to this situation and that your friends and relatives stand far and above participating in such behaviors. I can only hope this is the truth for you. However, over the years in my practice, I have acquired the knowledge that far too many people coexist with "invisible pain." I call it "invisible pain" because it is a vaguely sub-radar feeling that something is annoying, discomforting, or anxiety provoking. But it is "invisible" because it is not really conscious—not by the medical or psychological communities, not by society, and not by the victim.

If one studies the history and, consequently, the cure of physical or psychological illnesses,

3

it always begins with an exploration of not-yet-understood "invisible pain."

So, please, I beg you to stay open as you read further, for only with an open mind can new perspectives emerge. Only with an open and receptive attitude can we make the unknown, known.

And remember, admission of any type of pain never implies weakness, inadequacy, or brokenness. Rather, admission of any type of pain is the acknowledgement of discomfort and the elevated seeking-out of a richer, more rewarding experience on our glorious planet.

The remainder of this chapter is subdivided into three parts:

1. Thoughts and history about dating.
2. Specific categories of the downdatee.
3. The five constants required for a relationship to be a downdating relationship.

Thoughts and History About Dating

Dating appears in various forms in the twenty-first century. The stereotypical male-asks-female for a date on Saturday night is no longer the sole definition of, or requisite for, a date. Nor, paradoxically, is the couple who does this necessarily dating. Close platonic male-female friends

4

could have a "standing appointment" every Saturday night. They might even hold hands when walking into the restaurant or snuggle at the sentimental foreign film. This still does not necessarily constitute "dating."

For "dating," as self-explanatory as the term seems, is still a state of mind. And this state of mind is both determined by the individual independently, and the couple interdependently.

An objective observer may consider the couple to be dating, but only the couple themselves can verify the truth or falseness of this title.

This verification of the state of mind of dating usually has to do with friendship, obligation, attraction, sexual exclusivity, and some expectations around consideration and positioning.

But then again, dating does come in all shapes and sizes in the twenty-first century. Only you know if you are dating or are platonic with your partner/intimate other/pal, etc. Only you know the emotional difference between the two. For dating encompasses an elusive feeling that has yet to be deciphered by any text.

Overall, it should be understood that dating is a state of mind determined by the individuals of the couple. However, the concept of dating can only be applied to a couple within this heartfelt love connection. One truly cannot platonic down! That would take on another set of dimensions beyond the scope or desire of this book.

In Webster's dictionary, "down" is defined as "in or to a low or lower condition, amount," etc.

For a moment, I would like to bring to light some interesting facts from the animal kingdom and animals' behaviors around rank, or up/downness.

Most animals have an inborn concept of rank within their own species. If they move in or out of their rank, it is usually temporary, with the purpose of benefitting their entire pack, flock, colony, and so on.

An example of this lies in the bee colony. The worker bees, which are considered lower in the hierarchy than the queen, lick and feed off the queen's emanating pheromones. They in turn pass this on to their entire colony, enhancing smoother communications and less agitated bee activity. There is nothing "down" about this. Rather, it proves to be efficient.

Others in the animal kingdom have established their form of up and down.

We have all heard of pecking order. Hens truly have a pecking order. Their particular order is determined by aggression.

Similarly, swordfish have "nip order" where the most tyrannical swordfish gets the best food. (Interestingly, in this tyrannical hierarchy, the tyrant swordfish is usually overthrown. Its aggression will be tolerated only for a short period of time.)

Chimpanzees also have their internal ranking. The highest-ranking chimp is the male exhibiting the most strength and making the loudest noises. Nonetheless, what remains most significant in the chimp community is friendly relationships and physical contact. Although they might fight to establish rank, this behavior is short-lived.

Gorillas have up-and-down order, too. Refreshingly, gorillas have hierarchical importance through age. Older male gorillas, known as "silverbacks" because of their silver-gray hair, are the most respected in their particular hierarchy.

In our human societies of the present day, probably the most concerned with up/down stratification is the Hindu society. Here, no upward or downward mobility exists. One rarely sees co-mingling between priests, traders, nobles, and servants.

In view of the above, the only point I wish to make is that various animal and human societies recognize stratification of different sorts. It almost seems to be an organic necessity for efficiency and perpetuation of the species.

However, the down I refer to largely has to do with one word: IRRESPONSIBILITY (the behavior of not acting reliably and dependably)

It has a slightly different spin than the accepted caste system of India or the rancorous chimps on

7

the plains. With that in mind, it is applied to the following concepts.

Down/Irresponsibility in terms of:

- Communication skills
- Social standing
- Intellect; education
- Generosity
- Financial position
- Ambition
- Cultural sophistication
- Achievement
- Sensitivity
- Emotional maturity
- Psychological health

We can think of people who are born high and low in these areas. High, or up, usually because of following through on commitments, or living responsibly. Low, or down, because of not following through on commitments, or living irresponsibly.

For operational purposes of this book, we will be exploring the female-to-male paradigm. In other words, we will be observing the female dating down to the male.

Over the years it has been acceptable for the male to date or even "marry down." It did not matter, because in this type of relationship the female would unquestionably be up-ranked.

One of the most popular examples of this was when the Hollywood actress, Grace Kelly, instantly became Princess Grace when she married Prince Rainier of Monaco.

Another famous example of this was how little Bessie Warfield became the internationally revered Wallis Simpson when she married King Edward VIII of England.

Also, how Arianna Huffington and Georgette Mosbacher rose out of obscurity when they married, respectively, Michael Huffington (a G.O.P. congressman) and George Barrie (president of Faberge).

Along those lines, Donald Trump's wives all received immediate stellar status when they married him and marginal whisper status when they divorced.

A subtler example of "marrying down" was the secretly depressed, dysfunctional housewife of the 1950s, who opened canned fruit cocktail with a smile and secretly popped Librium with a vengeance. These women's progressive diversions into depression really created a down-marriage setting, but again, the "invisible pain" was never addressed.

Nobody pointed a finger at this couple. It was the norm. Nobody tried to help the solitary woman and nobody remarked about the man's poor choice—if that indeed was the case. Nobody remarked about anything because dating and marrying down didn't matter. For men, "stooping to conquer" was a given.

An example I am reminded of in my own life was the mother of my best friend, Isabella. Although we were only ten years old, I thought her mom was different from other girls' moms. She assuredly exemplified the stereotype I am describing.

Isabella's mother, depressed and unacknowledged, was in her bedroom with the door shut 90 percent of the time. When she might emerge, it was only to be critical or rude to Isabella or her father, take an "aspirin," and return to her chamber.

For Isabella's eleventh birthday, she distributed invitations to fifteen or twenty school friends. It was supposed to have been a Saturday afternoon luncheon. Her dad bought Isabella a new blue denim pantsuit with a red denim blouse and she polished her black *flatties*.

But when the kids arrived at her house, I remember that all her mother had for us to eat were pink iced animal cookies and lemonade. There was no lunch-appropriate food for fifteen hungry kids. The saddest thing was, Isabella did not even have a birthday cake.

I remember her dad ordering pizza at the last minute and apologizing for no cake. Isabella's mother stayed in her bedroom the entire time. Nobody said anything back then. Not her father, not the kids, and not Isabella. I remember watching her face throughout the party. She was having a wonderful time. She believed all was completely normal.

Had Isabella's father initially married down, or had her mother become clinically depressed after they married? I don't know the particulars. All I know is that dating and marrying down has slipped into our culture so unobtrusively that finding the forest for the trees looks like a futile endeavor.

This book exposes the reversed tables. No, not dating up. The reversed tables here are the females dating down to their male significant others. It is an odd reversal because it is both a backlash and a self-punishment. This type of reversal has never occurred in any culture or in any time period as it does today.

This backlash is causing heads to spin because there are no rules or set of behaviors on which to base anything. And this reversal's punishing component is strictly serving to break hearts and whirl one into boundary-less chaos.

Furthermore, this is a rather quizzical reversal, because unlike most long-needed reversals, nobody is winning.

And now, to define the downdating male.

You have begun to understand some of dating down. However, you may be asking: what, exactly, defines the male in this situation? What is a downdatee? How is he specifically defined while further understanding dating down?

What is a Downdatee?

A downdatee is a male dating or co-habiting with a female in an understood love relationship who possesses one or more of the following characteristics:

Repeatedly commits personal or social fraudulence. This is illustrated in chapter 1, "Could It Be Iceskate Introductions?"

Is a convicted or non-convicted career criminal or recidivist. This is illustrated in chapter 2, "The Three Marias."

Has a highly addictive personality, yet denounces any twelve-step or therapeutic support. This is illustrated in chapter 3, "To Call Upon My God."

Has no conscience about bringing the female's body and/or mind directly into an illegal and dangerous lifestyle. This is illustrated in chapter 4, "Drugs and Hugs."

Is from and stays connected to a substantially lower class than the female. This is illustrated in chapter 5, "Shoot the Cupid, or..."

Is physically or mentally abusive to the female. This is illustrated in chapter 6, "Some Dancing, Some Romancing."

Is chronically unemployed, has no aspirations of exceeding minimum wage, and/or is financially supported by the female. This is illustrated in chapter 7, "The Girl with a Silver Spoon in Her Wallet."

Has potentially dangerous psychosis or psychopathology. This is illustrated in chapter 8, "Beware the Shirtless Man in January."

Again, it must be emphasized that the criteria for dating down must be immediately dispelled if the male has unfortunately been thrust into crisis beyond his control. Also, if he is willing to seek necessary assistance within and beyond the relationship, and shows improvement over a reasonable period of time, he would not be considered a downdatee.

Consequently, for a relationship to be a "down" relationship, it must bear five constants. By keeping these in mind, dating down is more readily recognizable.

The Five Constants Required for a Relationship To Be a Downdating Relationship

Constant #1

The Female Frequently Takes on Full Responsibility for the Male's Unhealthy, Unproductive, or Harmful Behavior

"I will do the lion's share. He will come around soon. In the meantime, I'll take care of everything," is usually what I hear in the office from the over-functioning female. And most downdating women are over-functioners, at least in their love relationships.

The untrained or imperceptive observer may deem this woman responsible and energetic. In truth, her actions are two-pronged:

- She is working overtime to keep her denial system alive.
- She is obsessed with changing this man and how he behaves in the world.

As an aside, I must say "contribution" is the mainstay of any relationship. With contribution, the connectedness and good results of any relationship are far-reaching. But what I am referring to is an out-of-balance state. I am referring to

14

people who know in their hearts they've contributed 150 percent, but experience only a minimal return. This is not correct or spiritually laudable.

I am reminded of the age-old geisha in Japanese society. Starting in childhood, they are trained in music and dance mime, and are seriously versed in all social graces. As practicing adult geishas, they are respected and paid for their artistic social contributions.

The old myth that she is a long-suffering slave to the male gender is totally fallacious. Even the output of the hard-at-work geisha is far from the overfunctioning energy zap of the dating down female.

It goes without saying, there are times when one must bypass personal needs and take on full responsibility for another. This is true in crises and emergencies, and in some cases for the elderly, the infirmed, children, etc. This goes beyond what is purported in the twelve-step program that service is its own reward. Here, we are talking about full-out responsibility. This can and does occur at various times throughout everyone's life.

This is not at all the case with dating down, for there is no real crisis, no immediacy, and usually nobody is one wave shy of drowning.

The women who date down, however, experience their relationship as an emergency. The false perception and perpetual inner panic are exactly what keep her hooked into her own tidal wave (Who is really experiencing most of the drowning in the couple ?).

And so, we must ask ourselves here, are we contributing the necessary output a relationship requires? Or are we scurrying around in a solo mode of responsibility with little emotional compensation?

Constant #2

The Male in This Relationship Exhibits a Stubborn Resistance to Change His Maladaptive Behaviors

This is probably the main artery of dating down: the male is resistant to changing his maladaptive behavior.

Inclusive in this steadfast resistance lies irresponsible behavior. This resistance is co-partnered with avoiding responsibility in most areas of his life, not to mention old-fashioned selfishness.

But the female will not admit these truths when she is in the throes of dating down. She is too busy obsessing over repositioning his thinking to realize that she will never get anything from him.

I must underscore that we are not referring to the male who has been dealt an unlucky broadsiding in terms of illness, family circumstances, financial reversals, etc., but rather the male who has been dealt no "unlucky" blow, yet continues his self-defeating stagnation with other defeating abuses.

This stubborn male almost always possesses self-preoccupation, emotional inaccessibility, and/or overly consistent manipulation of the significant other.

In reading the forthcoming short stories, much of this will be illuminated.

Constant #3

The Female Endures Unmet Needs for Months or Even Years

In psychology and in lab biology, there is a concept called intermittent (or spaced) gratification. This means an animal is satisfied once in a while; intermittently. The laboratory animal eagerly keeps returning to its food dish because there is food "once in a while." If its dish were filled all the time, it wouldn't keep checking so often.

The same applies to humans. We energetically return to the source of the gratification when it is not always available.

In some instances of intermittent gratification, the prize is progressively less available. If this type of spacing becomes radically lengthy, some lab animals (and humans, of course) avoid seeking the gratification altogether. This learned behavior is called extinction. With extinction, the old source of gratification is avoided as if it never existed.

Not so with the dating down female. She seems to fly in the face of all behavioral psychology. Her built-in extinguisher is perpetually asleep.

And if a rare gratifying moment should slip through, she has developed a vigilance that now is always "in wait" for the other shoe to drop. She never truly exhales. Physical ailments begin to emerge or worsen at this point. Body pain, migraines, PMS, extreme exhaustion—all are potentially related to her increasing frustration.

For the most part, the female who has never dated down has a built-in device that blocks such energy expenditure. This woman feels thrown off her center when her needs are persistently unmet.

The dating down woman does not have such an internal thermostat. She must construct one somewhere, commonly in a therapeutic setting. I encourage my patients to voice their needs to their significant other. For starters, this eliminates mind reading. The unfortunate thing here is the woman in a dating down relationship rarely gets her needs met, whether they are voiced, texted, or broadcast over a loudspeaker.

To repeat constant #3—the female endures unmet needs for months or even years—we must see that the relationship is self-effacing to the female and poisonous to her soul. Again, is any-one really winning amid this denial, frustration, and "invisible pain"?

Constant #4

The Discrepancy or Mismatch Within the Couple Is Markedly Apparent to the Objective and Knowledgeable Observer

It is necessary that there is some degree of ob-jectivity here. As in any scientific classification, the researchers cannot predict the outcome of an event without previous knowledge or experimen-tation within the field. Likewise, with this portion of the definition, there should be some objectivity, some criteria, in classifying dating down.

Unfortunately, when tests tubes and petri dishes are not the method of experimentation, objectivity can hit too closely to judgement.

Yet, there has to be a degree of objectivity to avoid the rash categorization that every couple is a dating down couple. One may feel off balance in a relationship, but the reason for it may not have to do with dating down in the least. This is why there is a need for some objectivity—some. Truly, each person in the dyad/couple is the final gauge of whether she or he is dating down.

This constant is merely included as a watchdog for over-diagnosis.

Constant #5

And the Beat Goes On...As the Downdater Endures Frustration, Accepts Blame, and Blindly Tolerates His Resistance to Necessary Change

The most significant aspect of this constant is that a repetitive pattern has developed. It is not a one-time, short-term occurrence where the female must temporarily bypass her needs in order to render service.

This can and does occur. An example of this is the female supporting the male through medical school. In this case, she is usually in charge of all domestic and financial responsibilities. She is not dating down in this scenario. She is exercising an obligation while he does his share of the arduous bookwork.

However, if the supported medical student refused to pitch in once he became licensed, and presumed that she would continue to take care of his financial and domestic needs, we then would have a situation worth scrutinizing. And if the female decided to join in his selfishness—strictly for the purpose of keeping him close—we'd be observing the heartbeat of dating down.

Author's note:

So here we go with the following true-life stories. Perhaps you will recognize yourself, your friends, or family members—either whole or in part—as profiled by the women in this book.

If so, that is a good first step. This implies you are open to recognizing the repetitive behaviors and psychological makeup of those in our sisterhood afflicted with dating down.

Equally as important, readers, we must recognize the men who continue to perpetuate their position as downdatees. Again, for your learning process and for your enjoyment, it is suggested that you read the entire story first. Then go back and analyze it with the accompanying Red Flags.

This should prove to be both an entertaining and a most thought-provoking journey.

Self-esteem is the experience of being competent to cope with the basic challenges of life and as being worthy of happiness. Throughout history, self-esteem has not been a trait that most cultures have prized in women.

—Nathaniel Brandon

CHAPTER ONE

ILLUSTRATING DOWNDATEE #1 –

*Repeatedly Commits Personal
or Social Fraudulence*

Entitled...

COULD IT BE
ICESKATE INTRODUCTIONS?

It was December 24, 2007, ten a.m. I stood in the doorway of my office and laughed at how much I had chosen to express the holiday season this year.

The window was encircled with extra-large red and green Santa lights; atop the coffee table sprawled a manger scene, complete with "snow," smiling sheep, baby goats, and a friendly camel eyeing Mother Mary; the corner hugged an aromatic Christmas tree from which self-satisfied, fat angels dangled; a huge Jewish Star of David and a list of the Kwanzaa virtues swayed from the ceiling; and, of course, Christmas carols wafted exuberantly from the radio.

My patients absolutely delighted in the holiday ambiance the moment they stepped through the door. Anticipating the possibility of that probably was what prompted my hefty holiday expressions. It's all about spreading an inch more of cheer.

I was about to greet a new patient in the lobby. The lobby, too, was aglow with holiday décor since the other building tenants shared in my decorating frenzy this year. I was walking cheerfully down the hall when I first laid eyes on Mariska Dansko (last name similar but altered for patient confidentiality). Laying eyes on her made me stop in my jolly Christmas tracks. Visibly, she did not fit in with the gay and festive Christmas setting.

A very tall, large-boned, thirty-four-year-old Danish female sat staring at a magazine. Her thin, long brown hair practically obscured her face. Somehow, it looked as though she hadn't combed it today. The woman wore an expensive-looking pantsuit of brown wool, with a beige turtleneck, brown suede boots, and a thick, black cape. As she looked up, I observed far too much eyeliner and dark eye shadow for both such pale skin and such an early morning appointment.

Store that, I said to myself, and extended my hand.

"Mariska? How do you do? Very nice to meet you. I am Carole Field."

Through a mane of unruly hair, over a lowered chin, she eked out a smile and warmly received the handshake.

With an obviously Danish accent, she replied, "Thank you very much for being here on December twenty-fourth. It must be a busy time for you, Doctor...Miss...Doctor Field."

"I'm Carole, and it is my pleasure to be here for you," I replied, judging her to be rather empathic. "Please come into my office, dear."

She handed me the filled-out papers I had sent her in the mail. Then she rose and looked out the lobby window. I felt this was going to be difficult for this considerably sweet soul. I waited for her to move. She turned to me. All her five-feet-ten-inch, large-boned, rather overweight, over-dressed, and overly made-up self, trying to smile—rang out a silent scream that I pretended not to hear.

"Come, Mariska. Let's get to know you," I softly coaxed her, dodging the scream.

In our first session, I learned that Mariska moved to the United States in 1980, when she was six. Her parents, two-year-old twin brothers, and maternal grandmother settled in Pasadena, California. Both of her parents had been offered lucrative positions in the aerospace industry. When Mariska moved here, she spoke Danish, English, French, and German. She majored in education at UCLA and added Spanish to her list of spoken languages.

"But everyone speaks a multitude of lan-guages in Denmark," she humbly explained.

To help with UCLA tuition, she taught lan-guages to children around Los Angeles and the Valley.

Five years ago she and a friend opened a preschool in the San Fernando Valley.

"The word spread to the European community here," she said, "because I teach French to the children at our school. I love our little school and we are doing surprisingly well. My brothers come by to help out sometimes. When my parents come, the children refer to them as their 'school grandparents.' All the students' parents know each other. I love the community we've created. Actually, it is very Danish in feel. I have a very tight-knit family. No wonder the school follows suit."

REDFLAG
#1-1

She seemed animated and proud, talking about her school that now boasted forty students.

I assured her it was an impressive accomplishment to open a preschool in the competitive Los Angeles environment, and to be doing so very well.

"But I must say," she said, observing the holiday décor, "our school is not as decorated as this office. I have never seen such obese angels in my life."

"It must be all that good heaven cooking," I added. We both laughed.

Mariska reclined farther back on the couch, pushed the hair out of her face and looked at the twinkling Santas flashing around the window. I observed her gaze move from the window frame to the tree-tops in their December semi-blooms, to the streets below...the whole valley, some other place. Yes, some other place, some other time, some other "timeplace" I could not quite calculate.

I call her story "Could It Be Iceskate Introductions?" And we are observing downdatee #1: Repeatedly commits personal or social fraudulence.

Setting: November 1998, Grandmama Henrietta's living room in Los Angeles.

Mariska sat on her grandmother's floor, lacing up her new GAM 40 adult figure skates.

"Darling," said Grandmama, "it does not seem that long ago—when we were in Naestved. You were in primary school and your grandfather, rest him, bought your first pair of skates. You also sat on our living room floor with the same expression. Pure delight."

"But Grandmama, do you realize I have not bought myself a pair of skates in years and years?"

"That is what your mother told me. I think, just because you live in warm California, you should not give up what you loved back then. So, I thought it was time to buy you an early Christmas gift. How is the size? Do you like the off-white color?"

"The color is great. But the size..." Mariska immediately could tell they were too small. "Let me stand up in these. Oh...definitely too small, Grandmama."

Mariska sauntered around on the skate guards but shook her head.

Grandmama said, "So go, honey. Get a bigger size and you will be able to use them right away."

"I think I will do just that, Grandmama."

"Plus," Grandmama slyly added, "those sporting goods stores sure have their share of muscular customers, my love. Go meet a nice Danish skier or something."

REDFLAG
#1-2

"Grandmama!"

"Come, let us have a little tea and citronkage (Danish lemon cake). Then go meet your skier."

"Grandmama!" They both laughed.

The sporting goods store was bustling that Friday night in November. As she walked past the cash registers, she couldn't

32

help but notice the numerous displays of candy bars and candy bags. Thinking they were out of place at a large sporting goods chain, she picked up one of the candy bags she had never seen previously.

"Blueberry-chocolate reindeer? What?" She laughed aloud.

"They're good. Try them," a voice responded.

Mariska turned around and noticed one of the salesmen leaning against the counter.

"Really," he said. "Tasty little critters."

Mariska laughed. "Is that so? I have never seen these guys. How strange—in a sporting goods store. Anyhow, could you possibly point me in the direction of the iceskate department?"

"I will take you. You are returning something?" he asked, noticing her large box.

"Yes. They are too small."

"Let me take care of this. So, you still skate? And...you are German?"

"Thank you for helping me. It is so crowded in here. To answer your questions, I occasionally still skate. But I am Danish."

The salesman took the skates from her. "Allow me to carry them. My name is Neil." This man was an extremely thin, tall, dark-haired American.

33

She thought, *Well, he's not the muscular Danish skier Grandmama ordered. But he certainly might hasten the return process, so who cares?*

He did expedite the return process, but not without introducing himself and asking about her skating history.

"Everyone does winter sports in Scandinavia. It's no big thing. I just thought I'd like to get back into skating for fun. I taught ice-skating to little kids when I was in college. I loved doing that."

"Is that right? How much did you get paid for that?" Neil asked.

REDFLAG
#1-3

"Oh...it was always different."

"Could you teach an adult to skate?" he asked, snickering.

REDFLAG
#1-4

"An adult, like you?"

"Sure. I used to be into hockey. Do you have a card? Maybe we could get something up?"

Mariska scanned his thin frame. He did not look the least bit athletic. But he seemed eager, down to earth, and had a sweet face.

"Sure," she said. "There's a great rink a few miles from here. Why don't you give me a call? I'd suggest you find a class, too, if you're serious."

34

"I am serious. I will call you tomorrow."

They continued with the skate exchange, shook hands and parted. She really did not anticipate hearing from the congenial gentleman except for one detail: as she was exiting the store, she happened to glance back, and there stood Neil looking after her. Mariska felt flattered.

She self-consciously waved. He slowly waved back. And she happily left the crowded store with shiny new skates of the correct size.

"Neil. Neil, it's Mariska," she said into her cell phone. "I'm at the ice rink. You are forty-five minutes late. Are you coming? I will wait another..."

REDFLAG
#1-5

Then she saw him across the parking lot. He hurried over to her. She noticed he wasn't really dressed for skating and was not carrying a gym bag. She thought, *Oh, he's not really sure how to dress for a lesson.*

"Hi there, Neil. I was just calling you. We don't have much time on the rink. Did you bring your skates?"

"They're in the car. Listen, Mariska, change of sentiment here. Would you mind terribly if we got a drink, maybe a little dinner, instead of skating? Something

35

REDFLAG
#1-6

unfortunate just occurred and I think I need to be quiet. Actually, a kind ear wouldn't hurt right now."

"Are you okay, Neil?"

"Well, I will be okay," he replied, catching sight of the rink behind her. As he watched the skaters—from faltering novices to daredevils—he became still. She wasn't sure if he simply could not relate to the scene or if he was lost in thought over the unfortunate event that had just occurred.

"Come on, Neil. Let's go somewhere," Mariska sympathetically said, although she really would have preferred to give her lesson, get paid, and leave. She realized the evening was not going to go that way and acquiesced to extending an available ear to this mild-mannered, troubled gentleman.

REDFLAG
#1-7

"Thank you for being flexible, Mariska. You are very sweet. Let's go."

Neil reclined in the restaurant booth. He seemed more relaxed than at the rink. When the waitress asked if they wanted a cocktail, he waved her off. Mariska was glad to see him less anxious. He turned to her.

"My name is Neil Bonner. I am thirty-nine years old, am the manager of the sporting goods store, and just finalized a painful divorce."

36

"Is that right?" attentive Mariska responded.

"Yes...and...I was just talking to her. That's why our lesson didn't happen," Neil apologetically said, glancing away.

Mariska extended her hand. "How do you do, Neil Bonner? I am your new friend."

He looked in her eyes and held Mariska's hand with both of his. "So, my Danish ice-skater, tell me all about yourself."

She laughed. "I am a preschool teacher, single, very close to my family, and...um... overweight." They both laughed.

"Not as much as I am underweight, and it is harder for me. No joke."

They spoke about nutrition, life, preschool, his divorce. Nothing was said of the money he owed her for the lesson. She thought it inappropriate to ask, especially since he paid for dinner.

Neil walked her to her car.

"New Acura, Mariska?"

"It's six months old."

She noticed him becoming sullen, withdrawn, again. That same stillness he had in his eyes while watching the skaters.

REDFLAG
#1-8

Then he said, "Mariska, may I be so bold as to request seeing you again? I mean... actually...I mean, as an established date? You know—like, boy asks girl on the telephone. That old glorious radish. Is that possible?"

37

His brown hair and eyes looked the exact same color in the moonlight.

How did he master that? she laughed to herself. Neil stood there, vulnerable, awaiting a response to a date request. She liked this man. There seemed to exist a kind of strength within his vulnerability—maybe. She thought, *Even though he is no Danish skier, he is an ex-hockey player, I think. There might be many levels here. I would like to explore them.*

REDFLAG
#1-9

He thought for a moment and said, "In fact, next Saturday night I have a University of Michigan alumni dinner. It's at the beautiful Castaways Restaurant in the hills. Would you like to go with me?"

"Oh," she began, "yes, sure." She gave him her address and he warmly hugged her good night.

"Grandmama," she said into the phone the next morning, "I did meet someone at the sporting goods store. And it was because of your iceskates…oh, and some little blueberry-chocolate reindeer."

REDFLAG
#1-10

Mariska didn't like the way she looked in the white silk blouse with the black suede skirt. She changed three times and finally

38

settled on the dressy, black-beaded vintage sweater with the suede skirt.

She unwrapped her new Clinique blush and excitedly dabbed away beneath her cheekbones.

"Why not go out with a nice man?" she said to herself in the makeup mirror. "It's not like anyone else is on the horizon."

REDFLAG
#1-11

Neil picked her up on time, but as they were walking out of the apartment, he stopped in his tracks and said, "Mariska, could we take your car?"

REDFLAG
#1-12

She complied, not asking why, and they proceeded to the alumni dinner.

In the restaurant lobby, Mariska realized they were standing in the "T through Z" line. She remarked, "Neil, your last name begins with a B. We are standing in the 'T through Z' line."

"No, no. It's fine," he responded.

"What?"

"No problem. I have one of my friend's invitations. He was supposed to join us. He won't be here. Long story."

"Mariska," he said, as the first course was being served, "if there is anything I can do tonight, please let me know. I am so happy to be with you. It's just that I might encounter

39

a bunch of old classmates. I'm not sure. I just don't want you to feel left out. So, keep making eye contact with me and let me know if you are feeling in any way ignored. Okay?" He picked up her hand and put it to his heart. She felt wonderfully acknowledged.

The evening proved to be charming and comfortable. Great dinner, superb band, brief awards ceremony, and a most attentive date.

REDFLAG #1-13

As he walked her back to her apartment, she remarked, "Wasn't it odd, Neil? You didn't run into any alum from your graduating class."

"Yes. Yes, I guess so. But that happened last year, too. Funny—two years in a row." Then he took her face in his hands and said, "If there is some way we could spend Thanksgiving together, I would love that. Let me know." And he promptly left.

No kiss, she thought. *How refreshing to encounter an old-world gentleman. Feels rather good.*

She phoned her grandmother the next day. "Grandmama, I hope Mom and Papa don't mind if I bring a date to Thanksgiving at their house. Oh well, they'll just have to accept a non-Scandinavian for the eve-

40

ning." She laughed, "It's the muscle man from the sporting goods store."

A few nights later, Mariska was at home making lesson plans for her little students when the phone rang.

"Hi, dear. It's Neil. I just wanted to tell you we're having a special on skate socks at the store and I wanted to bring you a few—in appreciation for the Thanksgiving invitation. Can I stop over?"

He came over with an entire box of skating socks. Mariska brewed him coffee and gratefully made her selections. She noticed him looking at his watch more than normal and appearing somewhat agitated. Then his beeper went off and he abruptly gathered the discarded selections to leave.

REDFLAG #1-14

"Oh," Mariska began, "I'm disappointed. I didn't know you had to be back at work."

"Yes," he said. "As a matter of fact, I have to hurry. I'll see you this Thursday at Thanksgiving."

He grabbed her, nuzzled a good-bye in her ear, and passionately found her lips. Just as Mariska sank into his embrace, however, he pulled away and raced down the hall.

REDFLAG #1-15

41

The spoon against the cranberry sauce jar clanged loudly as Mariska scooped out the last few chunks. Her parents' house was already abuzz with people when the doorbell rang again. She went to answer it and this time, there stood Neil, barely visible behind a large bouquet, a pumpkin pie, and a Scandinavian aperitif. The other guests were impressed with his generosity.

"The turkey is delicious, Mrs. Dansko," Neil remarked over dinner.

"How kind of you," Mariska's mother responded in a thick accent. "But I really must defer to my mother, Grandmama Henrietta. She was on turkey duty this year."

"And roast beef as well," bragged Grandmama. "So," she said, turning to Neil, "you like my cooking, young man? Then you will have to come over for an authentic Danish dinner."

Neil looked as if taken by surprise. Nobody but Mariska seemed to notice. He put his fork down, leaned back in his chair and inhaled deeply. "I...I...would like that very much. Thank you, Grandmama Henrietta."

REDFLAG
#1-16

Mariska wondered why he responded to such a commonplace offer with such incredulity.

"So, Neil," Grandmama said, now having an in, "tell us all about yourself."

42

"Well, I am from Grand Rapids, Michigan. I went to the University of Michigan and majored in journalism and English. I was married briefly. I'm out of that. I'm now managing a Big Five sporting goods store."

"I see," Grandmama said. "Mariska said you used to play hockey."

One of the young cousins perked up and asked, "Did you really? Were you on the Red Wings?" Everyone laughed.

Neil responded, "I was pretty good, but not that good."

"What position did you play?" the cousin asked.

Neil replied, "Oh, forward, usually. Please pass the yam casserole."

REDFLAG
#1-17

"What is managing a sporting goods store like?" inquired Mariska's father.

"Oh, you know, just everything. I have to be on top of firing, hiring, the accounting crew, and the buyers. It is wrought with responsibility. And it's a large store. But for right now it suits me fine, primarily because I meet gentle and kind women there." He smiled and indicated Mariska. "You have a charming and lovely daughter, Mr. and Mrs. Dansko."

Johann, one of her brothers, jokingly replied, "Yeah, so you'd better be nice to her."

43

"I intend to, Johann. I fully intend to do just that."

Mariska stopped eating for a moment to take in Neil's response. Everyone around the table smiled and continued to banter. She made eye contact with her grandmother.

After dinner, Mariska walked Neil outside to his car before helping Mom with the cleanup.

"It's so cold tonight," she remarked.

"Cold? Come on, honey. We're from Michigan and Denmark. Toughen up! Forty-seven degrees in those places is a heat wave." They both laughed. He continued, "Why don't I come over tomorrow and keep you very warm?"

"Well, okay. I'd like that."

He stared at her in the crisp Los Angeles moonlight. Mariska liked the stare. She realized she was beginning to have feelings for this man. She just did not know him—yet. She thought, *It will take time. I can go slow.*

And she waved good night to this semi-mystery man in the foggy, chilled air as he sputtered away in his sixteen-year-old Datsun.

The next morning Mariska awoke early from the pounding rain on her bedroom awning. She opened the bedroom curtains and was actually pleased to observe the soothing rain. She sauntered into the bathroom and caught a glimpse of herself in the mirror.

"Sometimes being alone in the morning is good. What if someone saw me like this? My mouth even looks crooked," she laughed. She brushed her teeth, washed her face with the Danish cleanser she never did without, and looked at the time.

Between the cozy morning rain and the no-work agenda, Mariska decided to climb back into bed. As she started to drift off, she thought it must be raining exceedingly hard because the noise on the awning increased. She looked at the clock (eight a.m.) and realized it was not solely the rain; someone was at the door. She scampered to the door and looked through the peephole. It was Neil.

"*Velkommen*, Neil. Let me get a robe."

"It is pouring out here."

"Come in, come in."

"I'm sorry I didn't call."

He stood in the hall wearing jeans and a skimpy jean jacket. Not warm enough or substantial enough for this downpour.

"Do you mind, honey?" he inquired.

"Mind?" she asked, not understanding what he meant.

He walked back outside and brought in a duffle bag and a suitcase.

"Do I need to explain?"

"What?" asked Mariska.

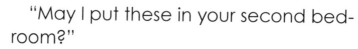

REDFLAG #1-18

"May I put these in your second bed-room?"

"Ah...yes...um," she said. "Sure."

He put them in her second bedroom, removed his wet jacket, sat down on the floor, and put his hands to his face.

"What is the matter, Neil?" the confused woman asked, not sure if she should be self-conscious over her morning persona, or attentive to Neil.

He extended his hand, beckoning her to sit by him. He pulled her to him and buried his cold nose in her neck. She did like the closeness, the smell of morning rain in his hair, and the sound of increasing drops on the windows. It was cozy, yet rather odd. They held each other until she said, "Are you okay? Should I ask?"

"Were you sleeping?" he asked.

"Dozing."

"Can I hold you in your bed?" he asked.

She led him into her bedroom, her bed, her welcoming arms. He did not kiss her and she did not kiss him. She stroked his back on top of his mildly damp Banlon shirt

46

and continued listening to the rain on the awning. Neil's breathing became deeper, his shoulders became softer, and she watched him sleep for the first time.

The next day he brought four suitcases and six boxes filled with personal belongings and moved in. She made a set of keys for him.

For a few weeks life was predictable. Neil would work most of the day, arrive home late at night, eat a light snack, and go to sleep—in the second bedroom. He'd go off to be with old friends on the weekend, but would return to her in the evening when they would usually catch a movie. He was fun and easy to get along with, and Mariska actually enjoyed her companion. She didn't tell her parents or anyone else that he had virtually moved in.

REDFLAG
#1-19

Had he? They weren't sleeping together. What was the definition here? A roommate? A boyfriend who was taking it slow? He was kind and considerate, and emphatically happy for her when she garnered a citywide honorable mention for her preschool.

"Let's go to a great restaurant Saturday to celebrate, Mariska. My treat."

47

REDFLAG #1-20

She thought "his treat" was somewhat in keeping, since nothing had been said about rent and bills, and thus far he had not offered her money for any of the above.

Aside from that, everything felt comfortable with Neil. She enjoyed waking up to his coffee making. The only thing that annoyed her was his beeper.

"I have to keep it on at all times for work. I am even in charge of foreign shipments which transect time zones."

She laughed and said, "Good thing you are sleeping in another room. I don't want to be woken at four a.m. by some mad Bulgarian soccer team that didn't receive its equipment in time."

The night they went to celebrate her award, Mariska chose an Italian restaurant on Melrose in West Hollywood. It was low-lit, infused with wonderful aromas, and fully had a European ambiance.

"I must show you around Europe sometime soon, Neil. Hey, what about Easter vacation? Why don't you take some time off? We could go to Denmark, and maybe France or England. You've never been."

REDFLAG #1-21

Just then, his beeper sounded and Neil excused himself. He never acknowledged her wonderful travel suggestion.

48

When they returned home that evening, Neil immediately turned on Ted Koppel's *Nightline* and curled up on the couch. Mariska, feeling both the romantic ambiance of the restaurant and the lingering Chianti, snuggled next to him and softly whispered in his ear, "Would you like to remove my necklace?"

He did so, but stayed focused on a rather uninteresting news segment on the show.

Mariska realized this, grabbed the remote control, clicked off the TV, and placed Neil's hand on the zipper of her dress.

"And now," she said, surprising herself, "please remove my dress."

"What?" he said.

"You heard me. Now remove my dress. *Vaersgof* (please)."

He did not do anything, so she led him to her bedroom and asked again, "Please remove my dress."

He then reached around her. All they could hear was the sound of the slow slide fastener dislodging from its tracks. He pushed back her long, thin hair and held it up with one deft hand as he cautiously removed the dress with the other.

There she stood, in bra, slip, and pantyhose in front of a man of which she was becoming increasingly fond. She tried not to allow her self-consciousness to fill the room; tried to be proud of her body, and their trust.

Neil sat down on the bed and looked at her. They did not touch and they did not talk. A sliver of moonlight shone through the window. It landed on Neil's left cheekbone. Mariska touched it and said, "Aha. Angel's light."

He took her hand from his cheek, kissed it, and pulled her on the bed to him. He wrapped his arms around her semi-undressed body and held her tightly. Mariska felt very close to him. He buried his lips in her neck.

But when she looked up to be kissed, there was no kiss. She placed her hands under his shirt but did not detect a response.

"It feels so good to be close to you, Neil."

"Same here, Mariska. But...I'm going to have to go to sleep soon. Too much Chianti."

She felt her body stiffen. She had to fight not to abruptly pull away.

"Do you want to go to bed now, Neil?"

"Soon, darling."

She loosened her grasp a bit. He followed suit without much resistance. Neil lay back and looked at the ceiling. The moonlight was on his pant leg now. But it didn't look like angel's light, somehow, just a break in the darkened room.

And then he said, "Was the red snapper too salty?"

She turned to look in his eyes. He was serious. He was truly pondering the dead fish's brine content.

She felt a cloying sensation rise in both her stomach and her throat. Fighting it, she responded, "Very American. When they don't know how to season, they salt. Strange, it was an Italian restaurant with Italian owners, but..." she trailed off.

"You're probably right, darling," he said, getting up. "Mariska, it was a beautiful evening. Good night, my sweet." He pecked her briefly on the lips and left the room.

Mariska heard him getting ready for bed and saw the light under his door turn off.

The next morning Mariska woke to the smell of Neil's Arabica coffee brewing in the kitchen. When she happily approached the kitchen to greet him, she realized he had already left the apartment. Instead, next to the coffee maker was a check for half the rent—for the first time.

REDFLAG
#1-22

"Sweetie," her grandmother's voice said on the answering machine, "it's Grandmama Henrietta. Well, the family firmed up

51

all our Christmas plans. Where have you been lately? No daily phone calls. Your mother wants to know if you moved back to Naestved. Call me. By the way, have you heard from that nice Neil chap?"

"So," he said, removing his tie after work, "I am sorry to state it that succinctly, but it is the truth."

"You will not even join us on Juledag? We celebrate December twenty-sixth, too."

"No," he said, surprisingly calmly as he pondered the shelf, choosing his midnight soup of chicken noodle or vegetarian vegetable. "I decided I just find it too difficult to do any holiday since I am estranged from my parents, and particularly after the divorce. No Christmas Eve, Christmas Day, or Juledag. I'll be working on those days and it suits me fine."

"The store is open on the twenty-fifth?" she asked, toasting a sourdough biscuit for him.

"No, but I can catch up on payroll. You can come by if you want, but I'll be hard at work. Come on, Mariska. I see you every night, including weekend nights. Is that not good enough?"

"No, I love being with you, Neil, but holidays—" She was interrupted by his beeper.

He excused himself and retrieved his message in the other room.

"So," he said, when he came back in the kitchen, "how was our school today?"

"Was that message important, Neil?"

"No, just one of the cashiers called in sick for tomorrow."

"One of the cashiers called in sick?"

"Yes, no big deal."

"I didn't think any of the store workers had your personal beeper number."

"No, some do."

"Oh. I bought some fresh marmalade. Would you like some for your biscuit?"

"That's my girl," he smiled, giving her a peck on the cheek.

"But you won't reconsider Christmas?"

"Nope. The only thing I want to consider right now is your promise to schmeer that brilliant marmalade all over this fine specimen of a biscuit."

Mariska eyed him and took a deep breath.

"Odd priorities, Mr. Bonner," she said, putting just the right amount of marmalade on the finely toasted biscuit.

Their life remained somewhat predictable for six months. They never argued. Mariska knew his routine and felt okay in this reliable scheme. Her family still did not know she had a "boyfriend" living with her. They never saw him. She told her girlfriends he was simply a casual roommate. Her feelings for him, however, dictated the diametric opposite.

One afternoon in June, he returned early from the store, and said he had a headache and was going to take a nap. Mariska ran some errands, came back in the early evening and checked on him. He was lying on top of his covers.

"Are you okay, Neil?"

"Come in," he beckoned. "Come in."

Mellow jazz was playing on the radio. Only an orange setting sun streamed through the curtains.

"Sit down, Mariska."

"Do you want some more water or something?"

"Water, slave."

"Yes, master."

She handed him a glass and he drank it, looking over the top of the glass at her as he did so.

"Thank you."

"Do you feel better?"

"One hundred percent. Now, do something else, slave."

"What, Neil?"

"Turn off the lights in the hall and come back over here."

She turned off the lights and walked over to the bed. He took her hand and pulled her to him. She was confused by this sudden show of affection.

He said, "You're good to me. You're good to me, Mariska."

He cautiously slid her down on the bed and swung one leg over her. She didn't know what to think, but decided to follow his dance.

He gently pushed her hair from her face, kissing her cheeks, neck, and collarbone, and amorously found her lips. She responded by pulling him tightly to her. This time he fully reciprocated, and she even thought she heard a soft moan of contentment. Mariska noticed the sun had set and the room was completely dark.

He sat up, tried to look at her in the darkness, and gradually began to remove her clothes. He asked her to remove his, and they made love for hours; until they fell asleep in each other's intoxicated embrace.

When they awoke in the morning, he kissed her and kissed her until he had to go to work. Mariska wondered if this was finally a turning point in their relationship.

But it was not. Their only intimacy in the ensuing months was a hello kiss in the evening. That one odd and unaccounted-for encounter had to serve to sustain Mariska. Every night she scrutinized his behavior, attempting to predict if another intimate encounter might spontaneously materialize.

REDFLAG
#1-23

Their second Christmas together quickly appeared. Mariska had resigned herself to his anti-holiday sentiment by now and did not broach the matter. He did have the momentary kindness of spirit to buy her a silver and turquoise bracelet and a romantic card.

At her parents' house on Christmas Day, her brother Johann pulled her aside.

"Maris, can I ask you a question?"

"What, Johann?"

"Whatever happened to that guy you brought to Thanksgiving last year? Neil, right?"

"Oh...um...I see him from time to time. He's doing well."

"Oh?"

"Why, Johann?"

"Because, Maris, Grandmama Henrietta said something funny in passing. You know her."

56

"What, brother?"

"She said she thinks you are secretly living with him. Isn't that funny?"

Mariska was not sure how to answer.

"And when I helped you move your TV last week, I could have sworn I saw a large Lakers sweatshirt on the bathroom door handle. Just a funny thought. Actually, Mom and Dad and all of us would be glad if you were. I just wondered."

She stared at him, and then looked at the large hutch across the room. That piece of furniture was one of the few that came over with them from Denmark. For a second, she reflected upon how it had looked in the living room in Naestved. A much simpler time, remarkably.

REDFLAG
#1-24

She looked back at Johann. He had a serious look in his eyes now.

"All I want, Maris, is to know he is meeting your needs. End of story. *Mange tak* (thank you)." He then leaned over, kissed her cheek, and left the room.

The following months were fairly predictable. Neil worked twelve hours a day, five or six days a week. And when he was home, the constant presence of the annoying beeper loomed over them. During the few hours they did spend together at night, he was curious and concerned for her

57

well-being, and generally seemed happy to spend time with her. They both saw other friends on weekend days, but reserved Saturday nights for each other. It was an established routine. She bought it with loyalty and with honor.

Mariska walked her two dear friends to the elevator. They were still laughing over the banter of their Saturday afternoon get-together at her apartment.

"We must do this more often," Mariska concluded before the elevator door closed. Just then, she saw a woman hovering near the elevator. She had never seen her before in the building.

"Good afternoon. May I help you?" she asked the stranger.

"Maybe so," the woman responded shyly, gazing at the carpet. The African-American woman was somewhat shabbily dressed, with a visibly tattered shoulder bag and coat, but had a gentle countenance.

"Are you okay, ma'am?" Mariska inquired. "What apartment are you looking for?"

"Um...201," she replied.

"I live in 201. What can I do for you?"

"Oh—are you Mariska Dansko?"

"That is correct," Mariska answered.

"My name is Bernice. I am Neil Bonner's wife."

Mariska felt her mouth snap shut and her shoulders rise. She stared at the woman in disbelief. What was this figure doing at her door?

"Wife?" She thought she had heard the woman say this, not ex-wife.

"That is correct," she replied with downcast eyes.

For a moment Mariska felt her body freeze. She voluntarily had to command it to move.

"My...my friends and I just had some freshly brewed coffee. Would you like to c...come in?"

"Very much, thank you," replied the soft-spoken presence.

Mariska led the woman inside, forcing herself to be cordial and not appear shocked.

"I am sorry not to have called, but Neil would not give me your number. I had the address from some mail and thought I'd take my chances and just come by, it being Saturday and all."

"Of course. Did you come a far distance?"

"I live in Downey. I took the bus. It took almost two hours."

"You poor dear. Did...did you come all this way to meet me?"

"Sort of," she said, sipping the coffee. "Mariska, may I ask the nature of your relationship with Neil?"

"The nature? Why?" She wasn't sure how to answer, but went for her own truth. He is my boyfriend, of course."

Bernice loudly banged the cup on its saucer and abruptly walked to the window. She stood there, clutching the sink.

"So," she began, "you aren't just roommates?"

"No. We are very attached. I'm pretty sure I love him."

Bernice turned around and leaned against the sink. "I guess you don't understand. And it is what I suspected. Oh...oh...I am so sorry."

"What, Bernice? What the hell is going on here?"

Bernice said, "We are not divorced, ma'am. He is living with you to prove to his parents that he is no longer married to an African-American woman. They think he's divorced and living with a roommate. They call him at your apartment and send his mail here all the time. His pager, that's them a lot. And me."

60

"What?" Mariska stood up.

"There's no divorce even hinted at between us. We have dinner every night and see each other on the weekend days, until I have to go to work. We will stop doing this pretty soon, I assume. At any rate, he is planning on moving back after the new year—parents' approval or not. We both have to be brave now, with the child on the way."

The room began to spin. Mariska suddenly did not hear another word Bernice said. There seemed to be more words in the air, but she could not catch them. Thoughts came to her in a dizzying eddy: no holidays with her, "estranged" from his parents, wouldn't go to Europe, the almost nonexistent lovemaking.

"Is he...is he really manager of the sporting goods store, Bernice?"

"Manager? Shit, no. Is that what he told you? Why did he tell you that?"

"So he could pretend he was more needed at the store than he really is," Mariska replied, as if piecing something together. The puzzle pieces started whirling through the air, just waiting to be retrieved. "He did...did all this, Bernice...so he could be with you more."

"Oh."

"I think...I think...I am going to have to be an ungracious hostess. Please write down your phone number and leave my apartment now. We must talk more. Right now I am feeling a little...tired."

As soon as Bernice left, the phone rang, but Mariska did not answer.

The voice on the answering machine said, "Hi, dear, it's Grandmama Henrietta. Something told me to call you. Nothing important. Just...that I am here when you need me. Okay? I am here. Kiss, kiss."

Mariska waited for the uncanny message to click off and ran to the phone. She made two phone calls.

"Johann, it's Maris. I'm so glad you're home. Can you come over immediately? And bring some large cardboard boxes."

The second call she made was to a locksmith.

As soon as the locksmith changed the locks, Johann and Mariska packed Neil's belongings and dropped them off at his locker in the sporting goods store. He was not there and Mariska decided not to wait around for him. Johann insisted that Mariska should sleep at his house the next few nights and not go to the apartment. But before they left the store, Mariska decided to compose a letter to Neil and leave it with his things.

> Dear Neil,
>
> Many months ago I discovered you did not attend the University of Michigan. Many months before that I discovered you never played hockey. I am from Denmark where everyone plays hockey. Your stories did not add up. But those are trivialities compared to my now knowing the truth. If I catch you around my apartment, I will call the police.
>
> How dare you be so injurious? Whatever gave you the right to deceive the world so frightfully? I do not need to explain myself. Just stay the hell away from me. The sad thing is, I think the strength I am obtaining from writing this letter is better than anything I have ever received from you.
>
> Thank you for teaching me so very much,
> Mariska

REDFLAG
#1-25

A number of weeks later, Mariska Dansko called my psychotherapy office for an appointment. I remember one of her first, and rather profound, pronouncements. It went something like the following:

"I am here to relate my story of love lost. I do not even feel grief yet. I do know, however, I have been deceived. But by him or by me? I am embarrassed and confused.

I have heard you might be able to help me. Maybe you can help distinguish what part of this was real and what part was a dream. I don't know how it all happened. Was I present?

REDFLAG
#1-26

Anyhow, I was trying on a pair of iceskates my grandmama had just purchased as a Christmas present for me when........."

64

DISCUSSION OF CHAPTER

"COULD IT BE ICESKATE INTRODUCTIONS?"

Downdatee #1 – Repeatedly commits personal or social fraudulence

One cannot say Neil did not repeatedly commit, in this case, personal fraudulence upon Mariska. He maintained the lie about his marriage and other lies for two whole years.

In legal terms, fraud is defined as intentional deception resulting in injury to another. Certain acts of fraud (constructive, collateral, inducement) have landed one in jail ever since sixteenth century debtors' prison. Woefully, there is no judge, jury, or jail for personal/emotional fraudulence.

However, we are here to address the dating down nature of this union, and how it proved destructive.

RED FLAG #1-1

In our first therapy session, Mariska said the most important element in her life was her tight-knit family unit. I want to briefly address this concept.

Nothing is more important to a child growing up. I might even extend this by saying if one does not have a supportive family structure (a village?), do not get pregnant. There exists a glaring correlation between supportive families and mentally healthy children.

Having said that, I must play devil's advocate for a moment. Sometimes, with that kind of closeness, the potential for emotional delayed development due to over-reliance on the family unit does loom.

The problem with this over-reliance is that it can narrow the person's vision. "The family is most important. We are your everything."

In Mariska's case, she was thirty-four and quite sheltered. Because of this, she hadn't dated much—gone outside her family unit. She was therefore ripe for someone like Neil to enter into her life and take advantage of her fresh, unsuspecting naïveté.

One other piece here. In terms of this specific downdatee (repeatedly commits personal or social fraudulence), the word fraud is a legal term, not a psychological term. In the field of law, it is defined as intentional deception resulting in injury to another. It usually consists of misrepresentation, concealment, or nondisclosure of a material fact.

We are reasonably sure Neil did not set out to intentionally hurt Mariska. What we are also sure of, however, is his concealment—of committing a huge act of social fraudulence.

RED FLAG #1-2

Grandmama said, "Go meet a nice Danish skier" at the sporting goods store. This had nothing to do with dating down; but we must be aware of the various forms of "programming."

Mariska was extremely close to her wise and loving grandmother. Would she have been as vulnerable to Neil's cajoling if Grandmama had not made the suggestion?

RED FLAG #1-3

Neil did not even know Mariska's name and was asking her how much she received for giving skating lessons. I believe that, unless one is close buddies with someone, asking about fees for service in that form is invasive. This should have been Mariska's red flag: Neil had a boundary issue. (Boundaries are defined in psychological terms as appropriate emotional "walls" between people where, if crossed, a sense of disrespect or invasion is experienced.)

RED FLAG #1-4

He went on to ask her, "Could you teach an adult to skate?"

So, not only was he exercising a boundary problem, he was exposing some immediate ulterior motives. These ulterior motives came on two levels. The first level was that he was asking her out, without asking her out. The second level was more serious, however. Here, Neil was checking out the landscape to see if it/she was ripe for his fraudulence.

I believe he was scheming, and probably regularly checked out all the women he met early on for their potential candidacy for his fraudulence.

RED FLAG #1-5

Being late for the skating lesson was negligent. Mariska did not have to wait as long as she did for him.

It was transparent that he had no intention of being her student. And even if he did, to be forty-five minutes late for a first lesson which is supposed to run one hour is inexcusable. In psychological dating down lingo, we call it jockeying for position, or passive-aggressive behavior.

(You possibly have heard the term passive-aggressive. This is not a technical term but psychotherapists do use it. Passive-aggressive behavior is defined as a set of behaviors that look passive or unremarkable on the surface, but really serve to hide much hostility below. These behaviors unleash odd and unaccountable attacks on unsuspecting victims and are commonly quite hurtful.)

Never stay cozy with people who are always late; it fortifies their need to be in control.

RED FLAG #1-6

Then, he professed the need to leave the ice rink. He clearly had another agenda—especially since he was not dressed for the lesson, and no skates or appropriate clothing ever appeared on the scene.

RED FLAG #1-7

Although she would have preferred to just give the lesson, get paid, and go home, she acquiesced to his dinner agenda because he was "hurting." What about consideration for her time, her schedule, and the agreed-upon event?

Many downdaters subjugate their needs, to the point of self-effacement, for their partners' needs. Nurturing someone is one thing. However, rescuing is about leaving your needs unnoticed. A large number of downdaters repeatedly rescue.

RED FLAG #1-8

She noticed him becoming withdrawn again. This was a clue that the man was either unusually depressed or had exceedingly low self-esteem.

Downdaters must fight the urge to "bring them up." Downdaters seem to deny the displeasure and difficulty of a depressed man. Their subtext usually is, "If he hangs by me enough, he will come up and everything will be wonderful."

None of the above EVER happens.

RED FLAG #1-9

He is an ex-hockey player, I think. Mariska knew from the onset there was some fraudulence. Before she even developed feelings for him, she went into denial over this instinctive hit (I have seen denial defined as "denying all").

70

Denial is a downdaters worst friend, but a close one.

RED FLAG #1-10

Could this all have happened strictly due to Grandmama's programming? Closeness and open trust in another even have their downsides, as they can engender programming. The problem with anything pre-programmed is, especially in the case of downdaters, people bypass their own instincts to incorporate the message of the programming.

We must all be alert for potential programming. However, there is a difference between this and coincidental reality. Programming, coincidences, and instinct sometimes have a fine line. The downdater always blurs that distinction.

RED FLAG #1-11

"It's not like anyone else is on the horizon," said Mariska.

When living things are acontextual (meaning, without a context, without a community, support system, etc.), they glom onto the closest likeness of what they need to survive. This is basic biological survival: all entities with a nucleus seek like entities with a nucleus to reproduce.

Man also gloms onto what is tangible and accessible rather than what might create more isolation from the species ("It's not like anyone else is on the horizon"). More isolation never bodes well for survival of any species. When these creations are created from lack (biological or otherwise), versus from choice, less elevated occurrences/offsprings are produced.

In dating behavior, a connection created from lack is a moderately dangerous position. This position often awakens the downdating in all of us.

RED FLAG #1-12

Neil said, "Mariska, could we take your car?" The problem here resided with Mariska. She immediately should have asked why.

One wonders what she did with his request. She seemed to neatly tuck it into denial.

RED FLAG #1-13

"You didn't run into any alum..." Going to an alumni dinner and not running into any classmates is a trifle odd.

The non-downdater would have questioned this phenomenon along with the car request. Between the two, some pretty glaring flags would be waving. Not in this case for Mariska.

These were clear indications at this point that Mariska was starting to date someone well below her integrity level.

RED FLAG #1-14

Neil appeared agitated and left abruptly after his beeper sounded.

Actually, this and the preceding two red flags would lead a non-downdater to perceive the fraudulence. But the downdater seems to deny these perceptions, step into these fraudulence ruts, and furnish them.

RED FLAG #1-15

Just as Mariska sank into his embrace...he pulled away.

Neil always pulled away when they would start to get close. It IS dating below you when your needs are consistently frustrated. Some women feel guilty or too "needy" for wanting physical closeness. This is ridiculous self-abnegation. It is

73

time to cease and desist apologizing for being human.

RED FLAG #1-16

Neil looked as if taken by surprise... Neil's over-reaction to Grandmama's simple dinner offer was also a clue of his fraudulence. He was not sure how to receive basic generosity through his web of calculated behaviors. When people are constantly calculating their behavior, basic generosity is actually experienced as an oddity.

Mariska noticed his overreaction, but did not catalog it consciously. A non-downdater would perceive this as something to discuss in the near future.

RED FLAG #1-17

Clearly Neil deflected this line of questioning by asking for the food. Anyone else would have loved to have shared sports banter—even for two minutes.

RED FLAG #1-18

First of all, he came over completely unannounced. Someone with a consistent boundary problem is difficult to predict. Secondly, his audacity in bringing his belongings with him would have been shocking to anyone. Mariska passively acquiesced.

On all accounts, this is considered "nervy," boundary-less, and classless.

For her not to notice this and/or not address it placed her right on a steep and slippery slope. Someone moving in on you—literally—is nothing to overlook.

RED FLAG #1-19

It is a common occurrence for downdaters to obscure the truth to their family and friends, for the purpose of keeping the relationship alive. Even people who are open and never tell white lies will suddenly change their spots, if downdating is their prey.

Rather than living in truth, the downdater lives so much in hopefulness that obscuring major facts, like Neil moving in, totally unannounced, seems par for the course.

RED FLAG #1-20

Whether Neil was a roommate, a boyfriend, or a sometime boarder, basic amenities like rent and bills should always be discussed.

When they are not, someone is manipulating. This is almost a constant.

RED FLAG #1-21

That he is not an experienced traveler is not why Neil is a downdatee. Rather, he is defined as a downdatee because he avoids all communication, honesty, evades definitions, and dodges the potential of any future plans.

It is the lack of integrity that takes the definition. Not how many museums in Prague he can name.

RED FLAG #1-22

Why Neil dropped a rent check after the preceding evening leads one to believe he was fully aware of his distancing measures and felt guilty for employing them.

A renowned family therapist, Virginia Satir (1916–1988), based much of her teachings on low self-esteem. She basically said low self-esteem has tremendous negative power on a relationship.

Mariska totally chose to put up with Neil's lack of communication. Dating down and low self-esteem are unfortunate first cousins.

RED FLAG #1-23

Downdaters keep assuming their partner will come up from some dormant, internally inspired revelation and change.

This refers to constant #3 in the introduction: the female endures unmet needs for months, even years.

RED FLAG #1-24

This is quite a supportive claim from her brother, Johann. The problem is, even in the face of such loving support, the downdater is too busy hoping her significant other will change - to even recognize the help. Here, Johann is banging at her door and expressing that he will help her in any way, and she disregards it to return to her mode of frustrating hopefulness.

RED FLAG #1-25

So Mariska did have more than an inkling of his fraudulence. But she continued to hang in there. She was, in effect, exercising constant #1: the female takes on full responsibility for the male's unhealthy, unproductive, or harmful behavior.

Downdaters tend to incorporate this unhealthy behavior as a kind of normalcy in order for the union to proceed.

RED FLAG #1-26

Her opening presentation to me clearly categorized her as a downdater: 1) Her needs were so unmet, yet she was so giving; 2) She took on full responsibility for his painful behavior; and 3) He continued to refuse to change or come clean after many months. She also continued to feel alone and not part of his sphere, and dove into solemn denial to keep it all afloat.

Since she eventually broke away and did seek help, we see a "red flag" of optimism, auguring the possibility of Mariska leaving her downdating orientation—hopefully.

It is possible one can fall into a dating down situation only once, even as seriously as this example demonstrated by my patient, Mariska. Or, one can fall into it twice—or be a chronic lifer.

The good news is that our instincts, which are our personal red flags, can wave over blind optimism. And this blind optimism never has to be further wrapped in the flimsiness of false hope. Rather, it can appear in a more tangible and secure covering. Frankly, I call this—choice.

78

CHAPTER TWO

ILLUSTRATING DOWNDATEE #2 –

*Is a Convicted or Non-Convicted Career
Criminal or Recidivist*

Entitled...

THE THREE MARIAS

Sitting in the West Hollywood living room of Maria Consuela (referred to as Connie), my former patient, it seemed as though I was in a college genetics class, observing specimens.

In front of me sat three of the most similar sisters I have ever laid eyes on.

My patient, Connie, age thirty-five, sat next to Maria Leticia (Leti), age thirty-seven, and across the room sat Maria Anna (Annie), age thirty-nine.

They were from New York City, of Puerto Rican descent. They all were five foot one, broad-shouldered, medium weight, with full busts and pretty legs. They all shared thick and shiny short black hair, similar facial features, and the same vocal timbre inside heavy New York accents.

They spoke quickly and spiritedly and continuously referred to each other.

The sisters possessed the same large brown eyes, huge smiles, and enormous hearts.

My Garcia sisters. The three Marias.

Annie and Leti were in from New York City, visiting Connie. When they heard I was embarking on this project, they flew in to be part of the interview process.

"We've been close our whole lives," said Leti, the middle sister. "Annie and I sort of suffered through this almost as much as Connie."

Connie was busy cutting up veggies and *queso blanco* when she said, "Annie, tell Carole your first few perceptions of America when you guys left Puerto Rico. It's so cute."

Annie laughed and said, "Well, Mom and Dad brought Leti and me to New York City when I was four and a half and she was two, and Connie was in Ma's tummy. I do have two early memories of that first day off the airplane."

"Please tell," I said, while testing the tape recorder and munching on a crisp slice of lemon-dipped jicama.

"I remember landing on the tarmac at the airport in New York and seeing snow for the first time. I recall running over to a large white snowbank and being really upset because it was too cold to play with and it stung my little hands. I asked my mom if the snow near where we were going to live was going to be warmer."

We all laughed.

"Tell her the second memory, *hermana*," instructed Connie from the kitchen.

"And," Annie concluded, "the second memory was at Connie's christening a few months later. We all shared the same white tulle christening dress, but Connie was such a fat baby that Mama couldn't button the back of the dress. So, we couldn't remove the christening blanket because everyone would see the no-buttoning and my mom was a master seamstress. I was in charge of keeping the blanket over her the entire evening. Aren't those cute first memories?"

Leti said, "You'd never peg her as a fatso by looking at her hot body now. ¿No, hermanita?"

Again the sisters laughed the same guttural, hearty laugh.

"They're great memories, girls," I responded, turning to Connie, who had been my patient for a year.

"Refresh me about your parents' beginnings, Connie. Could you do that?"

Connie poured herself some iced tea and reclined on the overstuffed sofa.

"Yeah, sure. Mom and Dad were from small coffee farms in central Puerto Rico. They worked and saved for five years to come to New York. They secured an apartment before they left and brought the

87

money they had saved. Little did they know they landed in the middle of El Barrio."

"El Barrio?" I asked.

Leti explained, "East Harlem, Spanish Harlem, El Barrio, Northwest Manhattan—same place."

Connie said, "I always wondered if Mama and Papa knew it was a rough area. They were a little different from the other Puerto Ricans of the area, Carole. Even though Mama was a seamstress and Papa was a manager for D'agostino's Grocers, they insisted on great educations for the three of us."

"So you went to private schools?" I inquired.

The girls laughed.

Annie said, "No way, Carolina. They couldn't afford that. But they had enough foresight to have a tutor come to our house once a week from the first grade to the twelfth. Do you believe they did that?"

"And," Connie said, "these tutors were wonderful. They would go over our lessons and wherever we were having problems, they'd fill in."

Leti said, "It worked. Annie went to NYU on a scholarship and became a lawyer. I went to Barnard on a scholarship and work as a translator at the United Nations."

Connie finished, "And I went to Columbia on a loan. But I paid it back."

Everyone laughed.

"As you know, I've been in theatre and television production since I left college." At that point, Connie went over to her hutch and brought back some pictures. "Here's me graduating from Columbia. And there's Papa hugging Annie at her graduation from law school. And, oh, here...here is..." Her demeanor changed.

Annie and Leti looked at each other. "¿Que es este, Chula?"

Connie was quiet. Her mouth went into a tight scowl. Her eyes softened for a moment and she shook her head.

"I didn't think I had this picture. I didn't think I had any of *his* pictures." She showed me a slightly tattered photo of a man in his early thirties, sitting on the Eighth Avenue subway railing, lost in thought, looking away from the camera.

I said, "This must be Tony?"

Leti said, "¿Aye, Connie, *por qué*?"

Connie said, "I didn't know I still had it. Don't worry, sweetie, it's only a photo. Here, Carole, is your tape recorder ready?" She

89

handed me the photo, looked at her sisters and asked, "Well, is everyone ready?"

Valentine's Day, about three years ago –

The recently married attorneys, Maria Anna (Annie) and Sam, sat in the front seat of the Checker cab. Annie's younger sisters, Leti and Connie, sat in the back.

"Excuse me, Mr. Taxi Drivah?" Connie asked in her Manhattan lilt. "Could you turn the heat on? It's freezing in here!"

Annie responded to her sister, "Maybe you should have worn some clothes."

At that, the unassuming cab driver glanced in his rearview mirror, due to the possibility of an unclad female in his back-seat.

Sam put his arm on the driver. "Relax."

Everyone chuckled.

Leti said, "I love what Connie's wearing. It's a Valentine's party. Everyone's supposed to show a little skin. Maybe you'll meet someone tonight."

Connie said, "I just hope people don't look at our feet." The cab driver adjusted the mirror in an attempt to see the back-seat ladies' feet.

"No," Annie explained to the driver as she removed a pretty silver high-heeled shoe.

"My mama bought us Valentine's shoes. She knows our sizes, but decided to get us the same style. Three for the price of two at Payless. Funny."

"Is a very nice shoe," said the obliging New York-Pakistani cabbie. He received a good tip for that run.

Sam introduced the girls to the senior partner at the law firm, who was the owner of the condo and was throwing the party. Sam then escorted them to the buffet. Leti and Annie filled their plates and found seats in the crowded living room. Sam and sister-in-law Connie were slower to serve themselves.

"Thanks for inviting me and Leti, Sammy. We love you."

"This is great! Glad you could come. Lotta food, huh? Oh, I want some of that Maguro sushi. You know what, Connie?"

"Yes?"

"This entire party was catered by a computer. Should be called robot catering."

"What do you mean?" Connie laughed.

"Well, one of the secretaries was in charge of catering and she did this all by checklists that supposedly defined the employees' culinary preferences. Then the computer configured the menu."

"You're kidding!"

"And," he continued, "in the middle of it, our entire computer system jammed. Just last night, the woman was sweating bullets, not sure if we were going to have food or not."

"¡Pobrecita! So what did you all do?"

"Well, it was on my shoulders," he said, admiring the hors d'oeuvres. "So I called this really terrific computer tech guy. God, was he adept...," and then he stopped.

"What, Sam?" asked Connie.

"I didn't even think of this. Whoa."

"What, Sam?"

"We had a lengthy conversation after he got the system running. Wait a minute."

"What?" she said over her sushi plate.

"Jesus, sister, wait a minute. You both love film, entertainment. He's a little younger. You like slightly younger dudes. He's a great guy. Just a minute." He went through his wallet and fished out the guy's card.

Annie walked over to grab some more hors d'oeuvres. "Whatcha doing in your wallet, love?" she asked him. "Paying my sister for her wisdom?"

"No, I'm looking for Tony Piccolini's card."

"Oh, that guy you liked?"

"Yes. And here it is." He pulled out his cell phone and called him. "Mr. Piccoloni? Hi ya. It's Sam Franklin from yesterday."

"What is he doing?" asked Connie.

"Not sure, sis," replied Annie.

"Tony, listen. I'm at the firm's Valentine's party on the Upper East Side. It looks like it's going to be happening for a number of hours. I'd like you to meet my sister-in law. She has very little clothing on and pretty silver shoes."

Mr. Piccolini must have heard Annie and Connie laughing.

REDFLAG #2-1

Most everyone was circled around the baby grand when Connie felt a tap on her shoulder. Sam was standing there with a well-dressed, brown-haired male. He looked to be a little younger than Connie and was rather short, but had the sweetest, warmest smile.

"Connie Garcia," said Sam, "this is Tony Piccolini. He thought he'd join the party. He's a friend of mine, so don't bite him. I gotta find my beautiful wife." He winked, and left the two of them to their own devices.

When Sam joined Annie and Leti, he realized they were watching. They gave

93

him the thumbs-up sign. So far, a two-out-of-three Garcia-girl consensus.

The following Saturday night was more or less Connie and Tony's first date—even though it was a bit crowded. The three sisters, Sam, Leti's new boyfriend, Lee, and Tony decided to meet for dinner at a quiet Italian restaurant in Sheridan Square. Everyone arrived before Tony.

Leti said, "It is very mucho far-out that Tony is joining us, Connie girl. He seems great. Hey, there he is." The five of them turned to the doorway to see the short, green-eyed, charming Italian gentleman approaching them.

"Hi, Tony! Welcome, Tony."

Tony immediately approached Connie, kissed her on the cheek, handed her a plastic bag from the Gap and then shook hands with everyone else. As the group took their seats, Connie opened the Gap plastic bag from Tony. In it was a turquoise and lime scarf with a price tag on it. Connie looked surprised. "Did you buy this for me?"

Tony matter-of-factly said, "Yes. I was passing the Gap before getting a cab and saw this pretty scarf in the window. I know it's going to be down to fifteen degrees tonight, so I thought I'd bring this for you." Then he reached for a menu. The people at the table all looked at each other.

"Tony," Connie said, "that was so considerate."

"Well," he explained, "if we all do go hear that group play at the club, we'll be getting home pretty late, and I didn't know if you were going to be dressed warmly enough— particularly in view of what you were wearing at the Valentine's party." He winked.

Annie grabbed Connie's hand under the table. An OK sign from a Garcia sister could rival the competition and scrutiny of a Pulitzer Prize committee. The squeezed hand said, "Congratulations. Good start."

The only aspect Connie regretted about the evening was the number of people at the table. She felt she couldn't get an accurate read on Tony: was he really quiet, or was he just quieted by the chatty group? However, the question was addressed the next day.

REDFLAG #2-2

Connie stood before the mirror in her bathroom lit by the morning sun. She looked at her thick black hair and large dark eyes. She pulled the brush through her hair, thinking, *I don't like my nose or my chin. I love my hair and my eyes. I wonder*

95

what Tony thought of me? She thought of his small but strong stature, his light, atypical Italian green eyes, and how much she had enjoyed him at her side last night. "Could I like someone I just met so much?" she said aloud.

Just then, her phone rang.

"Connie, good morning. It's Tony."

"Oh, hi again. What a nice person to start my day."

"Listen, are you free today? We didn't spend much time together—I mean, solo—last night. I wondered if you would like to meet me at the Frick Museum and have some lunch. They're lecturing all day on the hidden art of film lighting. Right up your alley. And we can spend some time together. Might you possibly be interested?"

They met outside the Frick Collection on 70th Street and Fifth Avenue. He walked up to her and, without saying hello, tightened Connie's new scarf around her collar. She smelled his freshly shampooed hair and looked into his clear green eyes. They both uttered a soft, "Good morning."

They walked through the unusual film lighting exhibit, had hot soup and shrimp salads for lunch, and spent hours by a fireplace in a hotel lobby. He was far from quiet.

He told her about his inordinate penchant for mathematics and how the computer field was such an easy and natural progression.

"But," Tony confessed, "my real love is film, TV, and theatre. You are really fortunate to be working in a promising position at NBC, Connie."

"I love it there, Tony."

"So, tell me more about your work and your aspirations," he asked, softly stroking Connie's hand. "And then, Connie, if you'd like, I will do the same."

And so the couple sat by the fireplace in some obscure East Side hotel, not knowing they were looking into each other's eyes "that way," and chatted till evening.

They left the Off-Broadway theatre, still laughing. "What a great, fun show. Thank you so much, Tony."

"My pleasure. And," he said, looking down the street and pointing, "I love that restaurant. Shall we?" They walked arm in arm into the cozy, unprepossessing eatery.

"Connie," Tony said, taking her hand and kissing it for the first time, "I'm really enjoying dating you, for many reasons. And your family, your blood community even turns me on. I'm an only child. I love how you and your sisters telepathically relate. I can see your antennas; I just don't see the code."

She laughed, but felt tingly from her hand to her chest. She wondered if it was the cold evening air that made her shudder.

Tony was impressed that Mr. and Mrs. Garcia had purchased the condo they had been living in for over thirty years. It was roomy, sunny, and comfortably decorated, despite their moderate income.

"But Connie," Tony asked as they exited the building, "is it safe enough? Your parents are getting on in years."

"Well, Tony, they've lived here this long and have never had a problem."

"Because if they ever do, Connie, let me know and I'll take care of it."

"What?" she asked, taking his hand. "What do you mean?"

Just then, as they were approaching the subway at 103rd Street, he pulled her arm and began to run down the street.

"Tony! Tony, what are you doing?" she asked. "Slow down, damn it."

But he continued to run and wouldn't let her break from his grasp.

"Tony, you're hurting my arm. Why are we running?"

"I hate this block and you are running away from here with me," he said, out of breath.

"What? Stop it."

"Piccolini! Piccolini!" someone said from behind them. "It *is* you!" At that, Tony finally let go of her hand. Connie lost her balance and landed on the sidewalk.

"Goddamn it, Piccolini, it is you!"

When Connie looked up, she saw two large, dark-haired men apprehending Tony. One had him from behind and the other stood in front of him, glaring down at him. Connie sat on the cement, shocked and scared.

"Listen, you bastard. We told you a year ago to stay away from this area. Do you understand? Go terrorize your fucking Guineas on Staten Island. I thought we cleared this up."

"OK, OK. Can you let me go? I'm with my girlfriend."

"And keep your fucking 'people' out of here, too. Got it, little boy?"

He said, "You'd better let me go."

The other man said, "Alberto, let him go. He's with some broad."

"Do you understand what we said, Piccolini?" the first guy adamantly inquired.

99

"Alright, Alberto, don't rough him up. It's really starting to snow. Come on."

The two men slowly pulled back and crossed 103rd Street, and were quickly out of sight.

Connie saw that her coat had become torn in the skirmish. The snow was really starting to come down. She stood up, collected herself and went over to Tony. He was standing there with folded arms, looking down. She put her arms around him.

"Are you OK, Tony? What was that? Are you OK?" He didn't answer. She just hugged him, keeping him warm as an onslaught of cold white falling stuff suddenly began to monopolize the entire scene.

REDFLAG #2-3

Connie chose not to mention the assault for a few months. It pre-occupied her waking thoughts, infiltrated her calm, tortured her sleep. But she chose not to say anything, and he chose not to offer.

REDFLAG #2-4

A few months later, Leti had friends over to watch the New York Giants play the Washington Redskins. Leti's boyfriend, Lee, was a devout Giants fan, so Leti thought she'd throw a fun Sunday afternoon lunch and football get-together.

"*Hermanita*," she said to Connie, putting an arm around her, "Tony is in my bedroom

100

talking on his cell. He wants you to come in."

The two sisters looked at each other, speaking only in Garcia telepathy-speak. Leti pulled back and walked away.

Tony was pacing in Leti's bedroom when Connie approached him. His cell phone was on the bed, taking on some odd center-stage status in the scenario. Connie slowly closed the door behind her.

Tony whispered, "Could you lock it, sweetheart?"

Click.

Connie looked at him, expressionless. He continued to pace.

"Connie," he began, both intently and hesitantly, "you see...you see...it was all about kickbacks."

"What, Tony?"

"Kickbacks," he reiterated, not looking at her. "See, they needed someone with excellent computer skills."

"What are you talking about?"

Tony stopped pacing for a moment, stared at his cell phone, and slipped it in his pocket.

"You will learn. It's been in our family for countless generations, from Staten Island to Catania, Sicily. I was...I was...er...in jail. We aren't really proud of ourselves. Funny, you

101

think I'd be happy enough with my really good I.T. salary, but it's odd. Family. History. There has been jail."

Connie stood motionless. "I have no idea what you are talking about."

Just then, a loud set of bravos, applause, and laughter came from Leti's living room. She looked at the door.

"Connie, I'm sorry. I'm keeping you from the party. But I have to tell you this 'cause I can't stay today. I have to leave."

"You can't stay? I thought we had today."

"Don't think that I don't want to. I'm sorry," he said, looking down, hands in his pockets. "But our family never partakes in the really big stuff. I mean—"

Connie interrupted him and unlocked the door.

"Go out through the kitchen. Nobody will know you have gone. Will you call me tomorrow?"

He clutched her to him and stroked her hair. As he did so, she felt two totally conflicting emotions: let me trust this embrace, and get away.

"Of course I will call you tomorrow. Have a good time with everyone," he whispered in her ear.

He held her for another moment. His familiar aftershave wafted around her head, the warm crook of his neck holding her up. Just as she was about to submit to this embrace, he pulled away, quickly left the room, and disappeared out the back kitchen door.

REDFLAG #2-5

For the next few months, Tony traveled extensively. Connie lost track of his schedule, denied the pain of his spontaneous interruptions, and progressively knew less of his whereabouts. She covered to her sisters, explaining that his tech skills were sending him out of town. Sam concurred; since he was such a capable technician, it made sense that he would be requested outside New York City. Few questions were asked.

She continued to date Tony for several months. One night they were at the Times Square McDonald's conversing with a tourist family from Tokyo.

"Yes," said the thick-accented, enthusiastic Japanese father, "we just go to South Street Seaport and garment district. Ver-r-r-ry wonderful!"

The young daughter crowed, "I bought a toy fish at the South Street Seaport that says 'New York City' on the fins. I show you."

Tony and Connie smiled to each other as the child excitedly dove into her bag.

"See. Big green fish."

"Wow," responded Tony, "may I see your toy? You are now an American angler. This sure is a swell specimen of a mackerel," he said, feigning interest to further delight the happy girl. "Where will you put it?"

"Above her bed," chimed in the keen older brother. "Not mine."

"And next we go to Central Park to build an American snowman," the child stated.

Connie asked, "Is that right?"

"But we must figure out how to get there," added the father. "Could you give us directions to Central Park, please? I know is nearby."

"Sure. You're right nearby," responded Tony, still holding the large rubber fish. "Just go straight up Broadway until you reach 59th Street and then..."

He dropped the child's toy on the table. She scrambled to retrieve it, almost spilling her Coke. Tony jerkily stood up, knocking over his French fries and gazed, wide-eyed, at the entrance.

For a moment he just stood there, staring. All momentum and friendly banter between the two tables came to a halt. Still staring at the door, Tony reached into his wallet, pulled out a twenty and handed it to Connie.

"Take a cab home," he quietly said, eyes glued to the door, and walked out.

"What just happen?" asked the tourist mother, concerned. "You boyfriend sick maybe?"

"Yes...yes," said Connie, staring after him and feeling a slow nausea igniting in her stomach. "He has been rather ill all week. I...um...I had better leave. So nice meeting you."

The Japanese father and son stood up as Connie gathered her belongings.

"Very nice talking to you," said the confused father.

Connie found herself bowing to the unsuspecting family, and then she smiled apologetically and hurried out. When she got to the street, she saw Tony one block away, bolting into a cab. It sailed up Seventh Avenue.

Connie did not hear from him for weeks. At her job, which she normally loved, she found herself being easily distracted and short-tempered. On the weekends, she'd stay at her parents' house for their everloving nurturing. She explained Tony's absence to them with variations on a theme of "he is in such high demand."

REDFLAG
#2-6

She realized she was more than mildly enamored with this man and was decidedly concerned about what the

105

future held. She related these disjointed and agonizing incidents to nobody.

One afternoon, during a patch of extended calm, they decided to attend a film lecture at Carnegie Hall. Connie, standing outside one of the entrances on 57th Street amid a crowd of animated film devotees, was excitedly anticipating the event. Unexpectedly, Tony grabbed her shoulder, sharply looked her in the eye and abruptly stated, "You are not to go to this lecture, do you understand? Call this number at noon."

REDFLAG #2-7

He handed her a piece of paper and quickly left the crowd, and his bewildered girlfriend.

She was baffled and frightened, but decided she'd better follow the directive. Connie collected herself, walked across the street to a coffee shop, found a table and sat down. She was immobilized. What was going on here? She thought it would be safer to call from a pay phone than her cellular. Listening to her intuition, she walked outside, found a pay phone and dialed the number.

A man answered. "I am Osvaldo. You must be Connie."

She gasped.

"Don't worry, lady, you're safe. Listen, these are the instructions from the big boss."

106

"Instructions? What? Do I need to write anything down?"

"No," Osvaldo replied. "Just listen. Too much is going on here, Connie. People aren't following directions." He laughed. "Not to worry. Tony Piccolini's safe and he will call you, but these are the instructions."

Connie felt her face go ashen, but steeled herself. "Go ahead. What instructions?"

"Do not try to call Tony anymore. Do not go to his house, or his parents' house. Do not expect to hear from him for at least a month."

"What?"

"You got that?"

"Why?"

"Jail and then some. Got it?" Osvaldo said.

"What?"

"And off the record, little lady, I'm not sure you want to be connected to him after all this."

"Who are you?"

"Look it up. England, Sicily, New York City. Bank fraud by computer hackers."

"What?"

"Any questions, Connie?"

"N-n-no. No."

"I have to get off now. Take care of yourself." He slammed the phone down.

She hung up the stinging phone and noticed a crosstown bus approaching. She boarded, not sure where it was headed. Ninth Avenue? Hudson River? As it pulled away, this third Maria saw the laughing revelers enter their safe Carnegie Hall.

It would have been a great lecture. It all might have been..., she thought, as she craned her neck to catch the final glimpse of a sweetly anticipated event, and watched majestic Carnegie Hall vanish into the exciting, energetic, now out-of-control Manhattan skyline.

Six weeks later an NBC position opened up on the West Coast which was offered to Maria Consuela. She packed a particular turquoise and lime scarf in her suitcase and flew out to occupy the new position in Los Angeles; exciting, escapist, cure-all? Day of Judgement? No sisters, big sunshine, out-of-control, vulnerable.

DISCUSSION OF THE CHAPTER

RED FLAG #2-1

I'd almost call this red flag a pink flag. Why? Because it is deeply subtle, without any kind of precedent. To be fixed up by a family friend, whom you trust, almost engenders passivity. One feels less of a need to seek out inconsistencies in this arena. It is not really a red flag, more of a warning. But no matter how we are introduced to someone, we must always go in with our antennas working.

The only red flag amid this pink flag is that brother-in-law Sam, as well-meaning as he was, knew Tony Piccolini from only one encounter. Maybe they talked for a while after Tony got the computer system back in order. How well can you know someone from such a brief meeting? A red flag amid a pink flag. Always keep your antennas working.

Yes, I know it is difficult and even unnatural to be on AMBER Alert in a safe environment. But just a drop of this awareness can augment growth and help reduce the possibility of future destruction. That's all we can do: augment growth in small increments. And in time, it is true, the antennas do expand.

RED FLAG #2-2

Another subtle red flag. If it is a first date and there is a group of people, after everyone is comfortable and some time has passed, the couple should attend to each other more than the group.

It seems as though Connie was shy or insecure in this setting. She did not get a good sense of Tony because she did not ask him enough questions. We also see that Tony was quiet because he was evaluating the Garcias. Could he continue to run his double life in this family? How soon would they be on to him? Et cetera.

In Greek mythology, there is a goddess named Hesychia who is the goddess of quiet. But there is a difference between Hesychia's quiet (being still until everyone is comfortable) and Tony's quiet (assessing to see where you can control). The way to combat this, readers, is through the mildly assertive position of asking questions.

RED FLAG #2-3

In an earlier encounter, after Connie and Tony left an Off-Broadway show, they went to a hotel lobby and talked for an extended period of time by the fire. Connie said Tony spoke much of his work; mostly, that his going into computers was a natural progression. What he didn't talk about was his other "work."

Here, finally, we have a blaring and glaring red flag. Nothing subtle or pink about this interaction.

Notice who walked over to whom after the frightening encounter with the two thugs by the subway. Apparently, Tony just stood there. Connie got up from the pavement, dusted herself off, and ran over to take care of him. The passivity of Tony's behavior was part mob-mentality (show nothing/tell nothing) and part manipulative male.

Now, here's an interesting wrinkle, readers. Connie was more interested in consoling Tony than in being sincere. If she were to have acted sincerely, she would have hurled a barrage of questions at him before she even rose from the pavement. Instead, she nullified all her instincts and her needs.

One of the problems here is that a covert setup is starting to take form. If the downdater

111

could voice this covert dynamic, she would say, "You do whatever you want. And do not worry, because I will work to make sure you get your needs met. We don't have to talk about it. I'll take care of you."

RED FLAG #2-4

Connie chose not to mention the assault for a few months. What? I ask, I scream. What?!

There is a concept in psychology that has come into very common usage—the concept of denial. "Denial" has already been addressed in Chapter One's red flags. In Freudian psychology, it is a defense mechanism. In the twelve-step programs, it is a disrespected behavior of those still addicted. Anna Freud, Freud's daughter and an honored psychologist in her own right, said, "Utilizing denial on a regular basis is immature. People must face life."

At some point, the only way for downdaters to maintain the connection is to go into as much denial of the facts as possible. When does this constitute lying?

Whatever it does, one can be sure of two elements here: the downdater will not get her needs met, and taking care of him starts to become a preoccupation.

RED FLAG #2-5

Of course, again Connie protected him. She should not have worked with him, as he implied. She should have confronted him and led him into the living room with the others to get her answer. But downdaters protect the downdatee, over and over and over.

Do you see how differently the afternoon would have gone had she confronted him? She would have saved herself months of grief.

RED FLAG #2-6

It didn't really matter what the future held for Connie. The present was an emotional hurricane. Her denial system was the prime mover here. That she told nobody about the incidents was another way to cement this denial. Where did this isolation get her? More upset.

One of the behaviors all downdaters exhibit is abnegation of the self. "I don't matter. What does matter is my giving enough so he will be OK." In psychology, we might refer to that as banishment of the ego.

RED FLAG #2-7

Come on, readers, this isn't an organic chemistry exam. If you are on a date for the first time, or with an established boyfriend, and he suddenly turns to you and tells you something as cryptic as "You are not going into this lecture; call this number at noon," you must stop him in his tracks and get specifics. Toe to toe. Eye to eye. "I'm not leaving this venue. What is going on?"

But at that juncture, there was so much water under the bridge in the form of denial, Connie felt she had to go along with the rest of the deluge.

One other note regarding this particular downdatee ("is a convicted or non-convicted career criminal or recidivist"). The word criminal is a legal term, not a psychological term. In the legal community, criminal is defined as: "done with malicious intent with a disposition to injure persons or property." A recidivist is defined as: "a second-time offender or habitual criminal."

We cannot say Tony had initially malicious intent toward the unsuspecting Connie. Nonetheless, figuratively speaking, one could not argue for a moment that Connie's feelings were not being "criminally considered." Criminality itself would have to be established in a court of law. Criminal consideration of feelings does not.

Connie had to know at this point she was dating a career criminal, and at best that she might have been headed toward a *camare*—becoming a career criminal's wife.

One wonders at what point people gain clarity, for we cannot predict what the straw shall be that finally breaks the dromedary's back.

What we do discern in this case is that she was never safe in Tony's presence. That concept alone, standing by itself—not being safe in Tony's presence—without the fluff of the particulars, defines this downdatee. And unfortunately for Maria Consuela, not much more need be said.

CHAPTER THREE

ILLUSTRATING DOWNDATEE #3 –

Has a Highly Addictive Personality, Yet Denounces Any Twelve-Step or Therapeutic Support

Entitled...

TO CALL UPON MY GOD

Los Angeles wavered between a semi-tropical furnace and a semi-tropical heat wave. Pick one.

I walked to the ladies' room in my professional building and splashed water on my clammy face and neck. It dripped all over my little cotton blouse, but, truth be told, I welcomed the momentary diversion from the 107 degrees. Even the air conditioner churned in struggle mode. Don't fail me now!

I would have to apologize to the new patient in the waiting room for my now wet outerwear. I begrudgingly dried the cooling droplets from my forehead, exited the ladies' room, and headed to the waiting area.

Thanks to her oblivious preoccupation with a magazine, Rachel Steinberg, my new patient, did not see me approaching. I was really grateful because I did not want her to see the look of surprise on my face when I laid eyes on her.

There I stood in a damp sleeveless blouse; there she sat in an ankle-length skirt, buttoned-up blouse with long sleeves, and a conservative hat. I waited a beat to collect myself and approached the sort of out-of-place and definitely over-dressed female.

"Rachel?"

She put down the magazine.

"I'm Carole Field."

"Oh, hello," she said, standing and extending her hand.

I liked her immediately.

I said, "Sorry to meet you in a wet blouse."

She laughed and said, "It's blazing out there."

"Please come into my office."

I noticed there wasn't a bead of sweat or a belabored inhalation to be found. I would've believed it if she had said, instead, "It's blazing out there for everyone but me."

Rachel was a tall, slightly heavy-set woman with shoulder-length black curls, light skin, and laughing blue eyes. I was amazed to learn she had just turned fifty. I would have pegged her as ten years younger. She said she had been married at twenty-five, widowed at thirty, and was an Orthodox Jew.

"That's why the clothes in the hundred and seven degrees," she laughed. She wasn't making excuses for her Orthodoxy, merely explaining, as she had done thousands of times before. She added, "Do you know Orthodox women have to wear sleeves below their elbows and skirts four inches below the knee?"

"I didn't know that, Rachel."

"Yes," she said, "and it is dictated by our *Poskim*."

"Poskim?" I asked.

"Yes, our rabbinical legal authorities. Did you know, once a girl turns nine, she must dress accordingly from there on in?"

"No."

"And collarbones must be covered and weaves of cloth must be simple."

"Why?" I asked.

"To remind us to remain humble and modest in every situation."

"I see."

She opened her purse and took out her wallet. "Before I go any further," she said, "may I show you my twin boys' pictures?"

"I'd love to see them, Rachel."

At that, she pulled out two photos of extremely cute, African-American-looking brothers in baseball attire. I looked up at her.

"I don't understand," I said. "They look African-American...and they don't have your blue eyes." We laughed.

"They are my Philip and Jacob. They came out of Operation Solomon. In 1991,

123

thousands of poor Ethiopian Jews were airlifted by, and into, Israel. They were saved from poverty and oppression and put into homes and absorption centers. Their mother gave birth a week after she landed in Israel. She was nineteen years old, had no husband, was now an immigrant, and was in desperate need. My best friend in Israel is a fabulous Palestinian woman named Alena. She is very connected. Through Alena and the proper sources, I flew to Tel Aviv and adopted these babies. That was sixteen years ago. The rest is history. They are my soul."

"That is an amazing story, Rachel."

"My boys and I always joke that their offspring will have my blue eyes."

"That's very funny. But Rachel, you are widowed? At thirty, did you say?"

She looked down. "Yes, that was before Philip and Jacob. In my community, they still arrange marriages. After I received my master's degree from Tel Aviv University and moved back to the United States, my uncle set me up with his friend. The man was twice my age. There was never a bond. He had a fatal heart attack. But that is not why I'm here, Carole. That's not it at all."

First, Rachel methodically removed her hat and slowly sat back on the couch. Her personality had been friendly and welcoming; now she was suddenly subdued and internal.

Then, she looked to the right, past me, and gave off an appearance of inaccessibility. I just watched her and preferred not to interrupt. She was clearly connecting to another time, not this place.

Philip and Jacob wanted to attend a conservative, or non-Orthodox, synagogue service that Saturday. So their mother, Rachel Steinberg, acquiesced and decided to attend beautiful nearby Valley Beth Shalom for a change of pace.

They were standing by the after-services kiddish table furnished with wine, juice, challah bread, and prettily cut vegetables when one of the elderly congregants approached them. The trio was used to the fact that the color of Philip and Jacob's skin attracted much attention.

"How do you do? Are you people new to the temple?" asked the friendly female congregant.

"Oh, hello," said Rachel. "We're the Steinbergs. We're just jumping ship for this Saturday. We usually go to Orthodox observances, but my sons wanted a change of pace."

125

"How lovely. How old are your boys?"

Philip said, "We're fourteen and a half, but I'm two minutes older than him."

"Fourteen and a half?" asked the friendly woman. "Well, well, well, my granddaughters are thirteen and they're here today. Would you like to meet my twins?" The boys' eyes lit up. The woman winked at Rachel and led the boys by the hand across the banquet hall.

Rachel laughed, delighted at the cordiality of this sweet older woman, and reached for a cup of grape juice.

"So you don't go to this temple, either?" said a male voice.

"What?" she asked, turning to see who was behind her. She saw a man about her age and height setting down a wine cup and picking up another.

"Hi, there. I'm not a congregant, either. My name is Rob Deniston."

"Rachel Steinberg."

"So what brings you here, Rachel?"

"We live a few blocks away and my boys wanted a non-Orthodox service this morning. We're Orthodox, but I do encourage their general exploration," she said, sipping her juice. "I commonly take them to church services also. We tend to really like Unitarian. What about you, Rob?"

126

"Oh, I live in West Los Angeles, but this synagogue has such a great reputation I thought I'd check it out. I'm half Jewish. Mom, yes; Dad, Catholic. We had no religion in our house. I wasn't baptized or bar mitzvah'd. All of a sudden, for some unexplainable reason, I'm getting serious about my roots. I've been exploring. I'm thinking of following the Jewish side, but I want to find which one and where."

"I give you much credit, Mr. Deniston. Say, next Friday night the boys are having some friends over to Sabbath dinner. Their friends are not Jewish, but they want to see a traditional Sabbath dinner. Why don't you join us? It would be our pleasure to have you, too."

RED FLAG #3-1

"That's so generous of you, Rachel. Would you be so kind as to write your phone number here?" he said, pulling out a small pad and a pen.

"No, I won't write my phone number down because we cannot write on the Sabbath. Writing is considered work. A day of rest is mandatory in Orthodoxy. But I'll recite it and you can write all you want."

On Rachel's and the boys' walk back home, she wasn't quite sure why her step

127

was a bit lighter and her voice was appreciably sillier.

The dining room table was covered by a white lace-braided tablecloth with blue ribbon borders. On top of it sat glowing blue candles and blue chinaware. The white roses in the center of the table came from Rachel's garden and sat there, in a blue china vase, looking proud.

Everyone remarked how the scent of the cinnamon chicken and carrot casserole filled the air. The lights were low and the conversation flowed. Philip and Jacob's friends were curious about the rituals, as was Rob Deniston.

"But why do we still need the Sabbath?" asked one of Philip's friends.

"Put it this way, Timmy," Rachel began. "Some people say, 'People keep the Sabbath,' but others say 'The Sabbath keeps people.'"

"That's really wise," Rob chimed in. "May I take another glass of wine?"

"Please, help yourself," she responded.

"Mr. Deniston," said Jacob with concern, "That's your third glass of wine and those are tall glasses. Will you be able to drive home?"

Rob stopped for a moment and looked at the concerned fourteen-year-old twin. "Of course. How kind of you. I require barrels of liquor to get me drunk," he laughed.

After dinner, Rob asked Rachel if she'd like to go for a walk. "So what do you do, Rachel, when you're not making fabulous dinners?"

"Believe it or not, I own a high-end bicycle shop. Odd, for an Orthodox Jewish woman," she laughed.

"Somewhat, yes," he nodded. "What type of bikes?"

"Treks, Cannondales, Serottas, and LeCorsas. The best. I love it. I bought it ten years ago and it is quite successful. And my manager takes over on Friday nights and Saturdays so I can observe the Shabbat and have special time with my boys. I have a master's degree in biblical archeology, so that's a natural progression. We all open bicycle shops," she sarcastically remarked.

They both laughed. "And your boys? They're so dear."

"It says in the Talmud," began Rachel, "whoever brings an orphan into her home is regarded as though the child had been born to her."

He looked at her and smiled.

"And you, Rob? What occupies your days?"

"Oh, I'm a workaholic stockbroker. I have my own firm in Santa Monica. I also jog, play with photography, and I guess I'm looking for my religious identity these days."

"Those are good things. So, any luck with the latter?"

"Yes. I've been to one church and three synagogues. I like Valley Beth Shalom, where I met you, best."

"Would you like to accompany us to an Orthodox service sometime, in view of your present pursuits?"

"Don't the men and women have to sit apart?" he asked.

"Yes, there is a partition."

"I'm not sure, Rachel, that I could be in the same room as you for two hours and not sit near you," he earnestly remarked.

She looked up at him and slowly averted her eyes. There was an awkward silence.

He broke it. "Why don't we go back to your house and cut into that beautiful watermelon I brought you? I think the boys and their friends would like that." She looked up at him again. For a moment, their eyes locked. When they walked back in the house, Rob sauntered to his wine glass and poured a fourth.

RED FLAG #3-2

130

Then he said, "Want me to get the boys for the ceremonial cutting of the watermelon? Certainly, there's some tradition or prayer over this fabulous pink beast."

Rachel replied, "Hey, don't laugh. That is my area of study, and would you believe there really were watermelons in the Nile Valley in the year two B.C.?"

Together they laughed again.

Just then, Jacob ambled into the kitchen. He eyed Rob holding the large glass of wine, filled to its brim. Rachel and Rob's laughter immediately died.

Rob placed the glass on the counter with the other untouched glasses, turned his back to it, and immediately started cutting the watermelon.

Rachel observed the silent communiqué between the two, but busied herself in searching out the perfect platter for the casserole leftovers. When the perfect platter was found, she remarked, "Look, guys. This was my grandma's serving dish in Russia. Isn't it beautiful?"

The two males in the kitchen nodded their heads, but continued to stare at each other. Eye combat.

RED FLAG
#3-3

"So, Rachel, darling, I have to ask, what brings you here today?" Rabbi Feingold asked Rachel.

131

Rachel adored Rabbi Feingold. Although he was Orthodox and operated traditionally, she felt she could confide in him more than her closest friends, her parents, or her brother and sister. He commonly looked at all angles of an issue and was admirably unbiased in his perspective and feedback.

She had asked his advice on adopting the boys, on buying the house, and even on purchasing the bicycle shop. It was one of those "ask the rabbi" times again.

Rabbi Feingold stereotypically looked like an eighteenth-century, Eastern European community leader. He was covered in the traditional black robe and sported a beard of which any man would be proud. He sat back in his overstuffed chair amid a paneled but humble office and squinted his eyes at Rachel.

"Rabbi," Rachel began nervously. "Rabbi, I have met a man."

"A man?" He lifted his heavily bearded chin in inquiry.

"He's a beautiful man, Rabbi Feingold. We've been on many dates. He's wonderful to the boys. This has been going on for four months, so I thought I'd better talk to you. You see, my kind friend, I am unsure. I mean…I am not sure about him. He's not Orthodox. In fact, only his mother is Jewish, and there was no Jewish upbringing. Unfortunately, he had no religious upbringing whatsoever. He's not met my parents. Do you begin to see the picture?"

Rabbi Feingold leaned back in his chair and stroked his beard. There was a long pause. Rachel just looked at him. Then he said in a monotone, "Did you know King Solomon loved the daughter of the Pharaoh? Rachel, I have known you and your family for years. They are ultra-Orthodox. You are moderate Orthodox. Would you like to know where I stand?"

"Please," she responded, wide-eyed.

"It is no longer the era of excommunication when someone dates out of religion or of religious sub-categories. I've known you for years. You are the best mother. You lost a mate far too young. Rachel, Rachel..." He leaned forward in a most non-rabbinic posture and said, or rather, demanded, "Fall in love."

A slow smile crept across Rachel's face. She put her hand to her heart and clutched her blouse.

"And now, my darling, I have real business to which I must attend. Do you understand me, young lady?"

"As my boys would say, Rabbi, you rock." They both laughed.

RED FLAG
#3-4

As she was leaving the building, she did have one remaining, haunting thought. *Oh, but I'm making too much of this one. It's probably nothing. What's a couple of drinks?*

She tucked away the thought, gleefully basking in Rabbi Feingold's "demand."

Knock, knock. Pause. *Knock, knock, knock.* Pause. On the third knocking attempt, Rob's door opened by itself.

"Oh, sweetie, it's me. Sorry, your door was open. Rob? Rob, are you here? It's Rachel."

Rachel walked into Rob's foyer and living room. "Sweetie, I'm here. Are you here?"

She looked in the kitchen. No Rob. "I'd better go upstairs. Rob! I'm coming upstairs."

Then she heard a sound. She wasn't sure where the sound was coming from, but walked toward Rob's bedroom.

"Rob?"

She entered Rob's room. The blinds were closed, emitting only one ray of sunlight that perfectly dissected his room. Rob was lying on the floor, running his finger back and forth across the ray of light on the rug. He began to laugh.

"Oh, Rachel. Come see our daystar on my carpet." And he began to laugh uncontrollably.

"What's going on here?" She moved quickly to him. Then she smelled it and saw it. Next to him was a half-consumed bottle of Stolichnaya, with the other half seemingly emanating from his breath.

"What's going on here? Rob? Are you OK? What are you doing?"

He tried to stand up, but fell down. "I sure like your hat," he said to her, laughing. She began to help him up. He fluctuated from feeling like dead weight to actively resisting her. She abandoned the notion and decided to sit down next to him.

"Just what are you doing, Rob?"

"Nothing, just taking a Sunday afternoon break from the cruel world. And, hey...look at this sun streak. It perfectly bisects my sleeping quarters."

She picked up the vodka bottle, paper cup, and pillow from the floor. "How long have you been drinking today?"

"Oh, I don't know. Maybe I started at two o'clock when I was bored. What time is it?"

"It's seven. We're supposed to go to the movies. I bought the tickets. What are you doing? I've never seen you like this."

RED FLAG
#3-5

"I have. Oh boy, I have," he laughed.

"Rob, are you an alcoholic?"

"I resent that," he said, lying on the floor. "And I would like to go to sleep for the night right now. Where did my pillow go?"

"Why are you doing this?"

But he closed his eyes, did not hear her words, and looked serious about his evening plans. Rachel brought the bottle downstairs to the kitchen, poured out the remainder and threw it out. She leaned against the counter and put her face in her hands. She took a deep breath. Small tears welled up in her eyes. Then she went back upstairs.

Rob had retrieved the pillow and was snoring on the floor. She stood and looked down at him. The sun streak had almost totally disappeared at this point.

She pulled the blanket off the bed and covered him. He was unaware of her protective behavior, ensconced in a dream, or perhaps just some banal, slovenly stupor.

Rachel slowly walked downstairs. As she approached the front door, she pulled out the movie ticket envelope which read: "Make your night happy! Come to the movies!" There was a yellow smiley face on the cover. She very slowly ripped it into little

136

pieces and scattered them all over Rob's living room floor.

"Excuse me, Mrs. Steinberg," said Elliott, Rachel's store manager. "Someone out front wishes to see you."

"Is it about the Trek bike in the window?"

"Er, no."

Rachel ambled to the front of the store and stopped in her tracks when she saw Rob. He had never visited her store unannounced. They stared at each other.

"Come into my office, Rob."

She shut the door and he pulled her to him. "I am sorry about last night. I didn't go to work today."

She didn't say anything, but pulled away and sat behind her desk. "Sit down, Rob."

He did so and looked at the floor. Then he said, "So now you know. It doesn't get in the way of my work, normally. I keep it compartmentalized. I went to rehab once. I don't need it. Was I bad last night? I found the torn-up movie tickets this morning."

RED FLAG
#3-6

"Do you remember me being there?" she said, somewhat mistrusting any response at this juncture.

He shook his head.

**RED FLAG
#3-7**

"Rob, I have a lot of book work to do. I also have to think. Are you still taking the three of us to the Dodger game Thursday night?"

"Of course, of course, sweetheart," he assured her. "Should I leave and just see you then?"

She looked down and nodded.

Rob, who looked like he was feeling a notch happier, left the bicycle shop.

It was an exciting game. Top of the seventh inning, bases loaded, and there was a tie. Philip and Jacob were keeping score on an erasable scoreboard, Rachel was drinking a Seven-Up and Rob was on his fourth beer. She tried not to notice and said nothing. She also tried to keep her feelings of anger at him under wraps for the boys' sake.

**RED FLAG
#3-8**

Rob went back to the food stands and purchased a fifth beer, and asked for it in the Un-Cola cup. The boys did not notice. They were too busy keeping score and making predictions.

Rob sat down with his new beer. Rachel didn't say anything, just stared at him. When the boys were definitely engaged in the plays, she took the cup out of his hand

138

and whispered in his ear, "We want to get home safely."

Then, she carefully poured the brew on the ground. As Rob watched it trickle down the sloping stadium, she noticed he looked sad, as though the spillage of his alcohol proved the death of some sentimental, precious memento. The remainder of the evening he was subdued, even when the Dodgers won.

The boys were taking a nap that Saturday afternoon after synagogue. Rachel was reading when the doorbell rang.

"Rob, what a pleasant surprise. I thought you weren't coming over till tonight. Well," she continued, "I'm glad to see you. Maybe you can fix the screen door..." Her voice trailed off. He was reeking of alcohol. "Wait a second, Rob. Let the boys nap. Let's go outside," she said, with the true intent of not wanting the boys to discover yet another bout.

RED FLAG
#3-9

"Guess what, darling," he said with slurred speech. "We got a really huge account yesterday. Want to know the particulars?"

"Yes, of course."

"Two millionaire families, cousins, want us to invest for them."

"That's astounding. *Mazel tov.*"

139

"Ow," he said, reclining on the chaise lounge. "Do you have any coffee, darling?"

She went inside to make him some coffee. When she came back out, he was fast asleep on the chaise lounge, in the sunlight, in the middle of the day. She stood there, holding the coffee cup, thinking to herself, *How can I help him? I really care for him. How can I help this man?*

RED FLAG #3-10

Just then, Jacob came to the kitchen window. Rachel didn't notice his observing Rob sleeping on the lounge chair. Jacob just looked down, shook his head in disbelief, and then quickly left the kitchen so his mom wouldn't realize that he had seen.

RED FLAG #3-11

Rachel detected a slightly pungent smell coming from the bathroom. She noticed she had left the light pink nail polish open on the counter. As she picked up the top to close it, she had a thought. *I would like to take this nail polish and paint a scene on the mirror before me. I would paint a very large house, maybe even a community. The lights would be on. There would be constant music and everyone would be happy. Everyone would be happy.*

She slowly replaced the polish top as Philip walked into the room. "Mommy, excuse me…er…Rabbi Feingold just called.

140

He would like to see you in his office this week."

"Oh, really, honey? Sure, I see."

She put the polish away and looked back at the mirror. There was no happily-lit, music-laden community in it, just a lady who needed a haircut—and maybe some other things. She went to the phone and dialed the rabbi.

In Rabbi Feingold's study, Rachel opened with a joke.

"So, Rabbi, you are calling me in for my advice for once, right?"

He laughed his fatherly, guttural guffaw. "Of course, Rachel. The greatest learning I do is from my congregants."

As his ancestors in Eastern Europe had done, he picked up a glass of tea—not a cup—and took a sip. Then, he looked into the distance and took a long pause. Rachel knew not to interrupt these pauses. She wasn't sure of their content, but knew they produced lush and fertile results.

"Rachel, darling, did you know that I met Gandhi at an interfaith?"

"Yes. Yes, I did know that, in fact."

"And that every sermon I constructed after that, for months, was based on our meeting?"

141

"How powerful, Rabbi."

"He has a famous quote, darling. Well, many, but this one must be relayed to you right now. He said simply, 'Hate the sin, not the sinner.'" She looked away. "But let me say this, too. Anais Nin, the author, said, 'The only abnormality is the inability to love.'" He looked at her. "This is a hard one, Rachel."

Rachel looked down and said, "Rob and I had so many great weeks together, and then..."

"What does he say when you talk about it?"

"We," she began, and hesitated. "We don't. I've not brought it up."

"Can't? Won't?"

RED FLAG
#3-12

"Probably won't. I don't want to hurt him. He's so good to the boys...and the way he looks at me."

"You have a choice, Rachel."

She looked up at him. His eyes were intense. It was the proverbial father, plus ten, about to speak.

"These are your options: Choice number one—you go to Al Anon meetings and send him immediately to therapy and Alcoholics Anonymous, or..."

Her attention was rapt.

"Choice number two—never see him again."

"What?" It was a knee-jerk response. "I could never do that."

142

"Which one? If there is one you could never do, do the other. I gave you a choice. Surely you can do one of those two."

She looked around the room, put her hands to her mouth, then began to twirl her hair and explain. "The only entity I've ever turned to in strife has been God. I'm not sure how to access any other intermediaries."

RED FLAG
#3-13

Rabbi Feingold sat back in his chair and stroked his beard. He waited a few moments, and then said, "Can I overload you with yet another quote, dear? The famous evangelist, Billy Graham, said something you might be able to use about now. He said, 'Millions of angels are in God's command.'"

Rachel faintly smiled and nodded. "Yes," she said. "By the way, Rabbi, how did you know to call me in? Certainly the community is not whispering about me."

"No, no. But I will tell you how I am privy to this information. Two of my congregants are young gentlemen of Ethiopian extraction. I have known them since babyhood and have always deemed them to be curiously wise."

A month had passed. There were no "incidents," but Rachel always anticipated the other shoe to drop. She so enjoyed being with Rob, but she was never quite at ease, always looking over her shoulder. Then, one afternoon as she was closing the shop, the phone rang.

"Mrs. Steinberg, please."

"This is she, but the shop is closed. Would you be so kind as to call back tomorrow after eight a.m.?"

"Um, ma'am, I'm calling from Cedars Sinai Hospital emergency room."

"What?"

"My name is Barbara. I'm one of the attending nurses in the ER. Do not worry. Everything is under control. But your boyfriend, a Robert Deniston, wanted me to call you."

"Is he OK?"

"He is OK. Apparently, he didn't go to work today, and I believe his secretary has a set of his house keys. From what I understand, she, luckily, decided to see if he was at home...in trouble...something. And, well, they brought him in about seven hours ago. He's sitting on the bed, talking, now."

"I'll be there as soon as I can. Thank you," Rachel said, hanging up the phone and trying to calm her pounding heart.

"And so," said Rob, sitting on top of his hospital bed, "my secretary found me. I'm so sorry to have put her, you all, through this."

Just then, one of the nurses walked in. "Mr. Deniston," she said, reading from a chart, "we do have to keep you one night until the tests are conclusive. We have to see if there's calcification from the abdominal x-rays and wait for the endoscopy results. Also, we have to be sure the effects are alcohol-related and nothing else. OK? So, stay comfortable and the doctor will be in later."

"A lot of tests, Rob." Rachel grabbed Rob's hand. She wanted to talk about it, but it didn't feel like the time or place. After all, they were holding hands and looking at each other like they usually did.

RED FLAG
#3-14

She handed him some more water and was smoothing his bed sheets when he said, "But you know, Rachel, this is all so odd."

"What do you mean, darling?"

"I don't really have a problem. I just have to drink a little less."

RED FLAG
#3-15

At that, she straightened her back from smoothing the bed sheets. One sheet corner was sticking up.

"You what?" she asked, not sure she had heard him correctly.

"I don't really have a problem, I just have to make a few alterations in my behavior— little alterations. No big deal. What's a

145

couple of blackouts? A couple of car problems? But right now, I really should call my office to get the stats on that new account..."

Rachel took a step back and just stared at him. She heard the people talking in the hall and the noisy clattering of carts, but she didn't hear him. Suddenly, everything Rob was saying had turned inaudible, like a TV set on mute—lips moving, no content. She watched his lips move, she heard less.

A nurse walked in to check some of Rob's vital signs. For a moment, the nurse shattered the screaming deafness. Crackling cacophony. Sound. But when Rob spoke, Rachel's hearing, or the TV, or something, clicked off again.

Millions of angels are at God's command.

Rachel thanked the nurse, collected her purse and sweater, kissed Rob, and slowly backed out the doorway. The last thing she heard Rob say was, "I'm telling you, this has been so awful. When I leave here, I might take up smoking..."

She inched into the long, brightly lit hallway and quietly strode to the elevator. The closer she got to the elevator, the more her heretofore perfect hearing returned.

Very ealy the next morning, the boys kissed Rachel good-bye and left for baseball practice. She returned to her bed, sat on top of it and pulled up her knees. The shades were drawn and the room was still dark. She scanned the room and looked down at her bed.

"And I thought this might be my future marriage bed."

Her discussions with Rabbi Feingold started to flood her. The quote by the writer, Anais Nin, came to her: "The only abnormality is the inability to love."

"But," she asked, "mustn't we love ourselves first? I am not truly sure how to do that. But I am sure of how to call upon my God. I do know how to call upon my God to lead me there. He or she shall light my path. He or she always does."

Rachel's eyes started to well up with tears. She reached for the phone and called her best friend across the world, Alena, the beautiful Palestinian woman.

When the conversation, and her tears, stopped a little—just a little—she leaned against her headboard, so grateful for

147

Alena, and said, "Millions of angels are at God's command."

Rachel Steinberg then picked up the phone again and stared at the lit numbers in the still-darkened room. This time there was no hesitation, no delay. A route, perhaps, to self-love. And—she dialed me.

DISCUSSION OF THE CHAPTER

RED FLAG #3-1

Rachel is a generous, giving person. However, she had little experience with the dating circuit. Even though there were going to be four teenage boys at her house for Sabbath dinner, it is never good protocol to invite a man to dinner, with such little knowledge of him, for a first date. I believe Rachel liked Rob immediately, but was not really aware of her feelings. She hadn't dated enough to be discerning.

Unfortunately, inviting a man to dinner after knowing him ten minutes might send a message that she is possibly indiscreet, overly trusting, flaky, or even male-hungry. Dysfunctional men thrive on this type of information. That was the rub. Well-functioning men receive this as it was intended: basically a kind gesture. Dysfunctional men, however, consciously or unconsciously pick up the vibe that she might be an easy mark.

It is with regret when I say that kindness is commonly misunderstood as scot-free weakness, wantonness, or fresh-baked material by downdatees.

149

Truly, their world lens is crooked. So this is my solution: continue to be kind and giving, but be watchful. And having a man to dinner after chatting for ten minutes would not be in the category of watchful.

RED FLAG #3-2

We are not sure if Rachel saw the fourth cup being poured. Apparently, she was busy in the kitchen and, at that point, had little knowledge of Rob's habits. Generally speaking, if one has a guest to dinner who drinks four glasses of wine— tall ones—it is fine to point out the "elephant in the living room." Lightly asking, "Hey, what's with four glasses of wine in one hour?" is all you have to say. Guests will either laughingly push the glass away and agree they've had enough, speak of their high tolerance level, or deny something about the behavior. Those really would be the natural response options.

It is important to know that most people are legally drunk after one and a half glasses. Of course, body weight and gender have to be taken into account, but for the most part, four drinks equal a 2 percent blood alcohol con- centration and that is legally drunk. It has been proven that two and a half drinks impair most people's judgment—despite their protestations.

Of this red flag, one last subcategory should be addressed. If a date is interested in anyone or anything else as much as he is interested in you (in this case, alcohol), this might be something to talk about in the future. Reason being, good manners usually preempts this type of behavior.

RED FLAG #3-3

OK, now we're really observing some specific behaviors. Young Jacob saw Rob with a fourth glass. Rachel saw them nonverbally communicating. At this point, she could not really express the kernel of what she was starting to feel. This was because of two reasons. One, she was not sure what to say, and two, she chose not to rock any boats at this site.

My theory, readers, is: if you are feeling that something is uncomfortable, imbalanced, etc., and cannot quite formulate the exact words, give it a little time and see what evolves. Time and expression can make a tremendous difference.

The main thing is, don't let the expression of the discomfort pass. Letting it pass will only feed the bad behavior. People are not mind readers. We must express what is upsetting us.

151

RED FLAG #3-4

In the twelve-step programs, it is common knowledge that the significant other of the alcoholic avoids her feelings about his drinking. This avoidance is referred to as denial. That word again. And this leads us to a double-edged sword.

The downdater utilizes denial to keep her downdatee close. If he is also an alcoholic denouncing help, she will be employing a double dose of denial. So it becomes two downward behaviors in one dynamic. Lotta work, here.

Rachel strictly wanted to talk to Rabbi Feingold about the Orthodox/non-Orthodox question. The drinking issue did not seem to be a priority for her—yet. Timing here is crucial. If the alcoholism is discussed soon enough, maybe help can be sought. If it is not discussed until much later, all different types of dysfunctionality can occur.

RED FLAG #3-5

"Are you an alcoholic?" I am baffled. Why would anyone ask a clearly inebriated person if he is an alcoholic? Did she really expect a rational response to anything at that moment? Interestingly, in some ways, Rachel was asking the inebriated man to rescue her. Her subtext really was,

"Please tell me you don't have this awful problem I see before my very eyes. Tell me everything will be alright." This is regrettable, in that she was opening up to a man outside of her Orthodox community and she certainly didn't want it to be a grand error.

Again, I refer to downdatee #3: has a highly addictive personality and denounces any twelve-step or therapeutic support. In this case, both.

And here lies the problem. Right here. It is not just Rob's drinking. It is also his denunciation of support.

Much of the problem here lies in this man voluntarily checking out of reality—not just checking in to his inert glass of vodka.

RED FLAG #3-6

"I went to rehab once, I don't need it." Again, I refer to this downdatee category—has a highly addictive personality with denunciation of any twelve-step or therapeutic support. Case exemplified.

The healthy behavior at this point would have been for Rachel to have confronted Rob. What was once? One day? One interview with a chemical dependency professional? One three-month stay at a center? What was once?

Even if Rob's drinking problem was not that far gone, his attitude surely was. And that is what we are battling with in all downdating: bad, negative, and impoverished attitudes that lead to malignant hurtfulness.

RED FLAG #3-7

Everyone has paradigms, mental cubicles, that define or compartmentalize one's life into categories. However, the less flexible these paradigms, the less our needs get met, because there is too much energy used in keeping them airtight—keeping everything as we have conceived it in the past.

This is layered with problems because in order to grow, we must look to the outside world for new information.

In this case, when Rachel should have been cold to Rob, she asked him if he was good to go for the Dodgers' game. Why? Because her paradigm of "boyfriend" was too airtight to allow in new (correct?) information. Rachel's true feelings were of hurt and concern, not, "Hey, let's break out our favorite baseball caps and rally around the peanut vendor."

We all have to observe our airtight concepts, paradigms, and so on. Sometimes, this requires unexpected work.

RED FLAG #3-8

Let's just add a little dash of insult to the pot of injury. Rob was on a serious bender a few nights prior and he tops it off by indulging in a few beers.

To enhance the insult, Rachel pretends not to notice. Readers, pay attention to who does not get their needs met in this group. The boys are happily involved in their erasable scoreboards and knowledge of baseball statistics. Rob is involved in getting slowly drunk. And, Rachel is pretending she is comfortable with the entire scene.

So, who is there for Rachel? Nobody. At this point, not even Rachel. We must be our own emotional advocates.

RED FLAG #3-9

Rollo May, the famous American existential psychologist, coined a term—*folie a deux. Folie a deux* is defined as both parties in a relationship supporting each other's bad behaviors. And this never gets verbally addressed. It is an understood, ongoing folly.

Rachel and Rob are practicing *folie a deux*. The unexpressed rules are: 1) there is some dysfunctional behavior occurring, 2) nobody shall address it, and 3) keep it going.

Left to their own devices, *folie a deux* could be serious, criminal, even deadly. If it surrounds alcoholism, we can be reasonably sure someone is eventually going to be pretty beat up physically or emotionally.

RED FLAG #3-10

The word codependent has not really reached into professional diagnostic vernacular. In many ways, it is too bad it hasn't, because it encompasses such a large panoply of self-defeating behavior.

One definition for codependency (there are many) is overreaching well beyond one's emotional grasp. When Rachel says, "How can I help this man?" she really isn't utilizing her most efficient thinking tools. Alcoholism is way beyond everyone's grasp, unless he or she is a professional.

What she should have said, what would have been a more apt expression, might have been, "How can I start getting him help?" There is a slight but significant difference in the questioning.

We must all recognize where we take on too much when someone else isn't doing his share. It goes back to the depiction of downdatee #6, who has a highly addictive personality and denounces any twelve-step program or therapeutic support.

Why is it, then, that we feel a need to step in and do the mending? Before we even need to answer that, it is best to simply recognize the behavior and, without further analysis, just stop the overreach.

RED FLAG #3-11

Jacob was taking on the family messaging. He seemed upset by the display before him. Again, instead of pointing out the elephant in the middle of the living room, he buried his thoughts and feelings and left the kitchen. This was an indication of his taking on the family messaging: In this case, the message is, "We do not talk about the behavior or our feelings regarding Rob's alcoholism."

But there is a bigger, more significant message here. It is, "You, Jacob, don't matter enough to express your thoughts and feelings. Concealing Rob's alcoholism is more important." Ouch.

RED FLAG #3-12

Rachel has been dating Rob for a fair amount of time and has successfully learned his covert command: "I get to do what I want, but it may not be addressed by you or anyone."

157

In marriage therapy, it is a fact that the lower-functioning person in the couple, unfortunately, slants the relationship toward his lower-functioning behavior. This is certainly happening with Rachel and Rob.

It is the job of the therapist to rebalance that skewed interplay, and how that is done, initially, is by talking all about the dysfunctional behavior. No more secrets!

RED FLAG #3-13

Rachel confessed to never having consulted with a therapist, support group, etc., outside her religious orientation. I am not talking about divesting oneself of one's religious orientation; I'm talking about being flexible.

Rabbi Feingold gave Rachel two excellent choices. They were bottom-line choices and therapeutically sound. Her first response was a knee jerk of negation. He had to rope her back into reality and openness.

It may be a crude analogy, but just because we have never called the plumber, does it mean we should allow the bathtub to leak forever? It is never good to be overly attached to any modality or paradigm in life. The wise rabbi said it from an evangelical source; truly, "Millions of angels are at God's command."

(I do beg the pardon of all my Orthodox and fundamentalist readers. I know this is not your paradigm. But, I am a psychotherapist, not a priestess, and can only come from my paradigm.)

RED FLAG #3-14

The amount of chemical changes in the body one experiences from being in love, and even from touching, is daunting. The dopamine release has been linked to a cocaine high. The hormones oxytocin and vasopressin almost make people addicted to each other. So, when Rachel says they're holding hands and looking at each other like they usually do, she is existing within the powerful tornado of neurotransmitters and hormones.

Really, that is the only thing that could keep someone hooked to an alcoholic after all this downward momentum. Not rationale.

In view of this biochemical tornado, it becomes even more apparent that we must stay emphatically alert and not date down, so as to counteract this involuntary chemical onslaught.

RED FLAG #3-15

What a pluperfect finale to a downdating example. Here sits Rob on a hospital bed, probably after a serious blackout, proudly proclaiming, "I don't really have a problem."

What does he need to believe he has a serious condition? How much confirmation does anyone need?

I repeat what we are illustrating: has a highly addictive personality and denounces any twelve-step program or therapeutic support. Denounces? This impoverished soul, who thinks he doesn't have a problem, is not even close to denouncing.

Instead of being strong and confronting Rob, Rachel has a minor dissociative experience. She did not hear a word he was saying. She had to dissociate from his fractured reality because it weighed too heavy on her heart.

I do believe in that hospital room, she finally came in contact with the objective truth of his condition, and that dating down can be a staggering breach to our souls, whereby–even religion–waxes impotently in the midst of such excruciating disappointments.

CHAPTER FOUR

ILLUSTRATING DOWNDATEE #4 –

Has No Conscience About Bringing The Female's Body and/or Mind Directly Into an Illegal and Dangerous Lifestyle

Entitled...

DRUGS AND HUGS

"GIRLS GIRLS GIRLS – SEVEN NIGHTS A WEEK." From her new Toyota, Lynda noticed the lights making the S in SEVEN had burned out. She made a mental note to tell the management, because it looked like "EVEN" nights a week, and that could impact business, her income, and the attention she garnered at the club. None of those would be good.

She gathered her overstuffed changing bag and entered GIRLS GIRLS GIRLS through the back door. The place had never had a legitimate name, even though the place was pretty legitimate. She laughed to herself.

She was the first woman in the dressing room that night. She pulled out her makeup, costumes, shoes, and beloved pink blunt wig—the wig that gave Lynda Goldstone the name "Pinky" at the club.

She pinned her curly brown chin-length hair into a bun and began her nightly transformation. *Lots of blue eye shadow tonight,* she thought. Her right finger dove into the little azure blue Maybelline tub. Lynda's stature was short, skinny, and small-boned. Lots of color on top seemed to compensate for the sometime feelings of invisible body and invisible soul. And so she smeared yet more azure blue on her eyelids and brows,

167

with lots of accompanied self-talk at her dressing table tonight.

RED FLAG
#4-1

"So what'll it be, Pinky? School? Therapy? Gotta make some changes. Church? Books? Something. I must consider a change."

But for this night, she just couldn't get enough blue eye shadow.

"OK, there you go again," she said, leaning back in her chair. "Lately, I just seem to be adding more and more blue..."

"SANTA MONICA ADVERTISING" announced a large, splashy neon sign encircled by retro-psychedelic paint. In front of the sign sat the two receptionists at the ad agency, Keisha Wilkins and Lynda Goldstone. It was a busy agency but an easy, cushy job. Lynda liked it because she didn't have to think much. Nine to five.

"Thank you for calling Santa Monica Advertising, how may I direct your call?" Although the dress code was pretty strict, everything else was breezeville.

Lynda, age twenty-nine, adored Keisha, even though the girl was ten years her junior. Keisha was African-American and in her second year of night school at UCLA. She wanted to be a physical therapist. Lynda enjoyed hearing about her classes.

168

College was going to be on the horizon someday, thought Lynda. Someday she would start to create that.

"OK, Keisha, gotta go. It's five o'clock. I just joined LoveMatch.com and can't wait to check my computer."

"Girlfriend, you deserve something fine. You really did that? Just don't go for any old dude, Lynda. You hear?"

"Alright," laughed Lynda, tucking her headphones in the drawer. "Not sure I know how, but I'll try."

Lynda hung up her blue jean jacket and excitedly turned on the computer. Then she went to the second bedroom and knocked on the door. Heaven's music came at her in all different melodious directions. Her "third career," raising cockatiels, evidenced itself throughout the second bedroom.

Two cockatiels to a cage, ten cages perfectly catalogued and spotlessly put together. She purchased the birds from breeders at six weeks, hand-fed and nurtured them for two months, and sold them to the highest bidder. Lutinos, Cinnamons, and Pieds, all types. Although she made money in the endeavor, it was really a labor of love.

"Good evening, everyone," she sang to them. "Your second feeding will be a trifle delayed tonight. I'm looking for a date!" She changed their lighting to the evening lamps, put birds three and four on her shoulders and returned to her computer.

LoveMatch.com came up on the screen. She typed in the screen name "julietcapulet" and retrieved one message.

"Yay!" she excitedly said. "This might work!" She ran into the cockatiel's room. "Guess what, everyone? The cute guy wrote back!"

She put birds three and four back in their cage and removed five and six. They didn't seem to want to shoulder tonight, so she put them on the top of their cage to walk around. She then returned to her computer and read,

> Dear julietcapulet,
>
> Thank you for writing back to me. I've never used this dating site before, so hearing from you is just great. You live in North Hollywood. I live in Hollywood. We are both 29. We both work in Santa Monica. We both like jazz. We are both short. My real name is Jason Samski. My phone number is 555-7225.

Feel free to call me as soon as possible.

Until then, your new friend, Jason

She left the computer room, smiling, and opened the fridge. She was about to retrieve the cleaned carrots and broccoli for the birds' dinner, but decided to head to the phone instead. She thoughtfully brought the phone to the floor and dialed 555-7225. It rang eight times. Lynda was about to hang up when a man's voice interrupted the ring tone by saying, "Lady Capulet, is that you?"

The coffeehouse was packed for a Sunday morning. Lynda luckily nabbed a table in the corner. She didn't want to over-dress for a coffee date, so she wore jeans and sandals, but decided to wear her new pink baby doll blouse. As she was about to settle back in the booth, she looked up and saw in the doorway a short, skinny guy with thick brown hair in his face. He wore a well-laundered, tight white T-shirt which showed his lithe and muscular physique. The sun was in his eyes as he squinted and cased the coffeehouse for his computer date.

Then, from across the fairly large and active room, they spotted each other. For a moment, they froze. Lynda stood up to greet him. As he approached her, there suddenly seemed to be no coffee revelers, no homey fragrance of freshly brewed lattes. Jason hugged her to him. If possible, everything fell silent. They had never met before, never uttered a word in each other's ears, yet they stood there, locked in a long embrace. Lynda closed her eyes and sank into his innocent, but strong, and desperately needed welcome.

RED FLAG #4-2

"So," Jason said to her across the dinner table on their second date. "We did a lot of laughing and chuckling at Coffee Haven, but we learned little about each other. Do please tell me about Lynda Goldstone."

Lynda looked around the restaurant. The Daily Grill on Laurel Canyon was a trendy and energetic Studio City haunt. She was so happy to be there on a Saturday night, on a date, with this new guy she had spent all of yesterday yapping about to Keisha.

"No," she said, setting down her wine glass. "You go first."

"Well," Jason replied, "you know I'm a car mechanic. I'm from St. Louis and I love jazz music."

172

"Any college?" she asked.

"Just one unsuccessful year of junior college in St. Louis. Then I went to a two-year occupational school to be a car mechanic, but only stayed one year. Didn't get the certificate, but it didn't matter because I know an extraordinary amount about cars."

"Could you build me a 1955 Cadillac with fins?" she laughed.

"I'd love to."

The waiter delivered their salads and Jason continued, "I have two older brothers who are also mechanics. They are still in St. Louis. Do you have brothers or sister, Lynda?"

"I'm an only child. My mother's a pediatrician. She's sixty years old and still works six days a week—and is on call." She looked down. "Nobody ever knew who my dad was, or tried to find out. I was largely raised by my aunt and a slew of babysitters and maids. Mom was always working."

"Is that right?"

"Yeah, Mommy was so rarely home. And you want to hear something really odd, Jason?"

"Go ahead," he said with concern.

"Guess what my mom bought me for a graduation gift from high school?"

"Go ahead."

"A house in North Hollywood."

"What? At eighteen?"

"Yeah. She put a hefty down payment on a house, slapped it in my name and said, 'It's your new house. You make the payments.' So I moved into my own home at eighteen and got a job. The payments were really small, but I had to do it. That was eleven years ago. And I never went to college."

"Didn't your mom want you to? I mean, being a physician and all."

"My mother is a wonderful woman, but she is not an attentive mother. Never was. She doesn't really approve of the fact that I've been a receptionist at an ad agency since high school, but has never led me in any other directions. It's odd. Mother is from a long line of physicians, but thinks as long as she buys me a new Toyota every year and I pay my house payments, my life is perfect."

"That's odd, Lynda. You are right."

"Oh," she began, "one other thing. I have another kind of career."

"Oh?"

"Yes. I raise cockatiels." Discussion of her third form of income was off-limits.

"I'd like to hear about that sometime, Lynda. I have another career, too."

"Oh?" she asked.

"Yeah," he smiled. "I deal drugs."

Digging into their romaine lettuce, they both laughed.

RED FLAG
#4-3

"And now, ladies and gentleman, Pinky!"

The lights are so bright tonight, thought Lynda, as she stepped onto the stage in her four-inch acrylic heels. *Lots of catcalls and whistles. Must be a full house. Let the lights help you in not seeing the audience and think about...what? What should I think about tonight? The new Laundromat on Riverside Drive that just opened. That's it, the Laundromat.* She stood in place and waited to hear her opening number, a Mary J. Blige song.

Ready, set, Laundromat.

"Lynda," said Jason, edging back into his seat in the bleachers, "I just put sixty-six dollars on Flicka Joe to win for us."

"Why sixty-six, sweetheart?"

He took her hand. "Because we have been dating for six weeks and six days."

She smiled. "Really?"

"Listen, remember I told you I had to meet someone here at the track? Take my betting ticket and finish my beer. I didn't know it was this late. I'll be back in twenty minutes. Are you ok?"

RED FLAG
#4-4

175

"Sure, go ahead." Lynda did think it was odd that he had a meeting at the racetrack. She watched Jason exit the bleachers and turned her attention back to the track. She could see the horses being saddled and the jockeys mounting in the paddock. She closely watched as the horses obediently entered their stalls at the starting gate.

"And they're off!" was announced with the starting bell.

Lynda jumped up and down, spilling Jason's beer all over the floor when Flicka Joe won. She ran to the betting ticket window and claimed $660 for Jason. When she returned to the bleachers, Jason had returned with a black briefcase.

She excitedly said, "Sweetheart! Sweetheart, you won! Look at this! Good call! Look! Here's six hundred and sixty smackers."

"I heard I won! What a trip," he smiled. "So cool! No, no, you keep it!"

"What do you mean? It's your money."

"No, it's OK. Good business goings-on. Keep it, Lynda, keep it."

"That's a lot of dough, big guy."

He put his arm around her. "I'm fine, Lynda. Get yourself some mad hubcaps for the Toyota and I'll put them on."

"Sweetheart, with six hundred and sixty dollars, I'm not going to spend it on my car."

"Just do me one favor," he said. "Come with me to Kevin's Halloween party next weekend. That's all I ask of you."

Then they heard, "And they're off!" Jason focused on the horses. Lynda shook her head in disbelief and moved the chipped, black leather briefcase that was between them over to the side to hug him very tightly.

Fred Flintstone pulled Wilma into the bathroom in Kevin's house. Lynda loved the fun and silly costumes she had bought for the party, down to the bones in their hair. She enjoyed darkening Jason's eyebrows and penciling him a five o'clock shadow that all good cavemen should possess.

"What, sweetheart? Why are we in here?" Just then, there was a knock at the bathroom door. It was Kevin.

"Hi, Fred and Wilma," he said, locking the door behind him and admiring his Dracula neck blood. "Looks real, huh?"

"Yes," said Lynda, wondering why they were locked in the bathroom.

"OK," said bloody Dracula, as he dropped to his knees and opened one of the cupboards.

Jason started to laugh and said, "Go, Dracula, my good friend."

"And blood sucker," added Kevin, pulling out a large plastic bag.

"The ice man cometh," said Jason, helping Kevin with a glass pipe, some white powder, and a box of matches. "Load up, Dracula. I need a hit, and so does Wilma here."

"What is that?" asked Lynda/Wilma.

"What is what, my love?" laughed Jason. "Ice, baby. You mean, you never fumed out over the ice, baby?" he asked, heating the bottom of the pipe.

"Are those drugs?" asked Lynda.

"She really doesn't know, Samski?" asked Kevin.

"I guess not. Wait, let me hit," Jason said, inhaling from the pipe. "Whoa, rush city, yes."

"My turn!" exclaimed Kevin. Grabbing the pipe, he inhaled. "Goddess! Great shit! Here," he said, handing the pipe back to Jason.

Jason handed the pipe to Lynda. "Suck, girlfriend!"

"I...I...I've never done any drugs. Just a little alcohol at parties, but—"

RED FLAG
#4-5

"Will you just try it, Lynda? Come on over to the other side of my life. There is nothing wrong with a little weekend fun."

178

"Go on, Wilma," said Kevin. "Take a walk on the wild side. It won't kill you."

"Just inhale! It's only methamphetamine. Do it!" pressed Jason, as he placed the glass pipe to her lips.

She looked at him and at Kevin, and put her lips around the pipe.

"Just inhale!" instructed Jason. "You might grow to love it." The two boys laughed. "This is good shit, Kevin. It might even make me clean your house. Ha! Go ahead, Lynda. It's your turn."

Lynda opened her eyes wide and inhaled from the tube between her lips.

"Now exhale, girl," instructed Kevin. "And give me some more." He pulled the pipe to him.

Lynda exclaimed, "Oh my god, what was that? Ouch. Shit! That's awful. Ow, give me some water! My throat hurts!"

"First-time user, for sure," said Jason. "Don't worry, you'll get into it. Go ahead, Dracula, my man. Suck!"

The boys laughed at the rank newcomer's response and Jason took another hit. "Yes," he said, jumping up and down. "Now this is a real Halloween party."

"Like the man said, Wilma, don't worry, you'll get used to it. Now, shall we join my party?" Kevin opened the door to loud music, flashing black lights, and colorful costumes, and faded into the crowd.

"Like it, baby?" asked Jason.

"It hurt my throat. And I'm a little jittery right now."

"That's about right. You wondered why I had such a clean house. Wow, this is good shit! Yabba dabba doo!" He grabbed her hand and pulled her on the dance floor. Lynda could not fall asleep until four a.m. that particular Halloween.

Lynda, morphing into Pinky, sat at her dressing table with bright red lip gloss in one hand and a letter from the club's management in the other. The letter read,

> "Dear waitresses, security, exotic performers, and cleaning crew,
>
> This is just a reminder to help keep our club on the map and doing as well as it does. Please never, ever come to work even mildly drunk or stoned. Also, if any drugs or alcohol are carried inside, they will be confiscated and you will be fired on the spot. Let's all keep a fine reputation as a legal and friendly atmosphere.

Thank you for your attention. Have a great Thanksgiving holiday.
Most sincerely,
The Management

Lynda, almost Pinky, looked around the room after reading the letter. Most of the other girls had just put it in their purses and carried on with their nightly transformations. Pinky slowly applied her lip gloss.

How odd and coincidental, she thought. *It's as though the club knew I've smoked meth with Jason five times after never having touched drugs in my life.*

She brushed her pink wig one more time and surveyed the dressing room to see if anyone was having the same response as she. Obviously not. She folded the letter and stuck it in her purse.

What's a little drugs? she thought. *I've never done them and it's not like I'm going to get hooked. And I get to share this for a while as I get to know Jason.*

RED FLAG
#4-6

She stood up and straightened the seams of her nylons as she heard the stage manager announce, "OK, Pinky. Sell it, sister! You're on!"

181

"Hi, perfect angel! Hi, baby!" She greeted the cockatiels. "Cage cleaning time! How are my babies?"

They sang their on-key and off-key sonatas to her. They were fluttering around and excitedly greeting the day as she opened the blinds and lowered the room heater. Today, she took out birds nine and ten, kissed them and played with them before she cleaned their cages, and doled out the morning rice, eggs, and apples. Then she took her own shower and left the house.

"Let's see," she said in the car. "Ah, here it is. Yes. South Vermont Avenue." She slowly walked up to the unsightly building and knocked on the door.

"Yes?" a man's voice said from behind the door.

"Uh, um, I am Jason's friend."

"Please go back to the sidewalk."

"Excuse me?"

"Go back to the sidewalk," repeated the man in sotto voce.

Lynda ambled back to the walkway. She saw a man's hand place a brown vinyl carrying case on the porch and disappear behind a half-closed door.

"Ma'am, thanks. Tell him he can pay me this week. Bye." And then he slammed the door.

Lynda picked up the case and returned to her car. There, she texted Jason, "I'm on Vermont Avenue. Did your favor for you, sweetheart. Can't you guys use nicer carrying cases? Adoringly, Lynda." She fluffed her brown curls, straightened her collar beneath the button-down cardigan, and prepared a shift in her demeanor for a day at the advertising agency.

"The switchboard is crazy this morning, Lynda. Thank you for calling Santa Monica Advertising Agency. How may I direct your call?"

"Sorry I'm a little late, Keisha. I had to do a favor for Jason."

"And while you're at it, you received three personal calls on the switchboard. Here, this one is a cockatiel customer."

"Oh, great, Keisha."

"And these just came in and—oh, by the way, I got an A on the anatomy paper, girl!"

Lynda high-fived Keisha. "And you didn't even need my mom's help."

"Speaking of your mom, she's one of the messages. She said Thanksgiving dinner will commence at six p.m. And the other one was from your new guy. It's an odd message, Lynda. He just called a second ago."

"What did he say?" she asked, trying to read Keisha's handwriting.

"He said," replied Keisha, "keep the stuff covered in the car. See you tonight."

"Oh," said Lynda.

Keisha stared at her. "Like what stuff, Lynda?"

"Um, I bought some groceries for Mom's Thanksgiving. Just to keep it fresh," Lynda said, turning away and scooping out her headset and writing materials.

Keisha looked at her with narrowed eyes, a furrowed brow, and a bewildered question mark on her forehead.

"Lynda, would you mind helping me in the kitchen with the dessert? There are twenty-five of us and I need a hand."

"Of course, Mom."

"Oh, and Doctor Goldstone," said Jason to Lynda's mom, "this is a great Thanksgiving. Thank you for having me."

Dr. Goldstone nodded to Jason and quickly scrutinized her daughter's boyfriend. She emitted a smile, but at half-mast of what she normally smiled. *Not sure of this boy yet*, she thought.

The caterers, Juan and Paolo, were already cutting up the four pies when Lynda and her mom reentered the kitchen.

"Oh, great! Thank you, guys. OK, we also have an apple cake that Aunt Rosie baked, and some vanilla frozen yogurt. Oh, Lynda, would you mind cutting and scooping the watermelon and honeydews? Here's the melon baller."

Lynda took the scooping utensil and started to laugh. "Whoa, this looks like a meth pipe. Ha. Like yo, a heating chamber and a tube. Are you sure this is for watermelon?" she laughed, and began cutting.

Dr. Goldstone stopped, looked at her daughter, and asked Lynda one of the few things she knew how to ask. "Do you have enough money, dear?"

"Sure, Mom, I'm about to sell a few more cockatiels and Jason just won me hundreds of dollars at the track." She neglected to tell her that customer tips at the club tripled around the holidays. "And, Mom, my mortgage is so low, thanks to you. I'm great."

"Well," her mother responded, leaning against the counter and watching her daughter cut and scoop. "Um, just go get fifty bucks out of my purse before you leave. A little holiday money. OK?"

The young, hip Mexican caterer, Jose, grabbed Paolo's arm. They shared a look and shook their heads. Lynda saw and Lynda scooped.

185

The room fell silent.

RED FLAG
#4-7

Lynda, Jason, and Kevin traveled in Kevin's car to the tattered building on South Vermont Avenue. "You gotta meet him face-to-face, Lyn. Then he'll let you help us much more," Jason stoutly announced.

"Uh, yeah," reassured Kevin. "We physical education teachers just don't make the bulky wallets, dude. Maybe I'll get a paper route. Ha! Man, if we keep bringing in all this filthy lucre, I might even be able to add a second bathroom to my casa. Right, bro?"

He and Jason slapped hands. "Yeah," said Jason. "We just need a trusty third. Good going, Lynda. This will help a lot."

"Yeah," replied Kevin.

Lynda glanced at Jason. Although his long brown hair was in his eyes, she observed him intently staring out the window. *He is so cute*, she thought. *Not handsome, but sexy and cute.* She took his hand and he kissed hers. Lynda really cared for this guy and all the attention he poured upon her. Since dating Jason, she even felt she needed less attention from the audience at the club, for some reason.

RED FLAG
#4-8

They pulled up to the building she had visited a few weeks prior.

186

"See, you gotta know this, baby. Meth is cooked. Cocaine is from a plant. So we need great cookers to continue our great buyer response. This guy, Korny, as we all call him, is one hot cooker. He just knows how to deliver the proper whatevers. We just need some more people to run. That's where you come in, sugar."

Lynda looked at him. She just wanted to be by his side.

"Babe. Babe," said Lynda on her cell phone. "Hey, are we gonna party tonight?"

He whispered back, "The shop manager is standing right by me. Just a second, sweetheart. Let me go inside the office. OK, listen, can you do Kevin and me a favor as soon as you get off work? We have to get some ice elsewhere."

"What, Jason?"

"Can you drive to Sylmar for us? It's a little rough there, but we need it soon. Are you comfortable? Big cook up there."

"Do you really need it?"

"Really, yes. Kevin and I have to go to San Diego and the other runners aren't available."

"But will I see you later?" she asked.

"Only if you do us this favor," he joked. "Of course you will. We'll give you a hundred bucks."

She thought about wanting to upgrade the heater in the cockatiels' room, and the new acrylic heels she needed for the club. "Um, well...I'll see. I don't want to take any money from you."

"No, you have to take it. Here's the address, Lynda."

"Will I at least see you tonight?"

"Now, for sure," he laughed.

It was really a back house; probably once a nice guest house in Sylmar. The time was seven p.m. on this brisk, windy December night. There were no street lamps aglow on this tucked-away side street.

What a perfect setting for a Freddy and Jason movie, she thought, laughing at the pun. She zipped up her coat and knocked on the door.

A woman opened the door and asked her to come inside. There was only a couch in the living room and one lamp.

"I'm Helene. How do you do?"

"I'm Lynda," she eked out, trying to be cordial.

"Come meet Korny." Helene led Lynda into the kitchen to see a man at the stove with odd paraphernalia around him. He did not look up at Lynda.

"You're Samski's runner? He's a good salesman," said Korny, doing his work.

"Would you like a cup of tea?" asked Helene, a rather passive and spent-looking woman.

"Oh, no, thank you very much. Just gotta get the stash and take off. Perhaps some other time." Then Korny looked up at her. From further away, Korny looked to be in his late forties, but up close he looked more like thirty. She thought, *Did the drugs do this to him? How long must he have been hooked?*

"Just a second," he said, leaving the room.

"How long have you been running?" asked Helene, lighting a cigarette.

"Oh, I'm just helping them out. Nothing formal."

Helene observed her through the cigarette smoke. "You're not a tweeker?"

"No, I guess not."

"You a virgin methy?"

"No, I use."

"But you're new, ain't ya?"

"Uh, yes, kind of. Just started using this year."

Helene got up and opened a drawer.

She pulled out a photo. "That's me, eight years ago. I was pretty. Fatter."

"You look beautiful in the photo, Helene. You still look pretty."

Helene looked in the doorway to see if Korny was coming back in. "Ever hooked on anything before?"

"Uh, no," answered Lynda.

"Grass? Junk? Squizzle?"

"Er, no."

"You are new at this shit, right?"

"Yes," replied Lynda, not sure what she was getting at.

"You seem like a very nice woman, Lynda. A little lost, but very nice. Listen to me," she said, again looking back at the doorway. "Quit while you're ahead. I'm not sure if Samski is your guy or not, but it don't matter. Believe it or not, I was Miss Orange County in 1990. I had two thriving nail salons and a beautiful condo. Please, please—" Then she was cut off as Korny walked in the room.

"OK, Lynda, right?" asked Korny.

"Uh, yes," said Lynda, looking back and forth between the two. She felt like she wanted to hear Helene's story, but knew it was verboten with Korny in the room. Helene's eyes looked pleading and drained.

"OK," he said, "this shit's gotta be delivered to Jason and Kevin tonight. The other bag goes to an address in Van Nuys and the other downtown."

"What? All tonight?"

"Uh, yeah. Maybe they didn't tell you?"

Helene walked over to an old breadbox and picked up the false bottom. Lynda saw greenbacks galore in there. "Here," said Helene, handing her a twenty-dollar bill. "Just take this for gas. You didn't know about all this driving. And you're paying our rent many times over tonight. But drive safely, and watch it at the Van Nuys address. He didn't tell you?"

"Tell me what?"

"Never mind. You'll be OK."

"Wow," said Korny. "You must really be into Samski or something. Wow."

"You'd better get going, sweetheart." Helene walked Lynda outside, stamping her cigarette out in the street. "Somebody buy you the new Toyota?"

"Uh, my mom."

"Yeah, you are between two or three worlds," Helene laughed. She noticed Korny looking out the window at them. "I'd better go inside, Miss Lynda. Remember my words. You wanna know one of the things I got to do as Miss Orange County?"

"Yes, of course."

"I got to go to schools and lecture against drug addiction. That was my platform in the contest. Who knew?" she said, looking into the cold black sky.

"Helene? Helene!" yelled Korny through the half-open door. "It would be a good idea to get back in here, dear."

Lynda slipped into her car and looked at the paper that had the address of where she suddenly had to drive. Lynda felt bad that the birds' evening feeding would be so delayed. She looked back at the house she'd just exited.

From behind the draperies stood Helene staring back at her. They smiled and waved to each other. Lynda felt her eyes well up slightly as she slowly departed from a self-imposed, iron-clad penitentiary.

"And now, ladies and gentlemen, a wonderful performer—for your pleasure—Pinky!!"

Pinky stepped onto the stage. She never bought the new acrylics. Instead, she used the hundred dollars toward a nicer Christmas gift for Keisha and a new air filter for the cockatiels.

It was a small crowd on this Sunday night. The lighting man surrounded her and the mauve lingerie-type costume in subdued pink lighting tonight. She took a deep breath. She was glad she couldn't really see the audience. She had chosen an Amy Winehouse song as her first number. Somebody told her the pole was too slippery tonight. She felt a little thinner than normal these days. Funny what she thought about tonight as she started her promenade down the runway. Helene.

"Girlfriend," said Keisha. "What the hell are you eating? Your birds' food? You are getting so skinny!"

"Oh," replied Lynda, "just holiday shopping and a little more exercising to the Pilates tapes at home."

"Oh, by the way, here. I stopped at Pierce College for you."

"You what?" asked Lynda.

"Yeah. I got you a course catalog and an application."

"You pumpkin."

"Wrong season, Lynda. Cherub would be more fitting. Fill it out, lady. Or do you really want to be here another eleven years?"

"No way. I'm not sure what's up, Keisha. It kind of depends on what happens with me and Jason. I'm sort of crazy about him and—"

RED FLAG #4-9

"What?!" shrieked Keisha, slapping down her Starbucks cup and spilling coffee on the desk. "What did you say?"

"Yeah," reiterated Lynda, "depends on what happens with us."

"You can't be serious. You're going to let someone else and the whimsicality of his life dictate your future—even if it is some muscular dude-guy?"

Lynda laughed. "Yeah, I guess I did say that. How do you know he's muscular? You've never met him."

"I don't know. Young car mechanic stereotype. Really, Lyn, just fill the thing out. Don't be led around by anyone—not Mr. Perfect, your mother, the Crowned Prince of Dubai, nobody."

"Now that you said that, Keisha, I'd have to admit, the only person who could possibly lead me around would be the Crowned Prince of Dubai. How did you know?"

"No, Lynda. Love those dudes, commit to those dudes, but leave your soul inside your body."

Lynda looked at Keisha. "Do you think I should call a shrink? I've never been."

Keisha nodded as Lynda's cell phone rang. It was a text from Jason: "Cannot see you tonight. Gotta do a run to Santa Clarita. Can you do a run for us? Kisses, Jason."

Lynda looked at Keisha answering the company phone line as she texted back to Jason: "Anything you need."

Jason lay back on Lynda's living room floor. "Crowned prince of Dubai...what?" he asked.

"I told my friend Keisha I'd only change my ways for one person in the world—the Crowned Prince of Dubai."

"Nobody? For nothing?" asked Jason, holding her.

"Not a soul on the planet," she said, kissing his cheek.

"Not even if someone has some excellent stash on them?"

"Uh, no, Jason. I gotta look at a cockatiel later and I don't wanna seem a little too electrified," she lied. She was really going to work at the club later, but still refused to tell anyone about her other job. Being stoned was against policy, so she declined.

Jason sat up. "I want to talk to you about something interesting, Lyn."

"Yeah?"

"Um, you know Kevin?"

"Yeah, what about him?"

"Well, um, you know he has really done a lot for me. We are making so much extra cash, it's unheard of. I might even do a little

195

long-distance jaunting for him, speaking of the Middle East. That was coincidental."

"That's intense, Jas."

He pulled away from her and walked to the window. "Cold night. Really cold December this year."

"Do you want me to light the fire, sweetheart?" she asked.

"No, no, I can't stay. Just a little thing."

She watched him staring out the window. "What, sweetheart?" she asked, lying on the floor.

"Um, he thinks you're really rad." Jason picked up the end of the drape and played with the tassel. She observed him intertwining the tassel between his fingers, but not really being in the room.

"What, big guy?"

"Um, he thinks you're a very sweet woman and, like, he thinks you have quite a rad little body."

"You're kidding!"

"No. He's done a lot for me. And you're having more fun partying and stuff. And so, like, he really wants to make it with you."

"What?" Lynda shrieked, sitting up.

"Yeah, like, specifically, he wanted to know what putting it to you would be like and I told him I'd ask you."

196

"What?"

"You deaf, my lady? I said, he thinks you're cute and cooperative and he'd like to have a night with just you and him. I told him I'd ask you."

"What are you talking about? What about us?"

RED FLAG
#4-10

"Nothing would change," he replied.

"Nothing would change?"

"No! We'd still be together, go out, party. You might do an occasional run. Nothing would change."

"Are you serious?" she angrily demanded.

"He's done a lot for me."

Lynda stood up, felt herself get a little queasy and turned her back to him. The room did a slight spin. "Um, you'd better leave. I gotta look at that cockatiel. Let's talk later," she said with her back to him.

"OK." He put his arm around her. "Good luck at your bird watching." He kissed her neck, hugged her from behind and approached the door. As he looked back, he noticed her back was still to him. He shrugged his shoulders. "Bye, ladybird," he said, letting himself out.

Keisha couldn't help but open Lynda's Christmas gift at the end of the day. It was

197

a red and black suede cropped sweater with a matching sash. "Lyn, I love it! I'm gonna wear it to Christmas."

"I'm so glad."

"All I could afford," said Keisha, "was a John Coltrane CD for you. But someday, when I'm a rich physical therapist, I will buy you ten in one fell swoop."

"Stop it, you. I wanted to learn more about classical jazz, since Jason likes it so much. That was very kind of you. But I gotta scramble. Jason and I are going to a Christmas party tonight. Can you do the last fifteen minutes without me?"

"What will the bosses think?" joked Keisha.

"Tell them I defected to open my own ad agency in direct competition with them."

"Have fun tonight, Lynda."

When Lynda arrived at Jason's house, she found Kevin on his couch.

"Oh, hi, Kevin. I didn't know you were going to be here," she said, realizing she hadn't acknowledged Jason's prior "request" for Kevin.

Jason gave her a hug and took out the smoking paraphernalia. "Anyone want to pre-party?" he asked, lighting up.

"Sure," responded Kevin.

"Not sure," said Lynda.

"Why?" asked Jason "You gotta. We all three have to be on the same vibe." He laughed. "Here, my lady. Use your aerodynamic lungs and suck."

She looked at him. She was not really in the mood for this tonight and was somewhat taken aback that Kevin was with them.

"Go," Jason said.

She put her lips on the glass tube and inhaled.

"Whoa," said Kevin after his inhalation. "Major crystal fire. I'm gonna get crank bugs just on this one toke," he laughed. "OK, to the party!"

Lynda and Kevin walked toward the door. The one puff had made her a little twitchy.

"OK, guys, have fun," said Jason.

"What do you mean?" asked Lynda.

"I had a killer day at the shop. Longer than usual. You two, you go ahead."

"OK," said Kevin.

"What?" asked Lynda. "You have to be with me tonight. It's a Christmas party and I left work early to be with you."

"Nah. I just wanna get high and try to do some bill payin'."

"Let's go," said Kevin to Lynda.

"No. I thought you were going to go. I thought you and I had a date."

"Not tonight, baby doll."

"Are you serious?" she disappointedly asked.

"Go!"

"Come on, Lynda. He'll see you another time," said Kevin.

"Please come, Jason. I can't be at a Christmas party without you," declared Lynda.

"Nah, I don't want to."

"Then can I just stay here with you tonight?" she asked.

RED FLAG
#4-11

"Hmm. Nah, I just wanna get sauced and be alone. No big deal, Lynda."

"But I want to be with you. Can't I just hang out with you tonight?"

Then Jason started to sing, "Chestnuts roasting on an open fire...," as he walked to the door and opened it. "Talk to you tomorrow. Have a great time. Jack Frost nipping at your nose."

"Please, Jas, please," she begged.

He kissed her on the cheek, turned his back and walked over to his pipe. "Have fun," he said, and waved back to them.

"Come on, dear," said Kevin, pulling her out of the house and closing the door.

Sounding adamant, he said, "Lynda, you gotta know this. When someone wants to get stoned alone, you gotta give them their space. It's important to them. It's not that he doesn't adore you. He just wants to be in his own space."

Lynda, in disbelief, walked to Kevin's car. "No, no. Wait. I'm gonna go home, Kevin. I'm pretty jittery. Gotta go home."

"You sure?"

"Yeah. Thanks, anyhow."

"You gonna do that little run for us tomorrow?"

"I don't know." She got in her car, slammed the door and drove two blocks. She pulled over and parked on Fountain Avenue and opened the window. She felt the brisk evening air on her face and decided to wait for her rush to subside a little. Then she called her mother.

"Mom, I'm so glad you're home."

"Hi, dear. I'm entertaining a lovely couple, a South African doctor and his wife. Where are you?"

"Mommy!" she wailed into the phone. "Mommy!"

"What? Lynda, where are you?"

"I'm in Hollywood. Can I come over?"

"Are you near Jason's?"

"Yes," she said, crying.

"I want you to get here immediately. Are you OK to drive?"

"Of course."

"Or do you want me to come and get you?"

"No," she said through her tears. "Mommy, I have a lot to tell you and to ask you and to yell at you and to love you. Can I come over?"

"I will ask my friends to leave. Come straight here. Do you understand?"

"We have a lot to talk about, Mommy," she said. "I'll be there soon."

She placed the phone on the seat next to her and noticed the community college catalogue. For a second, she stopped crying, picked up the catalogue and paged through it. She came upon a new curriculum called Veterinary Technological Assistant. Reading the specifics actually stopped her tears. She snapped the book closed and sighed heavily.

She decided she had an agenda tonight. It was a perfect night for this long-awaited agenda. She would show Mommy the catalogue, tell her about Jason, the drugs, and the third job, and ask for a referral to a psychotherapist. Finally, she had one more piece of the agenda, because continuing to be with men like Jason could be fatal. She saw the connection for a split second.

"What? Could that be snow in Southern California? No—just evening dew," Lynda said, entranced by the window sprinkles. Her last piece of the agenda became clear. If it took all night and if she had to greet the next sunrise, she was finally, after all these years, going to ask her mommy, "Why?"

DISCUSSION OF THE CHAPTER

RED FLAG #4-1

Is this a red flag or is it just an awareness enhancer? Or, are all the red flags awareness enhancers and this is a cousin? I will opt for the third choice. This has nothing to do with the man Lynda is going to meet— nothing to do with where he leads her. Nonetheless, it is a major reflection of Lynda, a stripper.

When Lynda came into my office, she said she had wanted to seek therapy for two years. How long do these promises go on? A day, a year, ten years? At what point do they scream so loudly that they have to be compartmentalized as guilt-producing annoyances? Or, at what point do the promises scream so loudly that the promisor finally listens?

This is just the beginning of Lynda's story. But we all have to ask ourselves, what type of character change is really necessary within all of us and why are we not making the change? If, in one sentence, we could say, "The reason I am not making this change is because...," we would learn a good deal about ourselves. What is your blank filler? What does it tell you about you? Our character here, Lynda, has a good amount to unearth. We learn more about her in the chapter.

However, one thing we do have to keep in mind is: how do we feel when we are at our dressing table applying eye shadow, promising ourselves something for the two-hundredth time, yet not even broaching the necessary actions for fulfilling the promise?

RED FLAG #4-2

I wish to address this "embrace." This embrace is both telling and emotional. Emotional because they immediately intuited each other's need for touch, and bravely proceeded. And telling for the following reasons: it has been proven that touch reduces blood pressure, lowers heart rate, and lessens cortisol (a hormone that is created during stress). Hugs also release endorphins in the brain. Endorphins are protein molecules that provide relief from pain, and also boost natural killer cells for attacking diseases. So, you can clearly see how hugs and touch are species' survival tools. Those of our cave brothers and sisters that utilized touch probably had a more successful survival rate. I do appreciate the naturalness of

Lynda and Jason's first encounter—a nonverbal embrace.

However, having said that, here's the red flag lurking in all of this: a prolonged nonverbal embrace unfortunately connotes too much premature or incorrect data. You can probably fill in the blanks on your own. Yes, it might connote: 1) Help! 2) I'm easy, 3) I'm indiscreet and need anything, and 4) I force intimacy and therefore might force boundaries, so be very afraid. Therefore, as much as it may seem brutally honest and supportive of species' survival, I would say on a first encounter, shake hands and make dandy eye contact. Unfortunately, that is the superior choice. Do not despair, for that will carry you quite a long distance.

RED FLAG #4-3

Does he? We all joke, goof on people, push our limits. But in an early dating relationship we must store all information like a squirrel stores chestnuts in November. Then, when the snow melts months later, the squirrel must analyze its stored goods. Either the chestnuts were consumed at the time or they weren't. But we must store at first. In fact, believe it or not, not doing that at all can render one flaky. While storing, never hurt anyone—particularly the squirrels.

RED FLAG #4-4

What? He had a clandestine appointment at the racetrack? Isn't the racetrack edgy enough? Talk about the daily double.

Lynda did admit thinking it was odd to meet someone at the track who couldn't even approach them. Frankly, I think it's somewhat rude that Jason left her alone at all. The red flag here is that his work, or his clandestine goings-on, or his self-centered activities, were put first—before Lynda, before his new relationship, before fully sharing an afternoon together. With such priorities, I would keep this as a bright red flag to address in the near future.

RED FLAG #4-5

This is absolutely dreadful. She just said she had never done drugs and rarely drinks. He did not say something like, "That's great. Keep up the good work. I did want to show you what I do so there will be no secrets between us," which would have been somewhat respectable. He glaringly presented himself as a downdatee #4: has no conscience about bringing your body or mind directly into an illegal lifestyle.

He does not think for a moment, "Hey, I really like this girl. Therefore it's my duty to keep her safe." Instead, his gargantuan self-centeredness, his addiction, and his immature need to party (if you call using drugs a party) prove far more important than Lynda's safety. In fact, if you look closely, she is suddenly no longer a girlfriend and sexual partner, but rather a buddy and a party animal with invisible or, at best, marginal status.

A definitive earmark of the addict, my dear readers, is that his drug high, drug jones, or bacchanalia is always more important than any relationship—unless, of course, the other person is also the supplier.

RED FLAG #4-6

Dangerous, dangerous, dangerous mind-set, Lynda. Nobody ever wakes up in the morning and proclaims, "Gee, I'd like to get addicted to drugs starting today." Unfortunately, one doesn't even need a genetic predisposition to become drug-addicted. Mere repetitive exposure can create an addiction in a previously disinterested individual. Also, one of the proven behaviors that create an addiction is having a best friend who is addicted. In this circumstance, Lynda really wanted Jason to be her best friend. Unfortunately, this best friend was an addicted, uncontrolled, reckless, locomotive.

209

For the record, the National Institute of Drug Abuse defines addiction as a repetitive behavior in the face of negative circumstances; the drive to continue something that is bad for you.

There is also some thought that women progress more quickly in drug and alcohol addiction because their dopamine levels (brain chemicals contributing to happiness) recede around their premenstrum. However, methamphetamine, cocaine, and alcohol slow this recession. The relief from premenstrual depression is so appreciated by some women that their body actually craves the drug to up-regulate their mood. This creates a vicious cycle of despair.

Also, in terms of alcoholism specifically, women get drunk easier and faster than men because they lack a stomach enzyme which prevents drunkenness.

So overall, Lynda's innocent pronouncements of "it's not like I'm going to get hooked" were really naïve, really disconnected, and unfortunately exposed how drugs have a will of their own, devoid of anyone's good intentions.

RED FLAG #4-7

NO PROTECTION HERE: perhaps, a logo for Jason's future T-shirts?

It is pretty obvious that he was fully intending to drop her into his uncharted existence. Did Lynda think Jason's getting her involved in his "business" was cool, fun, a fine entrepreneurial venture, or just another way to stay close to Jason? I would opt for the latter.

Whenever I observe anyone dating down in the form of seriously compromising ethics, I never see a happy ending.

Commonly, the way people couple at the beginning of a relationship (here, Jason and Lynda have been together about three months) is usually how they continue/end. The person in the relationship who is lower functioning, unfortunately, usually balances the scale toward himself—unless everyone is conscious. Meaning, if Jason had admitted he had a drug problem and didn't intend to pull her into his orbit, the tilt of activities would not have been in his direction. But here, the lower functioning of the two, Jason, actuated a full tilt directly toward him and his downward spiral.

RED FLAG #4-8

Was he really giving her honest attention, or was it somewhat phony attention because he needed another drug runner and she came across as lip-dribblingly absorbed in him?

Dating someone who needs you for an illegal act is patently dating down, no matter how you slice the pie. You are there for them, their base needs, and their out-of-control self-centeredness.

I ask: where are you, your needs, and your life in this three-ring circus? To reiterate an element from red flag #4-7: the person in the relationship who is lower functioning, unfortunately, usually balances the scale toward him—unless everyone is conscious, and trying to change.

RED FLAG #4-9

Ergo, is the nasty goblin of feelings. Although feelings are gut-based, they are darn incompetent predictors. We all have to be most cautious in this type of thinking; just because we have feelings for someone, it does not mean that very someone is going to be good for our higher self.

Lynda said, "It depends on what happens with me and Jason." Therefore, her life is on hold, based upon an unstable factor—Jason.

It was appropriate tough love that led Keisha to immediately confront Lynda. I think Keisha had an inkling the guy wasn't all that responsible. Dr. Goldstone, Lynda's mom, was instinctively onto him.

Let me backpedal a minute. I am not saying we should never make our lives contingent upon another. There are circumstances where one must, in fact. I am talking about making your life contingent upon a downdatee. That's the difference. And Lynda seriously needed to make some changes in her life.

Yes, her mom bought her a house and took care of her transportation needs, but Lynda was stuck and not growing. If not for her excellent orientation with the cockatiels, she would have had zero growth-producing outlets in the world. Such a stuck person usually has masked depression, confusion, and much unexpressed anger. To base that dysfunctional triplicate upon the lifestyle of an addict could be emotionally devastating. Thankfully, Keisha intervened.

Sorry she spilled her coffee.

RED FLAG #4-10

It has been said, "Drug addicts cannot or will not ultimately create attachments in a love relationship until they clean up from the drugs."

In the 1960s, a new school of thought in psychology began to emerge called Attachment Theory. One of the areas Attachment Theory studied was the different ways babies attach to their caregivers and how this attachment was duplicated in adulthood. In one style of attachment, the Avoidant style, babies seemed to

213

avoid their parents and pay more attention to their toys and other objects. This is not because the child is autistic, but rather because the caregiver tends to reject or minimize the baby's needs for closeness.

There seems to be a common thread between rejecting parents creating avoidant babies who morph into drug-addicted adults. What we take away from this is that the child can only relate to his "love interests" as his parents did to him. Therefore, when Jason callously pronounces something like "Kevin wants a night with you, but nothing between us will change," it seems commonplace to him. The bottom line is, men like this are in desperate need of help. This is not someone to date, readers. This is someone who needs to stop all momentum in his life and seek help.

I am open to the possibility that monogamy in certain couples is not the only viable lifestyle. However, this is not one of those exceptions to the rule. This is a form of (excuse the rough verbiage) being pimped out for the pleasure of someone else's gluttony. That is all Jason cared about: keeping Kevin happy so their "business" would continue to thrive (if the word "thrive" is applicable to any of these guys' behaviors).

RED FLAG #4-11

Just where is Lynda in Jason's life? Jason is more in love with his drug high than with her. Her feelings have little weight. The promise of their evening together is nowhere to be found and the togetherness of Christmas Present is immaterial for him. Is this anything but dating down?

I must refer back to the five constants in the introduction. Constant #1 was how the female endures unmet needs for months or even years. I'm not sure anyone would say Lynda's needs were being met by Jason. True, Lynda was not from the most nurturing of environments and so her "internal chooser" was a little handicapped. Therefore, she is someone who would have to be all the more careful. At this point in her life, she was drastically unaware of her handicap. The more challenged our family of origin, the greater must be our vigilance.

I would like to offer a light but applicable quote from Benjamin Franklin: "If Jack is in love, he is no judge of Jill's beauty." Applicably, if Lynda is in love with Jason, she is no judge of Jason's beauty—or mania.

My hope is that you now have a personally enhanced understanding of this treacherous downdatee: one who has no conscience about bringing your body and mind directly into an illegal lifestyle.

CHAPTER FIVE

ILLUSTRATING DOWNDATEE #5 –

Is From and Stays Connected to a Substantially Lower Class Than the Female

Entitled...

SHOOT THE CUPID, OR...

Thirty-three years old and slightly nervous, Jennifer McHale cautiously extended one foot out of her car. She immediately felt the stifling heat of the parking structure. The sweltering air stopped her for a second, putting a temporary halt to any nervousness. For some reason, a ninety-five-degree summer evening had a way of predominating over nervous energy.

Bright garage-type fluorescent lights beat down upon her left outstretched leg. The lights exposed a nyloned leg, extending down to a light peach-colored linen high-heeled shoe.

Jennifer thought, *Odd, how my shoes so perfectly match this skirt.* She twisted her leg back and forth, both admiring and criticizing the appendage. When she looked up, two men in the car next to her were smiling. One lowered the window and said, "You look great."

She laughed and blushed in the same response.

"Are you going to the singles' event on the plaza?"

"Yes," she responded.

"Well, we'll see you up there. I'm Ed and this is Armando."

"Jennifer."

They scurried out of their car and waved to her, leaving her alone for the last-minute tribal fixing of makeup.

Jennifer stepped out of the car and caught her reflection in its window. She approved of what she coordinated for the evening: light peach shoes and skirt, bright yellow lace-up camisole that really accentuated her tiny waist, and a bright orange Peruvian striped sash. She pulled out a brush and smoothed into place her short brown hair that still gleamed with the last remnants of a henna weave.

As she was placing the brush back in her purse, Jennifer noticed the evening's invitation. She pulled it out. It read,

> *Five churches of mixed denominations invite you to a Singles' Summer Fling on the courtyard of the Music Center/ Dorothy Chandler Pavilion. Five bands will be playing throughout the evening. $35. Dressy.*

She laughed to herself and tucked the invitation back in her purse.

Jen was discreet as to whom she had told about this event. Most of her friends were artists, fashion designers, or wardrobe coordinators at the TV studios, like she.

Fashion-forward semi-hipsters. Attending a church-created singles event called Shoot the Cupid was decidedly to be privileged information. Thinking of her clandestine discretion, she chuckled as her heels clicked against the concrete en route to the elevators.

On the front of the center elevator was a life-sized cardboard cupid wearing a crucifix. She walked in, throwing her head back in laughter, and rode to the courtyard level. When the doors opened, a man with a clipboard was there to greet her.

"Hello," he cheerfully said. "Welcome to Shoot the Cupid, an evening of dancing, food, and hundreds of religious singles just like you. And may I ask if you are prepaid?"

"Uh, yes," said Jennifer. "I am prepaid. And I see my name tag." She wanted to add that she wasn't religious, but decided to opt out of such intimate information so early in their relationship.

The man tore off her name tag from the master list, but looked befuddled as he tried to discern sufficient room for a name tag on such a skimpy camisole.

"Oh, here," Jennifer laughed. "Just place it on my right arm. A little creativity tonight."

"Ma'am," he continued, "take this ticket for the dance matchup event, and feel free to take a free necklace with either Cupid or Jesus as a memento to you from the five churches." Being a wardrobe coordinator at a major TV studio, she selected the cupid necklace and creatively threaded it through her sash.

"Clever," said the greeting man. "Now go in there, Miss McHale, and dance up a storm. But remember, Mr. Perfection is only a prayer away."

She smiled warmly at the efficient and well-meaning greeter and moved assiduously into the swarming courtyard of summerly-dressed hopefuls.

The Music Center housed three large theatres and the grand courtyard consisting of fountains and sculptures.

Jennifer walked over to one of the fountains and sat on a nearby chair. The water spewed up in a ninety-degree angle, and just as it reached its pinnacle, little rainbows of light seemed to twitter a language all their own. She smiled, trying to catch their gaiety. She noticed the dressed tables for sitting, talking, and eating on her right and the long buffet tables on her left. The large courtyard had taken on torches to light the night when the sun dipped. Overall, she thought the churches had done a wonderful job.

"I guess they mean business. Maybe everyone is here to 'shoot the cupid' tonight. Hi, guys. I'm just enjoying the fountain. Look what it does at its pinnacle. It rainbows. Have a seat."

It was Ed and Armando from the parking lot. "Nah," said Ed, scanning the crowd. "Armando and I are here to meet a couple of babes. We don't want to sit."

"I didn't know if you sat, you wouldn't meet babes. Good to know."

"Not that you're not a babe, Jessica," said Armando. "We just wanna meet...other kinds of babes."

"It's Jennifer. And I wish you luck tonight."

"Hey," said Ed, "one of the bands is playing some fifties' croony standards on the other side of the courtyard. Want to join us?"

"No, I couldn't handle two buff studpuppies with fifties' doo-wop. Too much excitement. I'm staying right here."

"Oh, got it. Well, good luck to you, Jessica," Ed said, joining in the moniker brain freeze. She watched them smooth their collars and walk off.

When they were in the distance and she had almost hypnotized herself back into the fountain, she noticed a man on her left who had been listening to her pithy conversation with Ed and Armando. He was snickering. She said to him, "Why are you laughing? The babes are all by the fifties' band."

"Not all," he said, pulling up a chair. "May I?"

"Please," she said, and gestured.

He said, "Those guys are great. What are the chances?"

"Slim to none," she laughed. "And where are you from?"

"Oh," he said, "my accent? I've only been here eight months or so. I guess I'm choosing not to lose it. I'm from outside of Birmingham, Alabama."

"I might have to strain for a few of your words, but I like that. It's a bit of a challenge. I guess understanding one's native language is not as second nature as we all thought."

"So, you're fascinated by the fountain."

She looked back at it. "Oh, very. How do fountains work?" she mused.

"Simple," he responded. "The heart of a fountain is both in the pump and in the electricity that forces the water out through the outflow fitting. It's simple. A few pressure valves, and voila."

"Uh, gee, thanks," she said. "I didn't really expect you to know that."

Just then, all the torches lit up and the courtyard illuminated the night.

"Oh, look. It's beautiful," she said.

"Probably the intense heat turned them all on. Didn't even need a master switch," he laughed.

"Is that possible?" she asked.

"No!"

They laughed.

"See? This heat is frying my brain. I live in the San Fernando Valley," she said. "It was ninety-nine degrees when I left my house."

"I love your outfit," he oddly countered.

"Excuse me?"

"What a beautiful combo of colors you assembled. And really, how'd you get the shoes to match the skirt?"

Jennifer looked at this man. She had gone from feeling like the not-flashy-enough babe with Ed and Armando to a remarkably coordinated lady in about twelve minutes.

"You noticed?"

"But it will be difficult for the rest of the evening," said the man, "because the sun is setting. So don't hold it against the other guys for not noticing." She threw her head back in laughter. "I guess my accent didn't bother you that time. You got everything I said."

227

"My name is Jennifer." She extended her hand.

"I can read your arm," he said, taking her hand and holding it.

"So, where's your name tag?" Jennifer asked.

"I didn't take one. I know the guys at one of the churches and they just let me in free. But my name is Jonathan Basil." He squeezed her hand, cupped it with the other and held it for three accepting beats. "Say," he continued, "it's obvious you are entranced by this fountain, but I'm getting really hungry. Would you like to accompany me to the buffet, Miss"—he leaned over to see her last name—"Miss McHale?"

"Pleasure. If I can continue to understand you through your drawl, maybe we can even eat together."

"That's a tall order, Miss McHale, but I'll try my best." He stood up, winked at her and assisted her out of the chair. The buffet lines were fairly long, but everyone was in friendly spirits and enjoyed bantering with each other.

"What line are we in?" asked Jennifer. "I think it's the hot food, but we can't be sure. It's too long."

"I don't really care," he said. "Whatever we pile on our plate is fine. I'm not on some

228

exclusive diet. Wait, yes I am. The Alaska diet."

"The Alaska diet?" she laughed.

"Yes, you eat anything to keep you warm, shy of snow."

"No blubber meat here, Jonathan."

"Oh, look, I see what looks like a chemistry class Bunsen burner," he said. "We are in the hot food line. Did you know, Jennifer, Bunsen burners have been around since the Civil War? It's true. There was a real inventor named Bunsen."

"How'd you know that?"

"All I know about in the universe is fountains and Bunsen burners."

When they approached the buffet table, he said, "May I serve you?" and made sure she was served first, before he took his dinner.

Jennifer and Jonathan had dinner and danced under the stars for hours. During the partner matchup event, they decided to hide behind the large Mark Taper Forum, laughing and conjuring up images of the frustration they were incurring upon their potential matches. After the dance matchup, they resumed their stance back in the crowd—holding hands.

At the end of the evening, Jonathan walked Jen to her car. Ed and Armando were just pulling out of their parking space.

"Well, Ed, did you meet any, you know, babes?" asked Jennifer.

"Nobody as babed-out as you, Jessica," said Ed. Then he said to Jonathan," Get her phone number, brother, and God be with you."

"And also with you," Jen and Jon chimed back as they all waved to each other.

"Where did you park, Jon?" she asked.

"I don't have a car and I live nearby."

She laughed at him, thinking it was preposterous not to have a vehicle in Los Angeles. Jon reached over, pulled off her name tag and stuck it on his hand. "Please write your phone number on here, m'lady," he requested. She pulled out a pen and accordingly scribed phone, cell phone, and email. He placed his arm on her back and slowly brought her to him. It was a warm and protective hug, appropriate for all intents and purposes, but too short. She hoped there would be more from where that came from. She was glad he had her contact information.

She drove off and he waved to her. *He knows so much about electrical things. He's probably an engineer who lives down here in one of those fabulous reconverted lofts. Maybe he even walks to work. Of course,*

230

he must have a car, she thought. *He's so funny.*

As Jennifer drove past the courtyard, she saw the final fountain blast of the evening. She was too far away to catch its rainbow twitter. Instead, she looked down at the grinning cupid enchained around her sash, patted his bald noggin, and joined him in rounds and rounds of laughter.

RED FLAG #5-1

Jennifer looked at Jonathan across the table. They were sitting on the floor, legs folded, drinking their after-dinner Japanese tea. Soft Japanese music played in the background and kimonoed women scampered around serving the diners.

"You know," Jon said, looking into his teacup, "it makes no sense."

"What doesn't, Jonathan?"

"Japanese tea is so prominent in Western culture. Yet, tea never did come from Japan. Tea is from China, India, and Sri Lanka."

"Is that so?"

"But aside from that," said Jon, "did you know that I can read tea leaves?"

"Would that you could."

"Give me your teacup, Jennifer." She chuckled and handed him her half-full cup of green tea.

231

"Well," he began, rubbing the cup, "first of all, the guy you are with tonight thinks you are pretty, sweet, kind, smart, and fun. But he knows you are not going to like what he's going to tell you."

She cocked her head to the right. He smiled, put the cup back on her plate and took her hands. Jennifer enjoyed the feel of this man's hands around hers.

"Listen, Jennifer, it's only fair that I tell you this. I'm having a great time with you and I want to continue seeing you, and I'm happy to take us to dinner tonight in Little Tokyo, being the first date and all, but you see..." He looked down and pulled away from her hands. "You see, after tonight, we'll have to go out Dutch—that is, if you continue to want to see me."

She looked perplexed. "Um, that's fine, Jonathan, but could you explain a little of this? I mean, I don't even know what you do for a living. I'd be happy to take care of my share, but you must admit this is a little odd."

He stood up, all six feet of him. She looked up at the tall man with straight brown hair as he walked to her side of the table and insinuated himself next to her. As he did so, she took stock of his attire. Being the perennial costume designer she was, she couldn't help noticing he wore the exact same clothes he wore the night they met—right down to the tie and shoes. She decided to stifle the observation, and instead reached over and grabbed his large, warm hand.

RED FLAG
#5-2

He piggybacked her statement by agreeing, "Yes, it is odd that a twenty-eight-year-old man should request a Dutch-dating connection. I agree."

She looked at him. He didn't offer much more in his gaze. It was a kind of can-we-table-the-rest-of-this-communication expression.

"No problem," said Jennifer. "I don't mind paying for myself at all." She picked up her cup and said, "But you forgot to inter-pret one more thing at the bottom of my teacup. It says, right here,"—she feigned a fortune-teller persona—"that the drinker of these tea leaves very much likes the guy she is with in return."

He took his index finger and ran a line from the teacup up her arm, up her neck and landed on her cheek. Then he turned her face toward him and kissed her softly on the lips.

"Green tea ice cream with coconut shavings?" interrupted one of the kimo-noed waitresses.

233

"Only if we can interpret the coconut shavings," joked Jonathan.

"So, you want to go, Jon?" asked Jennifer on the phone. "The Bolshoi Ballet only comes to LA every two or three years and I really want to see them. They have the largest costume budget of any European ballet company and they're so technically brilliant."

"Um, well, I love dance, but really, Jennifer, can I be honest?"

"Please," she said, putting the finishing touches of iridescent blue on her toenails.

"Well, part of my game plan is not to do anything radically extracurricular, um, for many reasons."

"No, you don't understand, Jon, I'll be happy to take us both."

"Oh," he said. "No way. You are not paying for me."

"Maybe people don't do that in Birmingham, Alabama, Jon, but I would be happy to have you as my guest for the night."

"Listen," he said adamantly, "the answer is no. Tell you what, dear lady. I think this is necessary. Why don't you come down to my place of business tomorrow, near Sixth and Main? You have the address."

"Why, Jonathan?"

"Um, there is a gas station and a large building on the block. You will find me. I think this is a good idea."

"Well," she said, "OK, I'll be by in the morning after I have breakfast with my parents. I'll show you my blue toenails.—providing they dry by then. I put on three coats."

"Drive safely downtown tomorrow and I'll see you and your blue toenails in the morning. OK, sweetheart?"

She hung up the phone and thought, *The engineer is probably in a large office suite. Whatever does this have to do with not wanting to go to the Bolshoi? Oh well, it'll be fun to go downtown and see him. No big deal.*

RED FLAG
#5-3

She looked down at her toes, commanded them to dry, and sat back on her bed thinking about what she was going to wear to visit the tall, darling Southern engineer tomorrow.

Jennifer sat at the kitchen table in her parents' house, finishing breakfast. Dad waxed boastfully of his pancakes made with Lactaid milk and nutmeg. Mom kept over-apologizing for her robe-and-rollers presentation.

Jennifer scanned the large eat-in kitchen. Not much had changed since childhood. The yellow duck-and-chicken curtains that deflected the morning Eastern exposure weren't even faded, after all these years. The "duckies and chickies," as she used to refer to them, still gave her a secret sense of security, when being at Mom and Dad's. Also, as usual in the morning, Mom's oldies station—from that old but perfectly fine transistor radio—softly delivered musical notes into the air.

"So, Mom, remember to sort through the bag I brought you. The wardrobe department just can't hold all the clothes the extras wore on the set. There are some nice pieces. Enjoy them."

"Thank you so much, darling."

"Mom and Pop, I have to cut this short."

"Don't you like my pancakes? I think the Lactaid milk in them is a great idea," insisted Dad.

"That's not it," laughed Jennifer, standing up and kissing them good-bye. "I met a guy."

"What?" asked her mother. "Well, well, well. When can we have him to dinner?"

"I guess I'll let you know later on today. He's from Birmingham, Alabama, and is an engineer." She left the house.

236

Her mother put a hand to her cheek, just in time to retrieve a falling roller. "You see, Henry, I was right. That's why she's been sounding so light on the phone. She met a boy *and* an engineer." She walked over to her husband and hugged him.

He said, "Let's cross our fingers, Mildred. Engineers are a good breed. They're hard-working, ambitious, and usually very stable. Let's cross our fingers. We could use an engineer in the family."

Jennifer stood in the lobby of the large building. She didn't understand. She scrutinized the list of tenants again, but found no engineering firm and no Jonathan Basil. Then she checked the address she had. "What? I'm two numbers off. I'm confused. Let me check the gas station next door. Maybe they can help direct me."

She left the building and approached the Chevron next door. She walked inside the station's Food Mart and converged upon the attendant's window. And there, inside the gas station booth, in a Chevron cotton shirt, sat Jonathan behind the desk. As he turned to her, the "Hi, I'm Jon" logo on his shirt cemented the scenario.

Jennifer said, "Jonathan, what are you doing here?" She looked around the Food

Mart trying to make sense of her disconcertedness. "Oh, Jonathan, do you own a Chevron Food Mart and gas station? How nice. You didn't tell me."

"Come inside the booth, Jennifer." He let her in and kissed her hello.

She tried to conceal her confusion. *Why would an engineer also own a gas station?* she thought.

"I'm so happy to see you, Jen," he said in his unequaled drawl. "In fact, wait a second." He picked up the intercom and said to one of the outdoor attendants, "Carlos, would you come into the booth for ten minutes? I need a short break." Then he hustled Jennifer outside.

RED FLAG
#5-4

"How long have you owned this nice place, Jon?"

He put his arm around her and walked away from the station. "Jennifer, I felt like you needed to see me here. I know we have only been together twice. Our connection is moving fast. We feel more than close. At least, I do to you."

She stopped and looked at her tall friend in the Chevron shirt. "I do to you, too, Jonathan."

"So, Jen, this is part of the piece. I'm a clerk at a gas station. I work nine to five, which is the sought-after shift. I get health benefits and one week off a year. That's all I need. I'm happy. I'll explain more later, but you see, this is me and I am happy."

She looked down. "There never was an engineer, was there?"

"What engineer?" he asked.

She turned away to hide her embarrassment. "And the Bolshoi?" she asked.

"If you go, Jennifer, I want to hear all about it. You see, I do not put money aside for concerts and shows. But I support your going, and no, you will never pay for me for anything I wouldn't normally do on my own."

"But I'd love you to be my guest," she earnestly implored.

"Sorry, Jennifer, my conscience, male ego, and Southern gentleman sensibilities couldn't handle it. I'm sorry. This is me. Walk me back to my booth." They walked back to the gas station in silence.

"Jonathan, I don't want to stop seeing you for a second. We'll work out our different orientations."

"That's exactly what I thought and hoped you'd say, Jen." He leaned over, smelled her clean hair and lightly brushed his lips against her cheek.

She took a deep breath and looked up at him. "I just thought of something, Jon. Our wardrobe department is invited to the County Museum's costume exhibit for a private tour Thursday night. Would you care to join us?"

Just then, a huge, noisy, rattling oil tanker drove up. Jen and Jon could not hear each other. He nodded in answer to her question and then pointed to her feet. Her blue toenails were peeking out of her sandals. He gave a thumbs-up and ran back inside. They smiled at each other through the glass.

As she drove back to the valley, she counted the Chevron stations and in her mind assembled the most adorable outfit for Thursday night.

"Oh, no! Look, Jennifer!" gasped Nancy, her co-worker. They were at the fascinating County Museum costume exhibit. "Panniers! Aren't they weird?"

Jonathan asked, "What are those?"

"Oh," laughed Jen, "we studied them in college. They were enormous hoops women wore under dresses in the seventeenth and eighteenth centuries."

"Are they authentic?" asked Dulsie.

Jonathan enjoyed how demonstrably punk Nancy and Dulsie were dressed. He was also impressed by how much they all knew about clothing history.

"Oh, yes," replied Jen. "Everything in this exhibit has to be authentic."

"So," asked Dulsie, "how long have you two known each other, Jon, Jen?"

"Less than a month," answered Jonathan.

"You're kidding," Dulsie responded. "You look like old friends."

Jennifer and Jon smiled warmly at each other. She pulled him closer to her.

"Oh, look at those, Jon! Tricorn hats. You'd look so cute in one of those!"

"Oh, I think he'd look better in the one with the feather," Nancy laughed.

As her eyes stared admiringly at the display of well-preserved hats, Dulsie offhandedly asked, "So, what do you do, Jonathan?"

"I work in the booth at a Chevron downtown."

"No, really," she implored. There was a short silence. "Really, are you on some fast track at CBS or something?"

"I work in the booth at a Chevron downtown."

"You can't get a straight answer from any of these yuppies nowadays," smirked Nancy.

"No kidding," agreed Dulsie.

"What on earth is wrong with working at a booth at a Chevron?" asked Jennifer.

"Absolutely nothing," said Nancy, "'cept that you'd never date one of those."

"Oh, look!" exclaimed Dulsie. "Full-armed silken empress dresses. We must be leaving the eighteenth century."

"I'm not so sure of that," said Jonathan, and he and Jen laughed.

Six weeks passed. The intense temperatures of an LA summer had finally dropped and everyone was pulling out light sweaters. Jennifer loved the early fall season because she could parade her self-designed knitwear. She and Jon continued to date—by his rules. They paid for themselves; if anything was too expensive, Jon simply would not go, and never would allow her to pay.

RED FLAG #5-5

He was not lying the night they met when he said he did not own a car. He took the bus and metro everywhere. Jonathan allowed Jennifer to occasionally pick him up, but never to drop him off after dark. He would bus home, exclaiming it was not the safest area. Jen did not understand why he chose to live in a rather rough part of town.

242

All in all, their relationship was uniquely constructed. Jen had never experienced a system of the sort. A part of it felt clearly communicated and up-front. Yet at the same time, it also felt inflexible and rigorously unyielding.

Jennifer parked the car across the street from Jon's apartment. She had picked him up many times, but had never been inside the building. He said it was time for her to do this, whatever that meant. The building appeared to have been built in the 1930s. From the outside, she couldn't get a sense if it was well maintained or not. The early art deco ornamentation was still intact and historically beautiful, but the chipping paint on the doors, windows, and front portal expressed quite another picture.

In the lobby sat two slouching and rather unkempt men. Jennifer walked down the long hallway to Jon's apartment. The lighting was inadequate and the wallpaper was peeling. The carpeting was in a prethreadbare state. Strong cooking aromas permeated the hallway and seemed to cleave to the peeling wallpaper.

She knocked on apartment 1-R and a happy Jonathan answered the door.

Scanning him quickly, because it was part of her job, she saw he was wearing the same slacks and shirt he always wore. They were clean and smart as usual, but a constant.

"You are my sunshine, my only sunshine," he started to sing in his drawl. "Come in. Come in."

"Jonathan, I'm happy to see you."

He opened the door and she was stopped in her tracks. Before her was a small converted hotel room with a fridge and a stove, and a tiny bathroom peeking out from behind the fridge. In one corner were a new-looking computer and an old-looking TV with an antenna. There was a bed with a brown chenille bedspread, a table and two chairs, a dresser, and a full wall of shelf space.

"Have a seat." He pulled out one of the chairs. There was no place to put her coat and purse, so she hung them on the back of her chair.

"Was your ride OK?"

"Yes, Jon, I love downtown."

"But I do not want you coming here after dark. Do you understand?"

"Got it," she said, truly not intending such high-wire feats.

"Do you want some tea or homemade applesauce, Jenny?"

"Nothing," she said, scanning the cramped living quarters.

"I'm happy to see you, pretty girl."

She smiled, still scanning the room for a secret hallway or a trapdoor to more living space. Nancy Drew might have been a welcome addition right about now.

"We need to do a little talking. You see, this is me, Jennifer. I'm happy. I'm content. I want no more. I wanted you to see it."

"It's organized and compact," she said, observing the old TV, wondering if it still worked.

"Jen," he said, taking her hand, "listen. Do you know what the Alabama Poverty Project is?"

"Clueless," she replied.

"OK. It was started in 1991 to educate the local citizens and eradicate the awful poverty in Birmingham. Did you know something like thirty-six percent of the population back then, in Alabama, lived below the poverty level?"

"I do know Alabama has great poverty."

Jonathan courageously looked into her eyes while holding her hands. "You see, dear, we qualified. You know I lived with my

245

mother and brother and occasional father. Well, we qualified. My great-grandparents were sharecroppers, the last of the great indentured white servants."

She looked away from him in partial disbelief and partial fascination. "And?"

"And I needed to get away from it for a while. But this is me."

"I'm sorry to tell you, Jon, there's a part of me that totally can't relate. And what do you mean, to get away for a while?"

"A year or so. I just wanted to see how the other half lives."

"What do you mean?"

"You know, bigger city, more culture, more sophistication, no Southern drawls."

"What do you mean, a year or so?"

"Yes."

"Yes, what? What do you mean, a year or so?"

"My life is what I know, Jen. I'm going to tell you a funny word." He got up and walked over to his window. His view was a cracked driveway littered with garbage cans. He turned to her. "Have you ever heard the word zoochosis?"

"Not since I was a child," joked Jennifer, impressed by his intellectual acumen, not really ever having heard the word.

"Well, it refers to weird behavior that animals exhibit when they are taken out of their environment and put into zoos. Now, the zoos might basically be safer, with more access to their animal friends, and excellent feeding conditions, but zoochosis still exists. It's what they know. The rhinoceros doesn't want lab-created rhino food. He wants marshy waters to roam around in alone. We can impose our rhino wishes on them, but..." He stopped.

"Thank you for the zoology lesson." Her gaze became intent. She raised her voice. "What do you mean, one year?"

"Marshy waters," he said.

"So, what, Jonathan? You want to go back to food stamps and handouts?"

"No."

"That's what you're saying."

"No, I just don't want to encumber myself with car insurance, flavor-of-the-week designer clothes, and impossible mortgages. Don't you see, Jennifer? With all this manmade stress, one begins to get possessive and territorial and neurotic, whereas I have libraries, sturdy jogging shoes, and an occasional church service. I need absolutely nothing more. I refuse to get manic over possessions."

RED FLAG
#5-6

247

"Manic over possessions?"

"Did you know, Jen, something like one in seven men have debilitating heart symptoms before the age of sixty? I can't fathom that."

"So what are you going to do, Jon? Detach from the world?"

"No, but I don't have to live like half of the Americans live, if you call it living."

"But Jon, man isn't built that way. I think man's natural instinct is to strive and grow and seek a better life..." She trailed off and started to cry. "And...and to love. To try to connect and to love."

She sat at the table and cried. He looked at her from the window. Her chest was heaving. She looked helpless and alone.

"Jon, you are only twenty-eight. I am thirty-three, and I live in a bit more sophisticated of a world than you."

"You do," he agreed, sitting down at the table.

"Do you know," she said through her tears, "how hard it is to connect? How hard it is to find someone who has the rapport we so quickly discovered? Frankly, I think it is more important to be open to the world than to live and die by some self-imposed standard."

"I am strictly coming from stress versus no stress," he explained. "That is not a weird standard. Going out of one's way to reduce stress? Nobody would argue that's a bad thing."

Jennifer stared at him through her tears. There was a light defiance in his eyes. She decided not to fight it, and turned away so he couldn't see the extent to which her lower lip was quivering. She thought, *How can he not see the goodness we could create?*

She slowly moved to the door with her back to him. A salty tear prickled her lips. She left the apartment and walked down the dingy hallway. Somehow the hallway looked darker now. The peeling wallpaper almost barked at her. And Jonathan did not try to stop her.

Jennifer loaded the last Snapple bottle in her parents' refrigerator. She was used to going to Mom and Dad's the day before Thanksgiving in the morning, to help them prepare.

"OK, Mom, I'll help you put the turkey in tomorrow morning and set up the folding table. And remember to try on the belts and sweaters I brought you from the costume department."

"Jen," her mother said, "are you OK? I mean, are you really?"

Jennifer stopped her momentum, looked down and stared at the familiar kitchen tiles. The yellow and white swirlyques looked back at her. "I just don't know why Jonathan couldn't wait to spend Thanksgiving with me. Why did he have to move back before the holidays?"

"Sweetheart," said her dad, "it's better. If he really meant what he said, the sooner the better."

"He wants me to visit him in Birmingham."

"To see how the other half lives?" asked Mom, sipping her morning coffee.

"It feels like such a dead end, Jen," said Dad, putting the turkey in aluminum foil. "We all have to be open. So, what is he going home to?"

"He says his natural habitat."

"And his stubbornness," said her mother. "Is he going to school, or what? You said he's very bright."

RED FLAG
#5-7

"I think he's going to check back in with the Alabama Poverty Project and tell them their golden boy has returned. I was really starting to care for this man, Mom and Pop. Where did I go wrong?"

Her eyes fell on the ritual cranberry sauce Mom had just blended, in its anticipatory Saran covering. "He would have

250

loved your cranberry sauce, Mom. Nobody makes it with peach relish. Maybe next year. Maybe another time. Maybe somebody else."

She watched her parents buzz around the kitchen. They were a complementary unit. Fine role models. They communicated, negotiated, and laughed. She looked down, saddened.

"Mom, I knitted a taupe shawl. I think I may wear it tomorrow night to Thanksgiving dinner. I'm looking forward to showing it to you. It's really glam."

Dad gave Jen a hug. "It's probably the most glam taupe shawl in existence—not that anyone knows what color taupe is."

Dad pulled out the kitchen ladder and climbed to the top cupboard where reserved-for-holidays-only platters lived. Jen watched her parents work in harmony and assisted them wherever possible, despite a forced smile. She soaked the holiday platters, took down their good wine glasses, and retrieved her great-grandma's silverware from the china cabinet drawers. Her thoughts, for once, were not consumed with what outfit she was going to coordinate for tomorrow. Instead, she was thinking about the grinning cupid on her perfume tray and exactly how she was going to discard him when she returned home.

Mom turned on her beloved oldies station. Out crooned Judy Garland's full alto voice. *"You made me love you, I didn't want to do it. I didn't want to do it."*

"Oh, and by the way, Jenny," asked her dad, "that dance you met him at, wasn't it called Shoot the Cupid?"

"Yes," Jen laughed.

"That's the problem, darling. You don't shoot Cupid. When you least expect it, Cupid is supposed to shoot you. No?"

Then, Mom, in over-exaggerated seriousness, turned up the radio, grabbed Jen, and started dancing. Jen laughed and cried and laughed, and it all got intermingled with Dad's philosophizing, his singing with Ms. Garland, the clanging food processor, their dancing, the "duckie and chickie" curtains—and for a very silly split second, she could have sworn, through her wet eyes, beyond the duckies and chickies and the frosty morning window, she saw the figure of a cupid.

Judy Garland now genuinely permeated the kitchen and joined the family with her song: "*I can't tell you what I'm feeling, The very mention of your name sets my heart reeling, You know you made me love you...*" ….....SHOOT!….....

DISCUSSION OF THE CHAPTER

RED FLAG #5-1

Jonathan is an intelligent man who understands some very basic concepts of mechanics and electronics. Nonetheless, there's no proof that he has an engineering degree.

Jennifer had little indication of anything about Jon, yet she wholeheartedly created a career for him, fantasizing that he lived in a chic downtown loft and conveniently walked to work at his engineering firm. How dangerous and disappointing for her when this rich fantasy subsided for reality.

This brings us to a significant aspect. There is an underlying myth of perfection that comes with dating. This perfection myth seems to work in conjunction with the savior fallacy. "When I meet Mr. Right he will save me, and maybe the world."

To elaborate upon this, it is really important we do not look to a relationship or anyone to reorder the world, or save us. This is one area where I see many relationships fail, when it has become patently clear that the significant other is a person and not a superhuman wizard/wizardess,

255

visiting Earth with the express purpose of exerting his or her magic upon our lives.

RED FLAG #5-2

Jennifer works in television costuming. Of course her orientation is going to be clothing and people's attire. This is her formal training and work focus, so she is not being superficial or critical when she observes other peoples' clothes and patterns of dress.

She said she decided to "stifle" her observation. Why? I believe we should observe whatever we can observe through our senses and always utilize that for information. The difference, however, is not to fall into judgment with these observances.

In this case, observations gave Jen necessary information. Where judgment comes in is when we put a good/bad, black/white, correct/incorrect tag on these observations. These tags limit our experiences, can prove unfair to the person observed, cage our growth, and lessen future interplay.

So I say, yes, tune up your five senses and your powers of observation on everything. Just remember to leave the judgment element out of your perception to ensure the pureness and fairness of these observations.

RED FLAG #5-3

A fair amount of time has passed since Jennifer met Jon. Their physical time together and their phone time could really have furthered knowledge of each other. Instead, Jen decided to flesh out her fantasy and decorate it.

This is largely related to the savior fallacy that jam-packs itself into new (all?) love relationships. True, we all should experience love and romance in our lives, but it must be balanced with reality.

Jonathan's career and where he lived were very basic information. Jen almost had a need to keep this obscured. How could she not have known this information? There are numerous reasons why people bury themselves into such early-on, unproductive fantasies, so that even basics about the significant other are overlooked. In Jen's situation, it came from "I like you so much and know you so little, please make all the pieces fit."

RED FLAG #5-4

Jennifer's savior myth became so firm-footed she actually had to substitute something else from her closet of accepted careers. So she asked him, "How long have you owned this nice place, Jon?" She never really asked him what he did for a living, and here she just substituted gas station owner for engineer.

It is true that sometimes our fantasies do keep us warm. Stepping outside of them is just feared as being too chilly. We'd rather fabricate. I say, put on a coat, give up the fabrication and step outside—quickly.

RED FLAG #5-5

Although Jonathan was up-front with his comfort level regarding dating, he should not be totally applauded. True, when people communicate their needs they are to be applauded. However, there is a major element amiss here. The element is the word flexibility. Jon stated, "This is how I date." Essentially, his implication was, "This is how I live." With such pronouncements there is little room for flexibility, and the problem with this is that the significant other's (here, Jennifer's) feelings and opinions do not factor into his equation. Everything is airtight.

His basic concept of "This is how I date, this is how I live. Want to hitch a ride? If not, sorry," is not a very well-negotiated connection, if a connection at all. This can only assign a fairly actualized female to the status of inferior minor.

Harry Stack-Sullivan, an American psychiatrist, theorized that two basic needs exist in humans: the need for satisfaction and the need for security. I think of Dr. Sullivan's theory in relation to Jonathan. It was deeply important for Jon to feel secure. In this case, he fought for security by constantly being familiar with his surroundings. And this familiarity produced control for him.

The snag with this is what follows, meaning, this need (ultimately for control) will be more important than the other need theorized by Dr. Sullivan—satisfaction. Control instead of happiness, control over satisfaction, control over living.

Again, this example of downdatee #5—is from and stays connected to a substantially lower class than the female—evidences how inflexibility wedges itself between the controller and the controlee, but mostly between the controller and life.

RED FLAG #5-6

We couldn't have a more potent example of downdatee #5. Again, this is not a class, religious, or racial prejudice. This is not all about Mr. Basil being from a poor family of origin. This is about Mr. Basil's attitude. He almost seemed proud to qualify for the Alabama Poverty Project. His attitude really looked like "once a projectee, always a projectee." In fact, this is not what national and state funding programs aspire to. Their goal is to get people and their families on their feet, stabilized, and out the door. So, at least sociopolitically, Jonathan's return attitude is incorrect.

259

Also, I beg the question, is there not some middle ground? Is it either a window with garbage cans littering one's view, or a cabinet stocked with Manolo Blahnik shoes? Does it have to be so extreme and final, Jonathan?

It does look as though Jon pulls no punches and states where he is. But if he were to be squeaky truthful, he would really approach women like this: "My name is Jon. I'm a very bright and rather nice human being, but I prefer to live around the poverty level, never strive for all that much, not own a car, and stifle any imaginable ambition. So this is me!"

It was really understandable that Jennifer was rather taken aback at his decision to "live down." Had she continued dating him with this attitude, she would have had to adjust her entire life's value system into dating down, and most probably, living down.

It is your decision if you believe all of that downward adjustment is worthwhile.

RED FLAG #5-7

Jennifer queried of her caring parents, "I was really starting to care for this man, Mom and Pop. Where did I go wrong?"

Before I address her question, I must bring up the American psychiatrist, Abraham Maslowe. Maslowe's main orientation had to do with man's hierarchy of needs—meaning, he theorized that man's most basic needs are food and safety.

When the needs of food and safety are handled, he seeks belongingness (in a group community, family, etc.), then he seeks self-esteem (respect, recognition, appropriate attention, etc.). And finally, he seeks self-actualization (growth, the helping of others, motivating one's talents, etc.).

For Jonathan to be so intelligent, yet to steadfastly cling to Maslowe's primary needs category—food and safety—is an unusual juxtaposition.

Therefore, to answer Jennifer's question, "Where did I go wrong?"—the answer is nowhere. She did not go wrong at all. He's the one who has to do the work; who has to lessen his clutch on an old identity that doesn't benefit him.

The even bigger problem is, if Jen and Jonathan hooked up long-term, in order for them to have harmony in this relationship Jen would have to "live down," what red flag #5-6 stated. It doesn't look like Jon wanted to leave his "view" of littered garbage cans rolling around on cracked driveways anytime soon.

So, taking into consideration this story alone, is it not more evident that dating down is not a win-win for ourselves, not for our loved ones, and, on a larger scale, not for the future good of relationships on this graced and permeable planet? I would vote NO.

261

CHAPTER SIX

ILLUSTRATING DOWNDATEE #6 –

Is Physically or Mentally Abusive to the Female

Entitled...

SOME DANCING, SOME ROMANCING

"A one, two, three, four, five, six, seven, eight. Again. A one, two, three, four, five, six, seven, eight. Pirouette. Pirouette. Step to the right. And, jump! No, gentlemen, no!" instructed Regina Tunkell to her men's ballet class at the community college in Los Angeles. "In order for you to turn, you must keep your hips together or the unit will fall off its center. Now, let's try it again."

The tall and conscientious teacher pressed her CD player and out wafted a sprightly Vivaldi flute concerto. Its sprightliness seemed to support the dancers and, consequently, her corrections.

"Back straight, please. And count to yourselves. Nobody knows you're counting, so use it. Ready? A one, two, three, four... good. Much better."

Since her two-year employment at the community college, Regina really had turned around the lifeless dance department. It had only offered one ballet class and one folk dance class. In two years, she now boasted four ballet classes as well as folk, modern, hip-hop, and ballroom, with a tripling of staff size and a quadrupling of enrollment. She had even secured an outside grant for a small performing company.

"OK, gentlemen, do it again to each side and we'll call it a day. And, Benjamin,

I want to see you after class. Ready? Pull up from your center and please jump with your legs, not your shoulders. And, a one, two, three, four, five, six, seven, eight." She watched the boys ranging from seventeen to twenty-seven years old. Most of them had never danced a lick before this class.

Amazing how a little proper selling to the phys.ed. department got so many guys off the athletic field and into dance classes, she thought, smiling to herself.

"OK, gentlemen, first position, deep bow with strong conviction, please. And applaud yourselves." Her astonishingly well-behaved Chihuahua, San Antonio, after having planted himself in one place for the entire class, would ritually run to the front of the room. The class would applaud the dog, laughing, and vocalizing praises to the teacher as they gathered their gym bags to exit.

"Thank you, Miss Tunkell. See you tomorrow, Miss Tunkell. Tough class, madame, a lot of jumps today."

And the boys would leave her class being yet more in touch with their masculinity. She saw to it.

Benjamin picked up his towel, wrapped it around his neck and approached Regina.

268

"Did you want to talk to me, ma'am?"

"Yes, dear. Let's sit on the floor and talk for just a moment." They both fell to the soft dance room floor, but this time San Antonio wanted to sit in Ben's lap. Regina caught a quick glimpse of herself in the long studio mirror. She saw a five-foot-nine, forty-three-year-old woman with thick, shoulder-length brown curls, big green eyes, a large nose, and beautifully high-arched feet. Next to her sat a short, skinny eighteen-year-old boy with a thick mop of blond curls and a booming voice which belied his body type.

"Benjamin, I wanted to ask you a few questions."

"Ma'am?"

"How long have you been dancing?"

"Oh, I'm mostly a long-distance runner. This is the first class I ever took. This and your ballroom class. So, I guess four months."

"And?" she asked.

"And I love it. I'm not sure I have ever been in such good shape. I think I'm running better, with greater stamina and everything, but I could never get serious about dance as a profession."

"OK, dear, I just wondered because men physically advance very quickly in this field—four times faster than women. You're both strong and adaptive to the art. You pick up combinations extremely fast. Just wondered if I could interest you in anything."

"Nah, Miss Tunkell. Thanks for the compliment."

"Just thought I'd ask. OK, Ben, go ahead. I know your biology class is clear across campus. I'm glad you're performing with us tomorrow night at the Chamber of Commerce dinner. It should be great."

"Thanks, Miss Tunkell. Oh, and by the way, my dad wants to see the three pieces you choreographed. He's sneaking in tomorrow night."

"Oh, I'd like to meet him afterward."

"OK. Tomorrow night should be fun. Lots of jumps today. Bye, San Antonio," said Benjamin as he ran out of the studio.

San Antonio went into the middle of the room and stared at himself in the mirror. Regina was amused by San Antonio's preoccupation with his reflection. She removed her ballet shoes and slipped on her flexible gym shoes to teach the hip-hop class. She smiled as San Antonio continued to state at himself.

"Come on, boy. Time to go to the dance studio across the hall." He ran to the door and waited for her to catch up. He took one last glimpse at himself and ran out to the other studio.

Regina thought to herself, *And if I didn't know better, I'd think he might be able to actually take a class.*

Regina stood in front of the Chamber of Commerce dinner in a long black skirt and a black leotard, her hair up in a bun and her back admirably straight.

"And so, ladies and gentlemen, the college is very pleased to have this performing group. Some of my dancers have just started dancing and others have studied their entire lives. I believe it's about the love of movement and performing, and so I merely adjust the choreography accordingly.

Our first dance utilizes classical ballet movements, but is set to a heavy metal song by Metallica. Our lead female is quite an advanced dancer.

The second dance is a full-out comic piece taking place in a men's weightlifting gym, with the men breaking out in occasional dance movements. The music is written by one of the students in the music department.

And the third piece is a salsa number sung by Celia Cruz. Sit back and relax, people of the Chamber, and enjoy the show."

271

Regina exited the stage, manipulated some of the lights backstage and loudly whispered, "OK, everybody! Places!"

At the end of the performances, everyone hugged each other backstage. Exclamations of "Good work! You rock! What a gas!" rang throughout the backstage area between students, Regina, and the stagehand, one of the kids' fathers. As Regina was tugging off a voluminous salsa cape from one of the girls, Benjamin tapped her on the shoulder.

"Ma'am, I'd like you to meet my pop."

"Oh, great!" She turned and saw a man about her age, short and thin like Benjamin and also with an immense mass of blond curls.

"Dad, this is Miss Tunkell. Miss Tunkell, this is my dad, Mark Howell."

"And your mom?" she asked, looking behind Mr. Howell.

"Nope," he said in Benjamin's same booming bass voice. "Not here tonight."

"They're divorced. It's Dad's night," explained Benjamin.

"Wow, that was quite a diverse and inventive performance," complimented Mark. "I think it's astounding that you have virtually non-dancers performing. Benjamin loves your classes."

"Oh, thank you! You know, he's really a bit of a natural dancer," she said.

"Yeah, she's forcing me to go professional," Benjamin teased.

"No, I'm not. I just think you're one of those physically innate dancers."

"Well, maybe next life, Miss Tunkell. I plan to be a web designer and to continue competing in long-distance running meets. And if none of that pans out, Plan B is to build schools and playgrounds in Cuba."

Regina and Mark laughed. "Not a bad idea," Mark replied. "Think of all the salsa classes you could take in Havana. Hey, Benjamin, get out of your salsa stripes and let's all go out for frozen yogurt. What do you say, Miss Creative Choreographer?"

Regina wasn't exactly sure what the protocol was for "socializing" with students, but thought vanilla frozen yogurt was virtually harmless.

"Sure," she replied. "We could all afford to unwind a little. But just a second." She turned back to the group buzzing around her.

"Everyone," she announced, "remember to hang up your rental pieces, be proud of yourselves, and keep your backs straight. A straight lumbar is not exclusive to dancing. See you all in class! Come, San Antonio."

273

The next day, Regina sat in her office with her feet up on the desk. She was revising a letter to the Chamber of Commerce, thanking them for giving the group an opportunity to perform. She looked down at San Antonio. He had picked up a ballet shoe and was carrying it across the room. He placed it in the corner, retrieved the other one, neatly put them side by side and looked up at Regina.

"So you're organizing my office?" she laughed.

Just then, the phone rang and he barked in its direction.

"And you're my secretary?" Into the phone, she said, "Yes?"

"Um, this is Mark Howell."

Finally the name registered. "Oh, Mark, hi! It took me a moment."

"Listen, Regina, I'm running late, but I wanted to call and quickly connect with you."

"Oh, gee," she said, smiling and sitting farther back in her chair. "I...I'm glad you called. San Antonio wanted to thank you for the yogurt last night."

"Listen, Regina, I was just wondering, if you are available Saturday night, would you like to have dinner with me?"

"Oh." Regina paused. "Yes. Yes, I'd like that."

"OK, I have to run. Could we fill out the particulars later in the week?"

"Uh, yeah, sure."

"Well, later. Bye." He hung up.

She sat back in her chair, put her feet on the floor and looked out the office window. *That was a fast conversation*, she thought.

"Hello?" A face peered in the doorway. It was Luke, one of the other dance teachers and a good friend. "Regina, my partner, Dave, wants to meet you. Dinner Saturday night? What do you say?"

"As a matter of fact, I just accepted a dinner date for Saturday night. So, can we rain check?"

"Anyone spectacular?" her good friend queried.

"Well, the father of one of my students."

"Your student wants a good grade so he put his dad up to it. I have it down."

Regina laughed and leaped down on the floor to San Antonio's level.

"San Antonio, I have to start class. Bring me my ballet shoes."

"I cannot believe your frickin' dog follows directions," smiled Luke.

"You should see him dance."

275

"So, darling, are you really going out with a student's papa?"

"Um, yeah. I mean, the invitation really took me by surprise and I already committed. Should I have declined?"

"Well," said Luke, leaning against the doorjamb, "if it was an eighteen-year-old student, I'd say you'd look perverted and silly. This way, you only look horny."

"Oh!" Regina picked up one of the ballet shoes and threw it at Luke.

He dodged the shoe and ran laughing down the hall, pronouncing, "Violence in room 102! Violence in room 102!"

And for a split second, Regina pondered if she had made the appropriate decision.

Regina looked around the bustling potted palm restaurant, flipped her long hair back and stood up. She discreetly demonstrated a *tendue* for Mark.

"That's all it is, Mark. It's a point on the floor with one foot. That's all. And I can usually tell how long someone's been dancing by that alone." She sat back down and scooped up another piece of cheesecake. She felt its velvety softness against the roof of her mouth.

276

"My Benjamin is truly enjoying your class. I know you majored in dance at the University of Illinois. Then what?"

"I've been taking ballet since I was four. After college, I joined a modern dance company in Switzerland for a year, danced with the Houston Ballet for three years, and with the Pacific Northwest Ballet for one year. Then I went back to Illinois, got a master's degree, and taught there for ten years. I sorely needed a change, so I applied to sunny California and lucked out as the chair of the dance department a few years ago. I love it."

"They love you," Mark said, with soft eyes. Then he turned to the waitress, sat erect in his chair, and in a reprimanding tone said, "Ma'am, excuse me, would you please continue to keep our water glasses and decaf filled here? Come on, now, you should have known better."

Regina put down her fork and looked at the blond man in front of her. She did not know this somewhat charming man, so she could not gauge what was typical and what was out of character for him.

He filled in some of the questions. Lightly, he explained, "I seem to be a little tough on two subcultures."

"Two subcultures?" she queried.

"Yes, my employees and women."

"So," asked Regina, "let's say the waitress was a waiter. Would your tone have been different?"

Mark looked down at his plate for a moment. "I'm sorry. Did I embarrass you?"

Regina stretched her leg out from under the table, feeling her *tendue* on the floor. "No," she responded.

RED FLAG #6-1

"Oh, by the way, my Benjamin doesn't know I'm taking you out tonight, but I think it only fair that I tell him tomorrow. Are you OK with that?"

"Of course I am," Regina replied to the older version of her student in front of her, fully aware that he didn't really answer her question. "Mark, you've got to try this cheesecake." She took one of his unused forks and cut him a piece. "So tell me, Mr. Howell," she asked, feeding him the cheesecake, "why are you such a success-ful building contractor? I know. Ben brags about you all the time."

"I love the cheesecake, Regina. He brags about me?"

"Yeah. He said despite this national recession, you continue to get contracts."

"It's simple. I keep a tight grip on everyone, from my project construction

278

managers to the secretaries at the architect's office. We have meetings galore and I'm very firm. I hope my projects show for themselves. Well, I do keep getting contracts."

"Ah," said Regina. "So you keep a tight grip on your employees."

"That's right."

"And Benjamin?"

"Nah, Benjamin makes me super-weak in the knees. I'm mush around him. I told you, I'm only tough on two subcultures."

Then they said together, "Employees and women."

When Regina was back in her car, she checked her phone for messages. There was a text from Luke. It read: "So, baby, perverted and silly, or horny?"

She texted back: "None of your goddamned texting business. But I will tell you everything on Monday. Ta ta."

"Alright, everyone," Regina announced to the class. "I have to end class ten minutes early because I have to be somewhere. Let me see the combination one more time. A little more energy, and please stop looking in the mirror at the person next to you. This is your personal growth process. Eyes inside your body. No comparisons. The person next to you is on a totally different journey than you."

She stood back and watched the young students execute her combination of five counts of eight. The "no comparison" admonishment seemed to really help. She curtsied to them, stood for the traditional applause for the teacher, and ran out of the room and down the hall.

Passing her good friend Luke en route, he said, "Well, well, Florence Griffith Joyner or Deena Kastor. Who was that?"

She yelled back, "Can't talk, Luke. I have a date!"

He volleyed, "Obviously."

Regina locked the door to her office, hurriedly unleashed her hair from its bun, applied gray eye shadow atop her outer crests and lined her lips with a maroon pencil. She told Mark she'd have no time to change for the wine and cheese event and would have to attend in leotard and skirt. A minor concession would be leaving San Antonio home for the day. She approved of her Houdini-fast mini-change and ran to her car, happily anticipating an evening with Mark.

Regina excitedly marched into the busy event, eyeing Mark in the distance. His head of blond curls was usually hard to miss. When she approached him, he had a wine glass and was talking to some of the architects of the just-finished building.

"Regina, darling, come here. These are the architects who so brilliantly charted the course of this building." The buttoned-up gentlemen acknowledged her, but were pulled away by other cohorts.

"How are you?" Mark asked, kissing her on the cheek. "I'm glad that you're here. I really wanted to see you, Regina."

A pang of excitement shot through her. She was very happy to see him and appreciated the reverse confirmation.

"Your building is incredible, Mark. You should be too proud of yourself."

He leaned down to one of the wine decanters and poured her a glass. "Is that so? Here, sweet woman."

She took a sip.

"But really," he began.

"But really?" mimicked Regina.

"Regina, come here." He pulled her away from the crowd and behind a pillar with an oversized flower planter. "You knew I was going to have colleagues here. I mean, no offense, dear woman, but for Christ's sake, do you also shower in leotards and skirts? Hmm?"

RED FLAG
#6-2

281

"What?" she asked. "Oh, my clothes? No. I told you I wasn't going to have time to change."

"Alright, alright," he replied. "I forgot. Let it go. That sparkly sweater under your arm, put it on. Quickly."

She put on the vintage cardigan with the beaded work, staring at him.

"Better. Better," he said, eyeing the sweater. Handing her his arm, he added, "Now, come with me, I want you to meet my design engineer."

Regina followed Mark across the room but felt confused. She wasn't quite sure what had just happened to make her feel so thrown off her pins. She thought, *It's really too stuffy and crowded in here to be wearing this cardigan, but I'd better keep it on for now.* And for another odd second, she could have sworn she felt her usually-straight back, slouch.

"Go out for a pass, San Antonio!" said Bethany, one of the dance students.

"He can't catch a football, silly," said Bethany's little sister.

Regina was delighted to have planned a dance department picnic. Mark was kind enough to secure a friend's large home in the Palisades. About seventy-five students, teachers, siblings, and parents showed up with steaks to barbecue, Frisbees, radios, and musical instruments.

Regina decided to leave the energetic crowd for a moment and found a large Mexican fan palm tree behind the property. She spread out her blanket and marveled at the cloud formations slowly stirring above her.

"There you are," said Mark.

"Hi," she said. "I just wanted some quiet space."

"Do you want to be alone?" he asked.

"No, no. I want you here."

"Regina, it's been a little difficult keeping my distance from you this afternoon. I'm pretty sure you don't want to blast to the department that you're dating Benjamin's father, but all the same, it's been a little hard."

"I'm sorry, Mark. Lie down next to me. Look," she said, looking up. "A cumulus. They are my favorite cloud type. So big today. Cumulus clouds remind me of Illinois snowstorms when I was younger. Big, puffy white stuff." She laughed.

"Do they?"

She added, "But unlike Illinois snowstorms, you wouldn't be drinking iced smoothies, nor wearing shorts. In fact, do you want to hear one of my secrets?"

"Sure," he replied.

"I love wearing shorts so much because it reminds me of the three months out of the year in Illinois when you were freed from awful weather."

"So, you really like wearing shorts?"

"Yes," she laughed. "It's a yearly rite of passage. I feel gratitude when I wear shorts. Isn't that funny? One of my little secrets."

"So, you really like wearing shorts?" he asked again.

"Um, yes," she responded, not feeling as though she needed to further elaborate upon such an esoteric issue as shorts.

RED FLAG
#6-3

Mark rolled over and said, "Regina, how heavy are you?"

"What?" she gasped and sat up.

"Well, I mean, can I be honest?" he asked.

"What do you mean?" she asked.

"You know I don't mince words, Regina." He scanned her body and sat up. "Let's be honest, dear. For an ex-professional dancer, well, for a very respected dance educator, you are really heavy. I mean, the average civilian would marvel to have your muscle tone, but as a dancer, you're what, fifteen,

284

twenty pounds overweight? Don't worry about it, I'm very attracted to you. I don't intend to stop seeing you. But is it such a big deal to be honest? Weight doesn't mean that much to me."

"I had to be skinny for so long. The company in Switzerland and particularly the three years I did with the Houston Ballet Company..." Her voice trailed off. She didn't want to make excuses for herself. She was not a compulsive eater, but being a little overweight was her choice and she knew it.

He continued, "I mean, Regina, you're not a big eater, but every time we go somewhere, you have to indulge in a sweet or two." He eyed the banana smoothie at her side. She picked it up and hurled it out.

He responded, "You didn't have to do that. I was just making conversation. I'm not putting a value judgment on you. So," he said, as he lay back down, "what do you hate about me?"

"Dad? Oh, Dad!" Ben's voice echoed in the distance. "Oh, hi, Miss Tunkell. I was just looking for you, Dad." Benjamin was stopped by Regina's quiet demeanor. He was used to her being upbeat and energetic. "Is everything OK here?"

"Sure, Ben," said his dad. "I'm just chatting up your dance teacher."

Ben looked back and forth between the two. Regina caught his savvy expression. He knew everything wasn't so OK.

"Um, alright, I just wanted to see where you were. San Antonio is beating us in football. See you later!"

Ben took off and Mark said, "What did I do to deserve such a love child?"

Regina looked at him lying in the grass. He had no idea he'd stung her. He reached over and pulled her closer to him, but she rejected the embrace. Then, she took the blanket she was lying on and covered herself.

She looked up at the white cumulus show. For a moment, their beauty and their float calmed her down. She glanced over at Mark. He, too, was entranced by the fluffy display. And, she realized, he hadn't a clue that on this warm day in June, at a happy picnic, the woman he adored was lying next to him, underneath a thick blanket, so as not to rankle his idea of visual aesthetic perfection.

"No, you cooked dinner. Let me do the dishes. And then I want to talk to you about something, Regina."

Regina watched Mark clear the table as she Tupperwared the leftovers. "Did you like the turkey loaf, Mark?"

"You are an amazing cook. Great, again. Couple of things. First of all, Ben is going to be with his mother over Labor Day. I was thinking I'd love to take you somewhere for the weekend. Anywhere you'd like—Laguna, Santa Barbara, Vegas, your call."

"Really, Mark?"

"We have such a great time together," he said, placing the silverware in the sink.

Regina liked the twangs and clangs of the silverware hitting each other. She was also happy someone was in the house besides her, doing the clanging. She was mostly happy it was Mark.

"How kind, Mark. You know, I've actually never been to Palm Springs."

"Oh, really? OK. Consider it done. Which sponge do I use?"

"Yellow."

"And one other thing. Regina, you know it's us. It's honesty time at the Howell-Tunkell ranch."

Regina stopped for a moment. The picnic came circling back to her. She never really did address the picnic remarks.

RED FLAG
#6-4

287

She wondered if he was going to drop another of his pain-induced comments. *No, she thought. He hasn't done much of that lately.*

"What, Mark?"

"You know," he said, loading the dishwasher. "I don't say this very much. But I have a good deal of money. Making money is not my weak suit. So please, Regina, ask for anything your heart desires."

"Mark, darling, that is so kind of you," she said over the loud kitchen faucet.

He turned down the faucet, turned to her and pointedly declared, "You know, like a nose job."

"What?"

"Oh, sweetheart, you're such a striking woman. But really, your profile."

"What?"

"Come on, Regina. I'm not exactly Brad Pitt, but if I'd had a large profile, I would have done something about it."

"But," Regina began to explain, "I always thought my large cheekbones and big hair balanced out..." She dropped the dinner napkins she was holding and looked down.

"Oh, darling," said Mark. "I'm talking the difference between striking and gorgeous. That's all. I'm at your command, captain.

Whatever you need, I'm here. You dropped the dinner napkins."

Regina's classes were done for the day. She ambled to the middle of the dance studio, lifted up on the toes of one foot and practiced her balance. She caught a glimpse of her other bare leg. She had gained over twenty pounds since dancing with the *Companie Moderne de Danse* in Geneva. She had hated having to stay reed thin, living on vegetables, Swiss cheese, and café au lait sans sucre. Perhaps she had gone overboard. Perhaps Mark had a point.

"All that and perfect balance, too?" Luke interrupted her from the doorway.

"Luke, I didn't know you were here."

"It's my latent Peeping Tom thing."

"Come in, come in."

"May I? You were so deep in thought. And I know those thoughts. They're not all about balance."

"You should put up a sign and become a professional psychic, Luke."

He dropped to the floor and tugged at her skirt. "Sit, woman."

She did so and looked at him. "What?"

"Regina, I am your friend. I'm just going to put this out there," he said, lying on his belly, stretching his quadriceps. "You went from

289

exuberant person a few months ago to an overly pensive, always-deep-in-thought ballerina. Are you feeling well, bunny? Are your parents OK?" He sat up, took her hands and looked in her eyes. "What is going on?"

Holding onto Luke, she looked away and explained, "There is something. I'm going to withhold from a specific explanation until I know for sure."

He took one of her hands and began massaging it. "Is this something spelled M-a-r-k?"

"Um, yes."

"Do you wanna talk about it?"

"Not sure."

"So, you'd rather balance on your toes on one foot in the middle of the room and talk to yourself than anyone else. Is that right?"

RED FLAG #6-5

"I think so. I just don't have the glitch figured out. Something is off, but I can't put my finger on it."

"I see," said Luke, pulling away and really staring down his good friend and co-worker. She really did seem at a loss as to what exactly was going on, and how she was feeling.

"You know what, Luke? He is taking me to Palm Springs this weekend. Maybe I'll have a clearer picture afterward."

290

"Listen," he said, getting up. It was nearly time to teach the modern class. "Just remember, Dave and I both are only a phone call away."

They stared at each other for a moment. She blew him a kiss, and he left the room. Regina sighed deeply and returned to her balancing practice.

There's probably nothing impermissible going on here, she told herself. *I'm just probably an oversensitive artist*. Odd, how right then she lost her balance.

Mark reached over and splotched some more sunscreen on his face and neck. "Let me do your back, Regina. The Palm Springs sun is intense, even at this seven o'clock hour. OK?"

"Thanks, honey. Lather away," responded Regina, lying on her stomach with an unlaced bikini top. Mark straddled her and squeezed more sunscreen on the well-exposed back.

"Your hands feel so good, Mark."

"Regina, can I ask you something?" he asked in an intent tone.

"Hmm?" she lazily responded.

"Well. Remember I told you, money is no major object for me? I'm not wealthy, but... remember?"

"Yeah, sure. What, Mark?" She turned slightly to look at him applying lotion to her back.

"Regina, I could have afforded any hotel in Palm Springs. The best room would have been no problem. Why the hell did you book us into a hole? Don't you follow directions, woman?"

"What? What do you mean? This is a very nice hotel. What are you talking about? And it's Labor Day weekend. We were very lucky to get anything. What don't you like about it, pray tell?"

"Just that there's a casino; that alone attracts the riffraff. You know, a lower element of guests with whom I do not usually associate," he said, dismounting.

"Mark, look around you. It's quiet families and couples and well-behaved kids. What's the problem?" she asked, turning over. "This is such a nice hotel."

RED FLAG #6-6

"Can I express myself, Regina? You've never been married, so you really don't know how to negotiate or follow directions in a partnership. Read my lips. I wanted something more luxurious."

"I'm...I'm sorry. I think it's...I think it's fine. Next time, I'll confer with you more."

"And we'll see if you can follow directions better."

292

For the remainder of the day, Regina was quiet. Mark didn't seem to notice, didn't seem to mind. She observed a degree of edginess about him she had never seen before. She had known Mark only four months and they had never been away together. Again, she wasn't sure what was typical and what was out of character. It didn't seem as though there were any extraordinary concerns in his life right now for him to be so verbally rough. Regina was perplexed and offended.

The next morning, his edginess appeared to have subsided, so Regina suggested a jaunt through the Palm Springs Living Desert Museum. Mark seemed to really enjoy the Western Art, Agua Caliente, and Cahuilla Indian exhibits, and the charming miniature rooms. They came upon a room of small stuffed coyotes.

"Oh, look!" said Regina, throwing her head back in laughter. "A room full of San Antonios!"

Mark looked at her. He did not laugh. Yesterday's edginess came bolting back to his eyes. Regina found herself stepping back, away from him. She thought, *What could he possibly be mad at in this coyote exhibit?*

293

"It is not a room of San Antonios. The coyote is from the species Latrans, which is far from the Chihuahua. I took lots of biology in college. I don't understand your correlation."

"I was just—"

"And what's more, to be honest, Regina, as long as we're on the subject, frankly it's a pleasure not to be around your dog for once."

"I really don't bring him out with us very much, Mark. I'm careful about that."

"Well, maybe you could be a smidgen more conscientious by tapping into my feelings." Then he raised his voice, moved in toward her and continued, "Did you ever begin to consider that I don't need the influence of a third party when we are together?"

Regina looked at him in the darkened room of the coyote exhibit. Dark purple evening-assimilated lighting cast a haunting glow over the desert scene. She wished some of the coyotes were alive.

In a soft voice, she said, "It is way too air-conditioned in here. I'm, um, going back to the hotel."

Regina left the museum, walked a few blocks, and stood under a store awning which spewed water from a mister. The soft spray on her shoulders brought a modicum of peace to her busy brain. She wished she could have just gone home, but they had one more night together and he had driven.

A few hours later, she was reading in the hotel room when Mark returned with two bags. His demeanor was undisturbed. There was no remorse in his eyes. Again, this confused Regina.

RED FLAG
#6-7

"Oh, there you are, young lady. One bag for you and one for my Benjamin."

She opened the bag, which produced a hooded aqua sweater boasting Palm Springs on the pocket, with little palm trees on the cuffs. She modestly thanked him, but found herself uninterested in much conversation for the rest of the day. Again, to her confusion, Mark didn't seem to notice, or to mind.

The next day, Regina was delighted to be on the drive home. To keep the atmosphere light, she decided to indulge in pleasant small talk.

"So glad we got away this weekend, Mark."

"Yeah, wasn't it a fantastic weekend?" he responded, seemingly honest. He continued, "I really liked the aerial tramway and all the swimming I got in."

"And come on, Mark. You enjoyed winning eighty bucks in the casino. You had a smile that lit up the room."

"Yeah, I did. Wasn't it a great weekend?"

She stared at him. He looked as though he really meant what he said. The whole weekend he was insensitive to her moods, needs, and responses, as demonstrated by his constant jabs—big and small. Did he really think it was a great weekend? She thought she'd test him. "Oh wasn't it just wonderful?" she lied. "I can't think of anything better."

He didn't respond to that, but said, "So, you back to teaching next week?"

"Yep. New semester. We're putting in a second hip-hop class. It got such a great response. Boy, that department has had a metamorphosis since I got there."

"Well, you're unusual, Regina."

"What do you mean?"

"Come on, Regina. Most dancers aren't ambitious or productive."

"Mark, have you an inkling of the years of dedication it requires to become moderately good?"

"That's not what I mean. I don't know," he mused. "I just kind of consider dancers a breed of overly trained, bitter children with no place to put their art. They're not very developed in anything else, either. No wonder my Ben just sees it as a healthy pastime. Anyhow, you're not like the rest of them. Or at least

296

I don't think you are. I have more to get to know." He reached over, grabbed her hand, kissed it and said, "Sit up straight, woman."

She was silent for the remainder of the ride home.

Regina wheeled her little weekend suitcase into the living room. The house had a decidedly still air. The shades were drawn and the windows were closed, both creating their own muskiness. And San Antonio was not back from the dog sitter's to joyously greet her, show off, and lend his energy to the quiet setting.

Regina felt the loud stillness. She opened her suitcase and removed the new cable-knit sweater from Mark. She hugged it to her and closed her eyes, smelling its newness, its never-been-worn attitude. She held it in front of her, then walked to the hall closet, stuffed it in the "Goodwill Donations – Thank You" bag, and tightly sealed the top.

Across the room sat a framed eight-by-ten photo from the picnic. It showed Ben's version of a sombrero made from a napkin being modeled by San Antonio, with Mark and Regina laughing in the background. She picked up the photo, rubbed her finger around the velvet frame, and noticed a teardrop on the glass.

"How could you do that? What was all that about, Mr. Howell? And who the hell are you, anyway?" Then, instinctively and without much thought, she picked up the phone and shakily dialed.

"Luke? Hey, dollface, it's Regina. Are you really a phone call away?"

"Where are you?"

"Just got back from Palm Springs."

"Are you OK?"

"I don't know."

"What are you doing now?"

"I don't know."

"Did you have an OK time?"

"I don't know!" she sobbed.

"Don't move a muscle. Dave and I will be there in twenty minutes. Make a pitcher of iced tea. That will focus you."

"OK," she managed.

"Twenty minutes."

"Twenty minutes," she repeated.

"Alright?" he asked one more time.

"I love you, Luke. See you wonderful friends soon, please?"

As she opened the living room window, she saw the elderly couple who lived next door. They were on their porch, hugging, laughing, and patting each other on the back.

She thought, *Is that possible?*

They saw her and waved. She waved back, but wanted to say, "Don't let me interrupt that embrace. It looks real, eternal."

She moved robotically into the kitchen and fetched the large pitcher, various herbal teas, ice cubes, and lemon juice. She had put the water on to boil when she caught a glimpse of another framed photo over the stove.

It had been taken at her first dance recital, and she was wearing that voluminous pink tutu. She had worn that tutu all summer—over her clothes.

"Wasn't everything supposed to be perfect as long as you wore that tutu?" she asked the photograph.

"Let's see...Mark likes his iced tea with lots of lemon juice and in a tall glass, but...not with much ice...and yes, those bendy straws. Better get them out. He loves those straws."

She scurried around the kitchen making tea for the boys, or Mark, or someone. A thought crossed her mind about a card she had on her desk at work for some psychotherapist.

She stopped in her tea-making tracks and stared at the tutu picture again.

"Little Reggie," she said aloud, "one of the hardest things to do is to distance people who once promised you great hope.

Wouldn't you say so? And whatever did Mom do with that tutu? Anyway...where is that box of straws? I could have sworn...oh yeah, now I know what I did with them."

She stood in the middle of the kitchen and took a deep breath.

"That's right, I gave them to Mark."

She found some vanilla Pepperidge Farm cookies, put them out, and cleaned the box of strawberries that was in the fridge.

She then wheeled her suitcase to the bedroom and removed the contents.

There was a note inside, written on the hotel's stationery. Mark must have snuck it in her bag when she wasn't looking. It read,

Dear Regina,

I could not have imagined a more fabulous weekend with you.

Looking forward to another little trip exactly like this one.

Mark

Just then, the doorbell rang. Luke and his partner, Dave, had arrived.

300

DISCUSSION OF THE CHAPTER

RED FLAG #6-1

If someone goes so far as to explain an aspect of himself, often it is polite and diligent for the receiver of the message to ask him to elaborate. Regina had a perfect opportunity to get deeper and faster insight into this man by asking what he meant by saying he was tough on his employees and tough on women. Do you know, even some grievous criminals give clues before they are going to commit a crime?

Regina really made a mistake by not asking him to specifically elaborate. She would have garnered much information so that she might have nipped the relationship in the bud, as opposed to prolonging it into heartache. It is one thing to prematurely pry into areas that are not yet pry-able. It is quite another to be given information and to throw it away. People usually do the latter because they believe the information is too delicate or too heavy. But for whom?

What's really going on here is the downdater, Regina, is protecting the downdatee, Mark. Do you see how downdaters discard their own importance? It was an ingrained reflex for Regina not to ask many more questions. It is an ingrained reflex for downdaters to protect downdatees.

So, if facts are presented to you that do not feel consoling, stop all engines and inquire. Do not discard these early bits of information. Remember, the early state of dating is the time to conduct discreet research, not to solidify denial.

RED FLAG #6-2

Regina did tell him she'd have no time to change for the cocktail party. This begs the question: A) did Mark really forget that she'd told him, or B) did he choose to forget? My response to A or B is the following. A: if he really forgot, why did he reprimand her in such a demeaning way? Pulling her aside and saying, "You knew I was going to have colleagues here…do you also shower in leotard and tights?" was uncalled for. If he was a gentleman, he wouldn't have remarked at all. This leads to response B: if he chose to forget and decided to lambaste her just for the heck of it, we have a pretty serious red flag here of downdatee #6: is physically or mentally abusive to the female.

Arbitrary lambasting is anger from past hurts that the abuser decides to let out on an unsuspecting present-day victim. One thing abusers do is dehumanize their victims, and unpredictably. He really talked down to Regina behind the plant pillar. She did not see it coming. It was the first time he did this, so Regina was not yet privy to his pitch-dark side.

Perhaps, readers, after reading this story, you will be able to catch these unpredictable slams faster in your own life.

Had Regina developed an awareness of this prior to meeting Mark, she might not have been so surprised or hurt at the cocktail party. Perhaps she might have handled his criticisms by returning an appropriate volley.

It is really important for us to be in touch with the behavior of critical, controlling people. Why continue to protect them? They are unpredictable and dehumanizing. With some knowledge, we can be aware of the unpredictable factor, at least. The dehumanizing is bad enough. I believe these people have to be verbally nipped in the bud, immediately. Something as simple as "that really hurts" goes a very long way.

RED FLAG #6-3

Buddha said, "Abuse is evil." So what is abuse? Certainly a rude comment at a picnic is not commensurate to sexual abuse or physical abuse. Yes, that is an obvious given. However, we must observe what the emotional abuser does, how he operates. The case of the picnic is the perfect example. One of the methods emotional abusers employ is that of slowly eroding the victim's sense of self-worth and self-esteem. Mark offhandedly threw this comment out to her as though he was asking her to pass the salt at dinner. If he really did not care about weight, why did he address it at all?

To women, weight generally is a very sensitive subject. Compulsive eaters, I believe, have a biochemical imbalance such that it is difficult to stop eating. Regina knew she was not in that category. Nonetheless, most women are socialized into believing their bodies are not and never will be good enough. Airbrushed magazine covers and sleight-of-hand TV commercials are the damnable culprits, and women are inundated with them. For a modern-day, intelligent man to be unaware of this is simple hogwash and deeply rude. And too much hogwash peppered with "deeply rude" adds up to abuse, my readers.

Here's the spectrum. On one end is the jerk; as we traverse down the spectrum, there sits the narcissist, then the abuser, and finally, at the other end of the spectrum resides the sociopath. Sometimes there are great distances between these categories. Sometimes their boundaries are blurred. I again refer to red flag #6-2 regarding his unpredictable dehumanization.

So, Mark is really collecting "admirable" character points. He is clearly an unpredictable dehumanizer and has proven he can produce piercing judgments at the expense of her self-worth. At this point, readers, I'd say this man has to be watched under a microscope.

RED FLAG #6-4

There are two reasons why Regina did not respond to the barrage of criticisms at the picnic.
1) She didn't see it coming and it really blindsided her. When she got on top of the "blindside," she felt too hurt and confused to address the criticisms. Instead, she just covered up her body.
2) It may sound weird, but she hadn't read this book. By reading this story, you have opened a tiny doorway of awareness that Regina did not possess.

The American Medical Association defines abuse as: "is regularly threatened, yelled at, humiliated, ignored, blamed, or is otherwise emotionally mistreated."

It is interesting, yet worrisome, that people have to be hurled against walls or have purple

305

bruises and broken bones for them to believe they are being mistreated. Regina had ample occasion to address her feelings of surprise and hurt. Never bringing it up gave Mark the message that his spontaneous outbursts were commonplace, no big deal. But Regina's sadness fully contradicted that possibility.

Emotional abusees commonly feel if they do not address the piercing assaults, then the assaults will magically vanish and the abusers latent humanity will grandly emerge. And so, the abusee maintains a nonsensical formula, stating, "If I withhold my hurt feelings, no doubt his true loving empathy will eventually spring forth." This is a pointless mind-set from a pointless formula.

Unfortunately, however, because the abusee allows such behavior to ensue for so long, the emotional abuser can morph into the purple bruiser and bone breaker. This is not far-fetched.

RED FLAG #6-5

"Something is wrong, but I can't put my finger on it."

I have expressed it before and I will express it again. We can't all be psychotherapists. Even highly trained and experienced psychotherapists cannot always figure out the inconsistencies in a couple-ship. So, when that "something is off" instinct rears its head and ruffles its feathers, pay full attention to that divinely created instinct.

Again, you do not have to figure it out. You do not have to be totally clear or eloquent when you express your confusion. All you need to say to your significant other is, "Something is off." Trust your instinct. Go with it.

Definitely allow a communication of your upset to fall upon the ears of the upsetter. Don't withhold, deny, or sweep it under the complicated Persian rug.

In this particular setting, inside the comfort of her dance studio, Regina still couldn't open up to her good buddy, Luke. Probably, Luke could have shed some light on her confusion.

I always suggest bringing your questions to a friend and/or a professional. But most importantly, be prepared to express it to the guilty party at large. You really must ask yourself what it is about you that needs to protect the guilty party's dreadful actions and emotionally abusive mode of treating the world.

RED FLAG #6-6

I need to come in on two fronts regarding this red flag.

First of all, abuse itself is universal, I regret to say. It is in fairy tales (look at Cinderella's

307

stepsisters, Hansel and Gretel's old woman encounter, etc.). It is all over Greek mythology. Hera flew Hercules' children into the fire; Apollo's wife had an affair, so he killed her and her lover; Andromeda's father chained her to a rock to be killed by a sea monster—just to name a few.

I bring this up because it begs the question if abuse is archetypal (archetypal is defined as a specific behavior and energy that exists in all mankind's unconscious mind—across every society and over time). And if it is archetypal, then all the more important for us to develop an awareness of it and banish it at its inception. Also, if it is archetypal, it still does not excuse or condone behavior like Mark's.

Part two of this red flag addresses people who carry out this abusive archetype. They are called narcissists. (Note: narcissists are created by a distinct type of parenting that is beyond the scope of this book.) The word narcissism is taken from a Greek myth about Narcissus, a youth who fell in love with his own image in a pool of water. In lay terms, narcissism itself is defined as vanity, and selfish self-centeredness.

To narcissists, life is perceived as consistently unpleasant and insecure. To them, intimacy and closeness will eventually bring about displeasure and pain.

This is the edginess Regina perceived in this narcissist, Mark. He liked her and was feeling close to her, but remember, closeness in a narcissist equals eventual pain. Unconsciously, Mark established a wedge between them to keep out the pain (I call it "ghost pain").

In this example, his wedge was a firewall of rude, unnecessary reflections regarding a rather nice hotel.

Congratulations, Mark, your wedging was effective. You did successfully distance Regina. But something else, Mark. The more you wedge with an abusive style, the more it will be apparent you are a blaring downdatee, the true persona non grata. You might need to learn, Mark, life is not about pain and control. For everywhere there exist beautiful souls and very safe women. Unfortunately for you, the more women (people) who read books like these, the more we will be aware of your mean-spirited schemes. Maybe someday you will learn humility, get help, and change. And then, oh joy, the world will be fortified with yet more winners.

RED FLAG #6-7

I hope you have been taking notes on these red flags. Here are some clues to look for in an abuser:

Someone who picks fights, blames, has abuse in his background, is cruel, ignores personal boundaries, or controls any situation possible. Abusers often do these things with little remorse or guilt.

Mark was most cruel and certainly guilty of picking a fight at the museum. Intelligently, Regina removed herself from his force field. When he met up with her a few hours later with the new sweater, he acted as though nothing bad had happened. This seemed to be a pattern with him. Again, narcissists believe all relationships end in humiliation, betrayal, or abandonment. Their motto is "Get her before she gets me."

A woman's or any healthy significant other's demands for intimacy are seen by the narcissist as a threat. Luckily, Mark didn't seem to exercise this behavior with his son. In this case, the narcissist was able to compartmentalize his dysfunctional behavior. (Remember? "I am only tough on two subcultures, employees and women.")

It is important for you to understand that dating an emotional abuser is dating down. If you have not seen a quick change away from the abusive behavior early in the relationship, don't expect to see it from him at all. For unless there is early-on, sincere apologizing and a behavioral shift, there will always be unpredictable anguish.

Therefore, what has to happen here cannot be your waiting for them to change. Remember constant #2 from the introduction: the male in this relationship exhibits a stubborn resistance to change his maladaptive behaviors. Rather, what has to happen here is your refraining from dating down.

It is strictly your choice, again. You may opt to take this short walk on our planet in comfort, or in unremitting heartache. At this juncture, it really looked like Regina was about to embark on a more comfortable walk...or dance.

311

CHAPTER SEVEN

ILLUSTRATING DOWNDATEE #7 –

Is Chronically Unemployed, Has No Aspirations of Exceeding Minimum Wage, and/or Is Financially Supported by the Female

Entitled...

THE GIRL WITH A SILVER SPOON IN HER WALLET

I pulled back the curtains in the kitchen and marveled at the unique and cozy display before me. Rain—not the most common occurrence in these parts—happily dominated my view.

I decided my favorite Sunday drink would be in order. So I concocted the chai tea, soy milk, and Stevia powdered brew I so loved and brought it and the Sunday *Times* to my couch. I was about to hunker down in this most relaxed setting when something told me to call my answering service.

"No," I said, on second thought. "No patient is calling me at seven o'clock on a Sunday morning." But intuition trounced logic and led me to the phone.

There were two messages. One was from an acquaintance with a rather inconsequential message. The second was not from an acquaintance, nor was it an inconsequential message. I put my steaming chai concoction down to take notes. The second message went something like this:

"Um...Carole...my name is Peter. I, um, I am calling about...er, for...my employer. Can you call me when you have a chance? The number is 555-2013."

I thought, *A little odd. This man calls me on a Sunday morning about his employer?* I reached for a pen and the notepad and dialed him right back.

"Hello," he answered.

"Hi, this is Carole Field, Peter. I am returning your call."

"Thank you so much for calling back so quickly. Um...one moment, please." Then he covered the mouthpiece and muttered something to someone. He then asked, "May I call you Carole, ma'am?"

"Of course," I replied.

"Um...well...you see, this inquiry is for my employer."

"OK, Peter."

"How soon can she get an appointment with you?"

"Well, let me check my appointment calendar."

As I moved to my appointment book, he continued, "I mean, Carole, like, the sooner the better. I mean, I hope you can squeeze her in tomorrow because, ma'am, let me tell you this right up front."

"Yes, Peter?"

"Money is positively no object. Charge us anything. She needs your services. I mean, it's not like she is going to die or—"

"I understand." So I said. In actuality, this type of desperation was somewhat unusual to my ears.

"So charge us anything," he reiterated.

"No. I won't do that," I said. "I will just charge you what I charge everyone else. Could your employer come by tomorrow at eleven?"

"Yes, yes," he said, leaping on my offering like a lapdog.

"You sound like quite a conscientious employee."

"I basically work for the family. I'm not sure I want to elaborate on the phone. We will be there at eleven sharp. Thank you. Bye," he efficiently responded, and hung up.

I stood staring at the phone through the now-lessened steam of the chai tea. I was aware of the fact that he had not given me his employer's name. Yet he had sounded either anxious or conscientious. I guessed more conscientious. And what? "Money is positively no object. Charge us anything."

I brought my tea and newspaper to the other side of the couch. It was closer to the window and I loved the clapping of rain on its pane.

Inside my house I felt cozy, safe, and protected. I was reasonably sure Peter and his employer, however, were not having the same feelings. I wished them peace and comfort, knowing tomorrow the pieces would begin to actualize.

Circa 1899

Twelve-year-old Isaiah Hamilton clung to his mother's arm. Mom and son were dressed in their "other outfits," their arrival clothes. He in woolen stockings, knickers, and a brown sailor shirt; Mom in a long tweed skirt and a waistcoat over laced-up boots. Isaiah enjoyed standing on the stern of the grand ship.

"I want to be the first person to see the port of Maine, USA, Mama."

"Perhaps you will be," replied the admiring mother, who had booked third-class passage for herself and Isaiah. "You have been first in many things, Isaiah," she laughed.

"I'm glad to leave that place, Mommy. You deserve a better life than the poverty of old Cornwall, England. We will have a better life. I will make it so."

She observed her son gazing at the horizon. She was always amazed by his insights and determination, despite the fact of his having had no father or consistent male guidance.

Suddenly, Isaiah opened his eyes very wide and began to jump up and down. "Mother! Mother, look!" he irrepressibly sang out, holding onto his flat cap, lest it blow off and into the sea. "Look, Mama. Can you see it?"

"I see something, darling," his mother responded, straining to make out something vague in the distance.

"Look, Mother, I can see it. I can see it. I believe, I believe, I do believe I see a tree!"

Nineteen years later, the Hamilton Logging and Timber Company became the largest company of its kind in Maine. Young Isaiah did see a tree and did see America first. He also gave his mother a better life—all as promised—or so the story goes.

Cut to 1996 Southeast Maine

Young Kristina Hamilton was escorted into her dad's office by the family driver. She loved sitting in Daddy's large leather chair. Above her was a grand ten-foot painting of great-grandfather Isaiah, the original founder of Hamilton Logging and Timber.

Isaiah the first - towered above her, surrounded by his wife, children, cat, and mother. He looked proud, humble, and determined, all in one. Kristina thought her dad had inherited Great Grandpa's deep-set eyes.

The furniture before her was eclectic, but comfortable. There were brown Italian leather couches, antique hutches that were whispered to be Heppelwhites, chairs that were whispered to be Stickleys, and a wonderful large antique rocking horse she had only recently outgrown. Dad must have just left the room, she thought, because the tape of *Evita* was playing.

Kristina wore a blue jean miniskirt, pink leg warmers, and a new pink Madonna T-shirt. Dad, Isaiah the third, walked into the room, head buried in a contract.

"Hi, Daddy, I'm here!" she announced.

"Sweetheart," he said, setting down the contract, "I didn't hear you come in."

She ran over and gave her dad a hug.

"How was school?" he asked.

"Fine, I just wish it didn't start so early, Daddy."

"I know, darling. Do you want something to eat?"

"No, Daddy, Mommy will have a snack for me."

"Then come and sit here on the couch. There's something quick I want to tell you, Kristina."

Kristina climbed up on the large leather sofa. The thick leather felt a little cold beneath her, so she pulled up her leg warmers. "You have a new plant in here, Daddy."

"Oh, do we?" her dad laughed. "I didn't notice." He walked over to the tape player as *Evita* was going into her final aria, turned it off, sat next to his only child and took her hand.

"Kristina," he began, "I want to talk to you about something. This talk is really from your mother and me." Kristina wondered if he was going to talk to her about the birds and the bees. She hoped not because she and her girlfriends were already looking into that subject.

"Kristina, look around this office." She did so. "Tomorrow is your tenth birthday and you are going to have a grand party. I wanted to get this in before your party because I thought you were big enough and smart enough to understand what I'm going to say." At that point, she was pretty sure the birds and the bees were not the topic. Dad reached over and picked up an ashtray.

"Do you see this ashtray?"

"Yes, Papa."

"Kristina, this ashtray alone cost one hundred and fifty dollars. Do you understand what one hundred and fifty dollars can buy most people?"

"Many birthday party favors."

"Oh yes, dear. Now, let me tell you something. Do you know what a trust fund is, darling?"

"Isn't it like your own bank account?"

"Good girl, sweetheart. OK, Kristina. Tomorrow is your tenth birthday. On your eighteenth birthday, in only eight years, you're going to inherit a, well, a rather large trust fund. Then on your twenty-eighth birthday, approximately twenty-five percent of this company will be in your name. It was set up that way. Does that make sense to you?"

She had a concerned look in her eyes. "But Papa, will I know what to do with everything by then?"

He laughed. "You never have to worry. We have numerous accountants and

business managers taking care of everything and keeping each other in check.
You will be well taken care of."

"I see, Daddy."

"I just have two requests of you in order to
keep these nice things, Kristina."

"Yes, Papa?" she responded respectfully.

"You must finish college," he said, and
lowered his eyes a tad, "and you must
always be kind to people. Nobody will be
able to check that one out, sweetheart, but
you will know it in your heart. That is what
we Hamiltons do. That is just what we
Hamiltons do."

"Of course, Daddy, we must always be
kind to people. Of course. But I just have
one question."

"Yes, dear?"

She looked across the room at the
antique rocking horse. "Will I be able to
keep the rocking horse?"

Dad threw his head back and laughed.
Just then, his secretary walked in.

"Oh, hi!" she said to Kristina. "Love your
Madonna T-shirt."

"Miss Lee," Isaiah said to his secretary,
"make a note for the lawyers to add as an
addendum in Kristina's trust fund."

"Yes, sir." She picked up a tablet of paper
to write.

"Make sure Kristina always has that rocking horse. OK?"

Miss Lee hid her smile and feigned great importance. "But of course, sir, of course. I will take care of that promptly." Miss Lee and Isaiah the third looked over at the about-to-be-ten-years-old Kristina. She was leaning back on the large couch that enveloped her little body, nodding her head and beaming a most contented smile.

September 2008

Kristina and her best friend, Polly, endured the university's long registration line. This year the undergrads were registering outside on the quadrangle. Sandy-haired, pretty, pixie Kristina and six-foot, overweight Polly were the Mutt and Jeff of Hollins University. Best friends, the odd couple, fiercely loyal.

"Whoa, Polly, I can't believe we're registering for the last year at Hollins. Where did the time go?"

Across from her, on one of the building walls, Kristina observed the September clinging ivy. She wasn't sure if the ivy was Japanese, Irish, or Persian. In no time, she thought, that ivy will be dusted with snow, then peeking out for spring, early summer, graduation, and life.

"I love this college, Polly, and I love Virginia."

"We all do, Kris. But have you heard the news?"

"News?" asked Kris.

"Yes," began her pal, "they're thinking of this being the swan song for undergrad girls only. Thinking of admitting male types in the fall."

"Are you kidding? How sad. This was one of the last holdouts. I rather enjoyed going to class in modifications on a theme of pajamas." The girls in line behind them laughed.

Kris and Polly paid their hefty registration fee and exited the crowded courtyard.

"So, what classes did you nab, Krissy?"

Kris responded, looking at her schedule as they sauntered through the green manicured courtyard. "I got Professor Johnson's coveted Ancient History class; Physiology II; British Poetry—ick, eight a.m.—and...Jewelry Making."

"Jewelry making?" asked a male voice behind them.

They stopped and saw a male, about their age, seated on a courtyard bench.

"Really?" he asked again. "Are you trying to bring back the hat stickpin?"

The two friends glanced at each other. It was odd to see a male on under-graduate registration morning. He was carrying a loose-leaf notebook and a textbook.

"Good morning," Kris responded, thinking the unusual sight was also an aesthetically pleasing sight.

"And a fine good morning to you register-ing co-eds."

"Registering co-eds?" asked Polly. "You sound like a timeworn character out of a 1940s movie."

"What 1940s movie, young woman? Per-haps a Dario Argento?"

"Who?" asked Kris.

"Dario Argento. He was an Italian shock, horror, and cult director."

"No," said Polly, "I'm thinking more along the lines of a Preston Sturges comedy. Listen, I gotta go back to the reg area. There's one class on my schedule that's not going to work. Kris, I'll catch you later," she said, giving Kris a hug. "Good-bye, director," she said to the young man, and she vanished into the crowd.

"And you've never heard of Dario Argento?"

"No," laughed Kris.

"Well, you should have. You have an excellent film curriculum on this campus."

"How do you know?" asked Kris.

The young man looked to his right as though he was looking for an answer—the correct answer. He looked back at Kris. "Just that my old girlfriend used to go to this university."

"Got it. Well, I really should get to my car and go to my apartment. Got a lot to do before school goes into high gear."

"May I walk you to your car? My name is Paul, or call me Dario," he said, extending his hand.

"Uh, sure," Kris said as they shook hands. "I'm Kristina, or Kris. Do you live around here?"

He did not answer right away. He glanced away and looked back at her three times before responding.

For a moment she pondered his slow reaction time to such a direct inquiry.

RED FLAG
#7-1

He then said, "I have a bevy of pals who attend Hollins University. Thought I'd drop by."

"Oh, how nice. Anyhow, my car's right here."

Paul/Dario eyed the white Cadillac Escalade. He looked at Kris. She did not feel the need to offer any excuses.

329

"I don't mean to be invasive," he said, "but is there something like a phone number whereby one might contact you? Emails are too cold."

She laughed. "I thought you'd never ask," she said, and removed a piece of paper from her just-purchased Hollins University spiral notebook.

"I will call you, Kristina. You seem very sweet." He took her number and saluted her.

"Nice meeting you, Dario."

"Oh, before I go, I must give you this information."

"You must?" She smiled.

"Yes. The number-one grossing film of 1940 was *Pinocchio*. Bye, pretty girl!" And his thin body in cuffed jeans ran off.

Kris stood there, smiling, thinking, "Yo, he is cute. I wonder if Polly really needed to return to the registration crowds? What an awesome friend." She threw her head back and chuckled.

"I just don't understand it, Polly," said Kris, nervously fiddling with her coffee stirrer. "Dario has called me three times, we have these extensive intellectual conversations, but he never asks me out."

"He's shy, Kris. Have him to dinner," said Polly, taking the stirring utensil from her and plopping it on her napkin.

"You think he's shy?"

"Well, at least it's one possibility."

The next night, Kris called Dario and asked him to dinner. He accepted.

Kris was putting the finishing touches on the yogurt parfaits for dessert. The salads and main course had gone well.

RED FLAG
#7-2

"Parfaits?" asked Paul/Dario.

"I hope you like them."

"What beautiful little parfait cups."

"Yes, my parents picked them up when they were touring the Lampang province of Thailand this summer. Thank you. So, Dario," she continued, dipping into her dessert, "you know, we've had lengthy phone conversations, but I don't know enough about the man sitting across from me. It's established that you are twenty-three, a year older than I am, but are you in school, or what? What occupies your days?"

RED FLAG
#7-3

"Well," said the thin man in a somewhat tattered (or was it just funky?) T-shirt, setting his spoon down and putting his hands behind his head. He looked to the right and into the distance. "It's not a gilded fairy tale."

331

Kris tilted her head in interest.

He began, "My dad was a traveling salesman for Xerox. He was never in town. My three sisters and I never saw him. The relationship between he and our mom progressively strained"—he picked up a cookie and demonstrated—"until it..." He broke the cookie and crumbs fell into his parfait.

"Snapped," Kris finished his sentence.

"That's right. Into crumbs. See?" He pointed. "And, well, the Cliff Notes version is, Dad met Nora of North Carolina. We call her NoNo. And that's where he's lived for six years."

"I'm sorry."

"Dropped—like a steaming hot potato—his family. Nothing. He sends no money. Mom works and I had to drop out of college and get a job."

Kris responded, "Oh, where do you work, Dario?"

"Here's part of the not-very-gilded fairy tale. I work nights at a hardware store. I've just been promoted to cashier. Days at our church, doing boy-Friday stuff, mostly janitorial work. And I tutor kids when I can mastermind my sisters' friends into paying me for the like. So that's it."

"You had to drop out of school? Where were you going?" she asked.

"Virginia Western Community College."

"How's your family doing?"

"I think all three girls have degrees of emotional fallout from His Fabulousness. I think *la madre*, however, is glad to be rid of him. You know, too much unpredictability."

"Well, where does she work?"

"In the office at the church," he responded.

A quiver of sadness cloaked in a cold sheath spiraled down Kris's solar plexus. She reached over and took Dario's hand.

He visibly acknowledged the empathy. "Kris, can I help you with the dishes? I should get going, but I would sure like to see you again."

"Of course we'll get together again," she said.

He stood up, carried his dishes to the sink and headed to the door. "Well," he said, "I am most seriously looking forward to seeing you again, pretty Miss Hamilton." Then, he pulled the small woman to him and courageously initiated the first kiss for both of their vulnerable lips. They tasted each other's parfaits—and timidity.

Before class the next morning, Kris called Virginia Western Community College.

RED FLAG
#7-4

"Admissions please," she asked, biting her nails and rocking back and forth on the dining room chair.

"Admissions. How can I help you?" said a friendly voice in a Virginia accent.

"Um, um, hello, good morning. I'm wondering if you have the ability to answer a very general question."

"We'll sure try, ma'am," said the voice.

"Um, generally, how much is a year's tuition at Virginia Western Community College?"

"Well, sure, ma'am. I wish everyone had such easy questions, ma'am. So, tuition rounds out to about four thousand dollars a year. Books and lodging are different per student, as you may well understand. And everything has to be in for this semester in one week because, you know, that's when we start for the year."

"Uh, yes, of course, I know, yes. Uh...uh, that's all I need. Thank you for your time."

After ending the call, she paced, eyes downcast. Then she stood in the middle of her living room, snapped her fingers and dialed another number.

A voice answered, "Maine Escrow and Trust."

"Mrs. Irving, please."

"One moment."

The one moment gave her more pause for deliberation. She came up with the same decision again.

"Good morning, Mrs. Irving here."

"Um, hi, Mrs. Irving. It's Krissy."

"Well, as I live and breathe. Now what's the deal here? You were supposed to call me as soon as you're settled in for the semester."

"I know, I'll call you next week and fill you in, but right now I have a pressing request and I have to be in class soon. So, well, could you do me a favor, Mrs. Irving?"

"Of course, Krissy. What is it?" said the old, loving acquaintance.

"I need you to cut me a check."

"Why? Your parents gave you a bunch of checks before you left for the semester."

"Um, no, this is from my trust fund. It's my own money. I mean, it's mine, like I don't have to get Mom and Dad's signature or anything, right?"

"No, of course not. What do you want me to send you?"

"Um, actually, make it out to Dario, er, Paul Dawson."

"OK, Kris. What amount?"

"Hmm, ten thousand dollars," she replied.

"You're sure?" asked Mrs. Irving.

"Yes."

"I'll get it in the mail today."

"I have to run to class. Can I call you next week?"

"You'd better, young lady."

"Love you."

"Love you, too, sweetie."

She hung up the phone, smiled, slipped into her blue Reeboks and bounced out of the apartment.

Dario took Kris's hand while driving her Cadillac Escalade. "I'm really going to miss you over Thanksgiving vacation, Kris."

"I know, honey, but my parents would have tortured me if I didn't come home."

"Slow, painful crucifixion," he laughed.

"At least you'll have my car all to yourself for a week."

"Um, yeah," he replied.

She shifted in her seat and looked more directly at her driver. "Dario, are you going to call Valley Western Community College back and find out why you weren't able to register?"

"Uh, yes. I'll try one more time to get a straight answer. Boy, that made me mad."

"It was all so weird. We got the money in on time," she said.

Dario leaned over and turned up the radio. "Nice clear day for traveling," he said over the loud music. She lowered it.

"And remember, Dario, my azaleas have to stay very moist. The amaryllis just needs moderate watering and the dracaenas even less, OK?"

"I know, sweetheart, I wrote it down."

"You are an angel, Dario."

He picked up her hand and kissed it. "Look!" he exclaimed. "The Roanoke airport already."

Kris put her key in the door. The Thanksgiving excursion home was wonderful, but the return flight was delayed for hours due to thunderstorms and she felt like she was catching a cold from Maine's early deep freeze. Dario couldn't pick her up at the airport because he had to work, and the cab driver had driven too fast and wouldn't stop talking.

RED FLAG
#7-5

"God, I'm glad to be home," she sighed.

She walked into the kitchen and noticed the juicer was in the middle of the kitchen table, where it normally did not live. She also noticed it had been used and not washed.

"What?" she exclaimed. "I forgot to clean the juicer a week ago, before I left?"

She walked into the bedroom and noticed three pairs of men's shoes on the floor.

337

"What is this?"

Then she saw a note in Dario's script on the bed.

> Kristina,
> I need to stay at your place through Christmas. Too much holiday goings-on at the Dawson pad. Hope it is OK.
> Can't wait to see you tonight, my lollipop.
> Dario

Kris put one knee on the bed. She then noticed some books that weren't hers in the corner. She walked over to them. *A Man's Simple Guide to Plumbing.*

She laughed and decided she would be glad to host Dario for a month, if his house was too holiday droning. But, she was confused as to why he hadn't previously alerted her.

"Oh well, Krissy, don't be so exacting. You dig him. It will be a fun month," she said, as she opened her suitcase and removed the beautiful Peruzzi leather jacket she had purchased for him in Maine.

RED FLAG
#7-6

Dario took Kris's hand. "It's jam-packed, honey."

338

She replied, "We are at a shopping mall and it's two weeks before Christmas. Of course it's jam-packed. Frankly, I love the cheerfulness. Oh, there's Polly now."

Tall Polly approached her two friends, loaded down. She had numerous over-stuffed shopping bags in each hand.

"Let me help you." Dario reached over and grabbed a few. "Hell's bells, what do you have in here?"

"I decided to get everything today. I refuse to go into my chemistry final with more Christmas shopping to be done. Come on, let me buy you guys some coffee. I need to sit."

"We're glad to see you, Polly," Kris warmly acknowledged her friend.

"Just don't look in the yellow bag." She pointed and they all laughed. "So, Dario, what are you buying Kris for Christmas? You have to buy her something nice because the holiday was named after her."

"Very funny," Kris laughed. When she looked at her boyfriend, he didn't seem to join in the joke. He looked away.

Brash Polly continued, "Certainly, with all the jobs you're working, you've been saving for something sweet for my darling friend. One small espresso," she requested from the barista. "Come on guys, it's on me."

The three of them grabbed their drinks and found seats. Dario was a little quiet.

Declarative Polly continued, "So, Dario, what happened? Are you going to enroll in VWCC this coming semester?"

"Oh...oh, yes," he replied, looking into his large chai latte and taking a bite of his biscotti.

"You didn't tell me, honey," Kris jumped in.

"It just didn't come up. Of course I am."

"What are you taking?" asked Polly. "And did they return the other check, by the way?"

"I'm not sure what I'm taking. And there was a problem with the other check."

"A problem?" asked Kris.

"Oh, no big deal. We can talk about it later," he said.

"Listen, you guys, I have one more gift to buy and I still have to study today," Polly said. "Kris, I'll give you a call tomorrow." Then Polly's eyes locked with Dario's. He couldn't read her, but did see the uncon-cealed steeliness in her gaze. Kris saw it, too, but it confused her. Polly took the final swig of her espresso, picked up her load, and disappeared into the swarming crowd.

"Dario?" asked Kristina.

"Hmm?" he replied, hungrily chomping on his biscotti, as if he hadn't eaten in days.

"What were you talking about? What kind of problem?"

"Well, not really a problem with the college. A problem..."

"What?"

"With my family."

RED FLAG
#7-7

"Like what?" asked Kris, concerned.

"OK, I'll just tell you. My dad sent no money for three months, and we had to pay the mortgage and the girls' dentist bills and for the broken furnace, and, well, I didn't use it for college. It's gone," he said, looking down.

"Oh," Kris responded, trying to stay calm.

"I didn't mean to spend it. Finances are so difficult at home."

Kris slowly stood up and walked over to Dario. She put her arms around his neck.

He returned the hug and said, "And I was so looking forward to starting school next month. But can you imagine a house without heat? I care for you so much, Krissy."

"Don't worry about it, Dario. I am sorry you are going through such upheaval. I hope the girls' teeth are OK."

"Um...yeah...better."

"Good. I'll see if my family might be able to assist you a little more," she replied,

341

already thinking of the best time to call Mrs. Irving tomorrow.

Kris and Polly went sloshing through the cold February rain. "I'm so glad that class was cancelled today, Polly. I can get more studying done at home than listening to our professor's dull assistant. He's like a human sleeping pill."

"I know. God, he's a bore. Here's your apartment. Call me later, Kristina."

Kris happily put the key in the door, looking forward to some quiet study time that just happened to fall into her lap when... legs folded, face up and snoring, lay boyfriend Dario, with a *Gilligan's Island* rerun whirring in the background. Turning off the TV still didn't stir the horizontally lollygagging figure.

"Um, Dario?"

"Oh. Oh." He started to stir. "Wow. Deep sleep," he laughed.

Dario did not move out after Christmas as he originally promised. She also could have sworn he had been in the apartment a number of times in the afternoons when he was supposed to have been at work, based on articles in the rooms being moved, but she couldn't be certain.

"Hi," he continued. "What are you doing home so early?" He sat up and rubbed his eyes.

Kris marginally contained her rage. "My class was cancelled for the day. Sick assistant professor." She stood and stared at him.

He looked up at her. Long pause. He smiled.

Then she asked, "You?"

"Oh, um, they didn't need me at work today and my class was cancelled, too."

She pulled up a chair. "Are you really working, Dario?"

"What do you mean?"

"Do you want me to say it in Portuguese?"

"Yes, Krissy, I'm really working. Just not this week."

"This whole week?"

"Well, the last two weeks."

"What? Why didn't you tell me?"

"It's not really important—temporary layoffs."

RED FLAG
#7-8

"What? Layoffs at the church? Is God taking a vacation for the week?"

"Now you're starting to sound like Polly," he said.

"Perhaps I should try to sound more like Polly. Just how long has this been going on, Dario?"

"Which job?" he slowly asked.

"What? Both. And the tutoring."

He got up, went into the kitchen and poured himself a Coke. While pouring his drink, he said, "I've decided I like Pepsi better. Plus, they never had cocaine in their soda like Coke did."

RED FLAG
#7-9

"Answer me, please."

"Um, the tutoring stopped months ago. It just dried up. Nobody called."

"Months ago?" she asked. "And the hardware store?"

"Same."

"What?"

"They had to let me go—the economy."

"You never told me. So you've just been working in the church for a few months?"

"Well, Kris, I'm laboring so hard in school—taking a full load and stuff." He took a sip. "So work had to take a back seat."

She took a deep breath, turned away, and stood up.

"Where are you going?" he asked.

"I'm going to the library to study. Enjoy your TV show." She went to the TV and turned it on for him.

And over the canned laughter of some banal dialogue between Gilligan and the Skipper, through the front door, she heard

344

Dario yell after her, "I'll have dinner ready for you when you return."

"Krissy, it's your mother."

"Hi, Mom, good to hear from you."

"Kristina, your father and I have been very worried about you. You haven't called in over two weeks. Now, those weren't the rules."

"I know, Mom. So much studying."

"Hold on, baby. Daddy wants to talk to you."

"Hi, angel food cake."

"Daddy, hey."

"Angel, what time do you get out of physiology tomorrow?"

"Um, why? Four o'clockish," she answered.

"OK, now listen. I don't mean to alarm you, but there will be a Mr. Constantine outside your classroom. Just look for someone who isn't nineteen, OK?"

"Dad, why?"

"I just want you to stay safe, angel. You know that. I have to go."

"Gee, you're cryptic."

"Love you." Click.

Kristina left her physiology class delighted that the assistant professor was

345

no longer assisting. The main professor was so engaging that she even enjoyed learning about aerobic respiration. As she walked out of her lecture hall contemplating how aerobic respiration and photosynthesis became linked, she noticed a handsome man around fifty, in a gray suit, leaning against the lockers and clutching a briefcase. He didn't look nineteen. She walked over to him, but did not say anything.

"Kristina?" the gentleman asked.

"You must be Mr. Constantine."

"How do you do? Call me Bob. Your dad sent me." He extended his hand and then pulled out a business card. "Can we go somewhere and be alone?"

"Of course."

"Can I take you for a snack, Kristina? Any quiet restaurants around here?"

"Just what is this regarding, sir? I don't mean to be rude."

"Let's talk, Kristina."

They found a juice bar across the street and ordered.

"I'm a retired policeman," he began. "All I do is private detective work right now. I love it. I fly around the country. I'm based in Maine and have known your family for years."

"You've worked for us?"

He laughed. "Oh, on and off, I might add."

"Have you seen me before?" she asked.

"Not since your big tenth birthday party."

"Oh my God, I remember you!" she exclaimed. "You have a son my age."

"There you go."

"Oh, Bob, excuse me. I didn't mean to be rude."

"Of course not. But I think we need to get to business." He unlatched his briefcase.

"Are my parents OK?"

He looked up. "They're perfect, and they're looking forward to being here with you at your graduation in a few months."

"Oh, good, wonderful." She took a sip of her carrot juice. It was too thick and she contemplated returning it, but was too mystified by the x-factor in front of her to leave the table.

"First of all," said Bob, "a note from your papa." Kristina opened a letter scribbled on his embossed business stationery. She read it aloud.

Krissy Angel,

I hope you don't hate your mother and me for this, but frankly, when you came for Thanksgiving we were very concerned. You weren't yourself, especially when the subject of Dario/Paul arose. We tried to pry some significant information out of you, but you'd clam up and look very sad. Then, when you decided not to join us for Christmas at the beach house, which you so love, we really became concerned. And your phone calls have not been like you.

So, we decided to put Mr. Constantine lightly on the case. Please understand we were worried. You've been tight-lipped and we felt at a loss.

I will never do this again, I promise, but you are only twenty-two and very far from us. Call me tonight, please. Oh, and Kristina, kindness comes in various forms. Remember that.

All my love,
Papa

She set the letter down. "So, what else, Bob?"

He took out a large photo of Dario. "Do you know this person?"

"Uh, yes."

"Is it Paul Christopher Dawson?" Bob asked.

"What? His middle name is Christopher? He's a Chris, too? He never told me."

Bob had an intent expression. "Apparently he hasn't told you many things."

Kris leaned back in her chair. "Go on."

"First of all, not to worry. He doesn't have a prison record; no pedophilia, drug dealing, none of that high drama."

"OK." She feigned the fact that she was somewhat relieved.

"Now," began Bob, "he lives with his mom and younger sisters when he's not living with you."

So far, so good, she thought.

"Um, did he tell you he goes to school, or works, or what?" he asked.

"Sure, yeah, both," she answered, trying another sip of the undrinkable carrot juice. She wasn't sure exactly what influence in her life right now was making her queasy.

"When did you meet him, Kristina?"

"Um, at registration on Reg Day."

Mr. Constantine took out some more photographs.

"Oh!" Kris said, flinching. "That's the three of us at the mall last Christmas. And who are these people?" He had three photographs of Paul with three other women.

"Diana was last year. This is Bonnie Susan the year before. This is Bebe, the year before that."

"So he had girlfriends," she shrugged.

"Not girlfriends, Kristina, not girlfriends." He leaned forward in his chair. "Supporters, sugar mamas, human loan institutions."

"What?" she inquired.

"That's right, dear. He and his family have it down. He stakes out women every registration day at this pricey girls' college and is set up for the year."

"What, Bob? How did you contact them?"

"Are you kidding?" he laughed. "This kind of work and low-tech surveillance are my specialties. It's quite routine, dear. Anyway, Mr. Dawson apparently has the same rap for all his prey. Sisters' dental bill is the big one."

"What?"

"And one of his sisters blazes the same scam. She just does it at Semper Fi Academy for Boys. She's sixteen."

"I don't believe my ears, Bob."

"What did Mr. Dawson tell you about his father?"

"Um, divorced, took off with another lady, never sends child support."

"The first two are correct."

"He does send child support?"

"Damn straight he does. He's an executive at Xerox. He could have his wages garnished in a wink. Oh, and as an aside, he's the first family member to put on a white shirt. He's from a long line of coal miners. Plus, he doesn't want to incur the wrath of his wife. Guess why."

"I...I don't..." Kris just shook her head.

Bob said, "She's the ringleader."

"What?"

"How much money did you give Mr. Dawson this year?"

She looked down. "In total, about twenty thousand dollars."

"Ouch. But you got off light. Huh."

"My head is swimming," she responded. "I graduate in two months. What should I do?"

"He's not a full on criminal. This doesn't really fall under the rubric of extortion because there would have to be a threat or fearful coercion involved. But if he ups the ante, remember, extortion is a felony."

351

"What should I do from here?" wide-eyed Kris asked.

Mr. Constantine sat back in his chair and placed his arms behind his head. "Well, let's keep it local and present, Kristina. Why don't you start by asking the guy behind the counter for a better carrot juice?"

She eked out a smile.

As the audience slowly filtered onto the courtyard, Kristina waited with the other graduates in her cap and gown, wearing Great-Grandma Hamilton's silver bracelet and cameo necklace.

She had purchased three guest tickets for the event. Two for Mom and Dad, who proudly flew in from Maine, and one for Dario.

She continued dating Dario after her revealing meeting with Mr. Constantine. She never told Dario about the meeting, but she did request that he immediately move out. He did so without much negotiation.

RED FLAG #7-10

Her feelings for him were clearly waning, but she wasn't quite ready to initiate a final breakup.

She had stayed in touch with her mom and dad after the meeting with Mr. Constantine and they brokered a deal with her. These were the conditions they made for her to continue seeing Dario as long as she was completing her studies at Hollins University:

RED FLAG #7-11

1) He had to move out. She agreed to that.

2) Her parents basically had to know of their whereabouts. Again, agreement.

3) She was to give him no more money. Yes, understood.

4) She was to expect an inevitable communication or even confrontation between her parents and Dario. She mildly acquiesced to that. She, nor her parents, knew what form this communication was going to take, but Dad said it was inevitable.

Those were the conditions or she would immediately have to stop seeing him—and they would know.

Isaiah Hamilton the third insisted upon these conditions because he was certain his daughter was not going to stop seeing Dario, despite Bob Constantine's findings. The Isaiah Hamiltons were all very clever men.

RED FLAG #7-12

Mr. and Mrs. Hamilton pranced out of the auditorium with flowers and gifts for their deserving daughter. They hugged her and congratulated her many times.

353

"And the man standing behind you is Paul, I assume?" asked Isaiah.

A rather thin, underdressed man with his hands in his pockets came out from behind Kris.

"How do you do? We are Kris's parents," Isaiah said, extending his hand.

Dario was slow to extend his in return. "Hi." Dario managed a smile and slowly turned away from them.

"These are the great people who flew all that way to see me accept a scroll of paper, Dario. My parents, Mr. and Mrs. Hamilton."

Kris noticed her father pulling back and folding his arms. His eyes took on a squint she wasn't accustomed to. He took a breath from someplace deep inside and puffed out his chest. Kris's inclination was to step back and observe.

"And so," Isaiah began. Suddenly, Kris remembered the last clause of their deal. "Mr. Dawson," continued Isaiah, exhaling, "are you coming to dinner with us and Polly's parents? Or, should we discuss here and now exactly how you are going to repay my daughter the twenty thousand dollars she so kindly lent you?"

The air turned to ice. All high-gear, post-graduation buzzing seemed to come to a screeching halt. Kris opened her eyes wide.

"We do not mince words in our family, son. I'm fully aware of your goings-on and I intend to put a stop to your 'career' immediately. Do you understand?"

Kris's mom actually came forward. "Sorry, young man, but we will be watching you and you will never be able to pull this off again. Last round."

Kristina looked at her mother. She felt both a sense of relief and a sense of disbelief.

Isaiah relentlessly hung in there. "You see, Paul, in my business we get all business dealings on the table," he explained. "This way, there's no mystification. Contracts are triple checked and every T is crossed. That's why I have a squeaky clean background and possibly why the Hamilton business has done just fine over generations. I do find it is necessary to teach you something. Perhaps way past due."

Paul looked permanently immobilized; nailed, exposed, and cornered. His eyes screamed he wanted to run. A thick, naked silence enveloped the four of them.

355

Isaiah continued to stare at Paul. "And one other thing, young man," he said, taking a step toward him and leaning in, "you and your family should be deeply humiliated and ashamed of yourselves. Integrity and kindness come in different forms."

Isaiah stepped back and looked away. He seemingly focused on the now-overgrown ivy enveloping the west wall. Then he returned his gaze to the group, slowly folded his arms again over a most inflated chest, and pointedly inquired of the scared-looking sometimes Paul/sometimes Dario, "Dinner, everyone?"

July 2008

Monday, eleven a.m. Indeed, the morning following the phone call arrived. Kristina Hamilton stood in my waiting room. She was a little too thin, her eyes a little too timid. But she was charming and unquestionably sweet. With her was Peter, her driver, and the voice from the early Sunday morning phone call.

In that first session, I learned that Kristina had recently graduated from the university and moved to Los Angeles, just for the summer, to work in her dad's West Coast satellite office.

She explained to me that her dad was paying her four hundred dollars per week plus any accrued overtime. She would not get any perks and had to perform the same duties as the other secretaries in the office, nine hours a day.

She also brought in a binder of photographs she wanted me to see.

"If we are going to work together," she sweetly explained, "I wanted to show you some photos of my family and stuff."

She removed a stack of eight-by-ten glossies.

The first photo was Kristina and Polly at their recent graduation; others were Mom and Dad building a snowman in front of their Maine home; the family's two tabby cats; her beautiful (opulent) bedroom in Maine; her personal vegetable garden; favorite antique rocking horse; antique brush and comb collection; Peter (her driver and family assistant) and Kristina cooking for her mom's surprise birthday party; and finally, a photograph of the ten-foot oil painting of her great-grandfather, Isaiah.

I was rather transfixed by the last photo, largely by Great-Grandpa's eyes.

"Oh, are you looking at Great-Grandpa's expression?"

Held by his eyes, I slowly responded, "Why, yes, actually."

The eyes transparently communicated.

They said—commanded—from that painting, over the years, over the miles:

"We can all do whatever we want. You just have to hang in there, work on it. Believe it." I heard him.

Behind him in the painting was a window with one pine tree. Just one. That is all you require.

I looked up at Kristina. She had a soft, demure look on her face. She nodded. Somehow, I received what she wanted to tell me. Somehow.

And then, the work of our sessions began.

DISCUSSION OF THE CHAPTER

RED FLAG #7-1

It is so very important to pay attention to our instincts—particularly from the gate. Kris asked a straightforward question, "Do you live around here?" For most people it is unusual to hesitate in the face of such simple directness. She did wonder why his response time was so slow. But these are exactly the tiny things we must store in our own retrievable thoughts in order to avoid future problems.

Also, there is an entire science around communication cues. A study out of UCLA recently reported that 55 percent of all communication is nonverbal. That study implies no matter what or how we say something, our body language is going to be the judge and jury of our truth.

Again, when we ponder someone's unusual response to a simple question or situation, the pondering alone is storable for future examination.

RED FLAG #7-2

Our protagonist's close friend, Polly, implied the reason for them not getting together was due to Dario's shyness. And so, I find it very giving that Kris picked up the ball and made the first move toward getting together. However, in this case we have quite the mitigating wrinkle: the boy was not shy at all—he was just secretly scheming. He was gathering information and waiting to discover where and when she was most vulnerable. At this point, one even questions if he had romantic feelings for her at all, or if she just looked like an excellent, fresh, and naïve mark.

And so, at the expense of sounding too traditional, here is my "educated" suggestion: don't ask him out, ladies. Rather, tell him it would mean a great deal to you if he would ask you out sometime! That really puts the ball back on his side of the court in a most confirming way.

Again, this is not to say that everyone who does not ask you out is looking for your cash cow potential. I am coming from the angle that women feel really good when the guy initiates a date. Yet oftentimes it is up to us to make it comfortable for them to activate that initiation.

RED FLAG #7-3

In 1921, the Swiss psychiatrist, C.J. Jung, coined the term extroverted personality type. This personality type typically acts in accordance with external demands—meaning, they are very keyed in to cues from their environment, other people's requirements, etc. In other words, they are fairly well tuned in to other people's needs—not just themselves. (Now, whether they decide to act on it behaviorally is another layer.) Extroverts also feel a bit safer to self-disclose more, at a faster pace, than the introvert.

In our case, Kris is not a classic extrovert. Her best friend, Polly, might be. Yet, Kris was rather quick to expose the fact that her parents bought the little parfait cups when they were touring Lampang, Thailand.

It is important to see that this is not a situation coming from friendly extroverted banter. Rather, this is an illustration of someone who was so accustomed to a particular lifestyle (luxury at every turn) that all facts about it just fell trippingly off her tongue.

So, here lies the point of this red flag: be conscious and selective regarding what you want to expose to early-on lovers.

Did Dario really need to know her parents took exotic holidays? Not at all. Did it add to his arsenal of Kris-as-a-good-target information? Absolutely.

This is not to say that everyone who exposes family information is going to be a victim of such a maniacal ruse as Dario's. But I think you get the point.

RED FLAG #7-4

And we are off and running: classic behavior of a downdater is to over-function for her downdatee. Here, Kristina is looking into Dario's college, figuring out where she can fill in for him.

When Person A is higher functioning than Person B in a love relationship, Person A must be careful not to over-function for Person B. In the twelve-step programs, this type of filling in might be referred to as a form of enabling. The up-down behavior is observable because the lower-functioning person usually sits back and allows the higher-functioning person to carry the lion's share of the load.

Kris's calling the college for Dario is a perfect example of this type of over-functioning. She did not even tell him she was going to do this research. And he was totally capable of performing the task without any assistance.

362

She also withdrew money from her trust fund for him. Was this "being kind," as her father always directed her to be, or was it enabling, over-functioning?

I shall leave this up to the reader to personally define—and soul search.

RED FLAG #7-5

At this point, Kris had known Dario for about two and a half months. She offered him the keys to her Cadillac Escalade, her apartment, seemingly her life.

Downdaters think they need to be loved more fervently. They have an overwhelming, incorrect assumption that they are separate from...what, I do not know. These assumptions that they 1) need to be loved more fervently, and 2) are separated from the "vital mass" lead them to prematurely hand out the keys to their life.

Her hope was that if she extended herself enough, Dario might be a better boyfriend, and a more responsible citizen. This is typical down-dating rationale. Her behavior was not a part of her dad's direction to "at all costs, be kind." Rather, it was from a false sense of separateness, with the ultimate goal of keeping him close.

RED FLAG #7-6

"Don't be so exacting." I beg your pardon. Dario moves into her place, basically unannounced, and suddenly SHE is the demanding party? I think not. It is common for the downdater to be hard on herself in a false attempt to correct the imbalance. The problem is, she is not the problem! So the situation will not correct itself.

The downdater usually acts in accordance with a silent demand from the downdatee. The demand usually comes in the form of "We do not question my motives around here. Back off!"

Personally, at this juncture I would cease to feel safe with Dario or any of his decisions. Assisting someone through hard times is different from allowing him to bulldoze through boundaries. This distinction must be understood.

RED FLAG #7-7

The implicit understanding was that Kris's generous check was meant to pay for his college tuition. Dario sidestepped this understanding. To add insult to injury, he only fessed up to this sidestep when pressured. Kris knew nothing of this obfuscation of the truth until she questioned him. The self-assured dater immediately would have questioned Dario about the misuse of her check.

364

Instead, Kris surprisingly threw her arms around him and contemplated when she would send him yet more money.

I believe we must all adhere to our original contracts—written, nonverbal, etc. We must question all parties concerned to make certain everyone has the same take on said contracts. This way, trust begets an appropriate flow of activities, there are no surprises, and everyone gets his or her needs met. Put another way, if we do not stand by our word, what have we? Obviously, Dario and his family did not subscribe to that ethical mind-set.

RED FLAG #7-8

And Dario's attitude unquestioningly bumped up against constant #2. He refused to change his maladaptive behavior.

RED FLAG #7-9

Perfect time for Kris. Perfect time. She was alone with no place to be. He just offered up a boatload of information. And his pouring of the Coca Cola was really body language anticipating discussion. But she overrode the shining opportunity.

However, I do believe Kris was both confused and at a loss for the appropriate words. She was also twenty-two years old, sheltered, and fairly new at relationships. (My heart goes out to the novice here.) So, reader, if you are in this position it really is quite simple. Here is the key: talk.

Stay calm, centered, and talk. Merely gather information. Do not accuse him of lying or even sidestepping. He will paint himself into a comfortable corner without your help—watch!

So, I would say, what a lost opportunity. The setting was primo. Not seizing the moment at a time like this only prolonged the questioning and deepened the subtle throb of "invisible pain."

RED FLAGS #7-10 and #7-11

Red flags #7-10 and #7-11 will be combined. Let us go back to what this story illustrates: downdatee #7: is either chronically unemployed, has no aspirations of exceeding minimum wage, and/or is financially supported by the female.

At this point in their relationship, it is patently clear that he has been living off her. Bob Constantine, the private detective, verified and clarified this information. And she still said after yet more proof from Mr. Constantine, "I am not sure what to do."

Here, her lack of experience was at play in a big way and her over-functioning was blaring.

366

Over-functioning is synonymous to codependent. Codependents always over-function for their love interest and cannot see their dating down patterns. No matter what good information downdaters learn or what proof of irresponsible behavior they come by, they continue to disinherit their own instinct, intellect, and good judgment to stay in the false state of flimsy possibilities.

RED FLAG #7-12

There are numerous reasons why people stay in a relationship past its obvious conclusion. Sometimes friends or family consider the significant other rather spectacular (they are not in the relationship with him, remember) and their prattle keeps one over-involved.

But in the case of downdaters, two elements keep them overly connected:

1) They maintain a kind of internal passivity and low self-esteem whereby they do not feel they deserve a more loving connection.

2) They pick up a nonverbal cue from the male which seems to command, "Do not leave. There will be no questioning. Just go through the motions and do not alter our status quo."

In this case, Kristina exercised both of these elements. If she had been in touch with then what she is in touch with now (and what this book is promoting), none of this would have ever transpired.

CHAPTER EIGHT

ILLUSTRATING DOWNDATEE #8 –

Has Potentially Dangerous Psychosis or Psychopathology

Entitled...

BEWARE THE SHIRTLESS MAN IN JANUARY

Upon entering Mimi's apartment for the purpose of this interview, I was struck by the obvious coordination of, well...color.

Her living room couch and dining room chairs were upholstered in the same light pink canvas, the lampshades boasted pink and lime green floral patterns, the walls were trimmed in lime green, and the throw rugs were pink with lime green in super-cool geometric patterns.

Mimi's waist-length strawberry blonde hair set off her small but piercing green eyes. That day, she wore lime green skinny jeans, a pink T-shirt, and a pink hoodie sweatshirt.

I said, "Congratulations, Mimi, for you have virtually invented peppermint." Yet, despite the delightful and pleasant ex-perience of walking into Candyland, and despite the soft-spoken and gentle coun-tenance of this woman, I wondered how much of the public perceived her edge, her wounded-ness, and her time-honored wisdom.

At that point, I had seen Mimi only a few times in my office. I knew, however, I was going to get the interview I needed. None-theless, my internal voice whispered, *Tread lightly, Carole. This is going to be a little tough for her.*

As a psychotherapist, I know the difference between gathering pertinent information (ultimately for the patient's sake) versus committing psychic trespassing. I chose to do the former by letting Mimi lead the interview.

At the time of this interview, Mimi was thirty years old. She was the youngest of four children from a Protestant, upper-class Indianapolis family. She had been modeling professionally for twelve years in Chicago, Los Angeles, New York, London, Milan, and Rome. Although she never reached the upper ranks of modeling, she always worked, securing a good to rather excellent income.

The photographs she was most fond of were discreetly framed over her fireplace. There was nothing exhibitionistic or self-aggrandizing about Mimi. She accepted her pretty face and tall, willowy frame rather matter-of-factly.

Modeling allowed Mimi to pursue her other loves—learning languages, studying music history, and playing three instruments. She was presently fluent in Spanish and

German. Her future plans included modeling for five more years, then returning to college (hopefully in Italy, she said) to study European music and business.

As "Peppermint Mimi" described her family of origin, she suddenly became guarded and low-key. She remarked that curfews, orderliness, and "correctness in public" were highly valued by her parents. Love seemed to be obscured by regimen and spontaneity suppressed by criticism.

"I started modeling locally while in high school. It was a wonderful departure from the over-control at home. From ages eighteen to twenty, I kept getting called to Chicago to do catalog work. My parents didn't really value higher education for their daughters, so my Chicago jobs didn't impede any longed-for college plans. My being a straight-A student was irrelevant to them. At any rate, I got to leave Indianapolis and my restrictive home for days on end to do something kind of creative."

This direct, intelligent woman went on to say, "Modeling was not the most mentally stimulating career and I was always aware of that fact. But what eighteen-year-old isn't a little taken with the glamour, the excitement? And I did love the hum of creativity about it, and I got to use my five-foot-ten, one-hundred-twenty-five-pound body."

Mimi continued, "The summer of my eighteenth year, I was living at home, running to Chicago often, and working as a hostess at a supper club restaurant in between modeling jobs. I would go to work an hour early each night just to tinkle the keys of their baby grand. It was a really OK job to tide me over until I could move out at the stroke of nineteen years old. Mom would not allow such a thing—sans husband—beforehand. Dad wasn't as strict about it. He saw I was responsible and was saving money to move out, but Mom had this arbitrary 'nineteen' thing. So I obeyed—shy of two months."

At that point, Mimi changed position in her chair. She flung one leg over the arm, broke eye contact from me, and sighed heavily. Talking about her family appeared relatively smooth for her. Perhaps we had a change in store.

There was an extended silence. I chose not to fracture it. *Let Mimi lead the interview,* my internal voice directed.

"I remember the night," she began. "I remember it so well. I have an elephant's memory, Carole. It was a freezing Saturday night in January. Snow littered the porch of the supper club where I was hostessing. The coatroom floor was slushed with wet boots and galoshes."

She went on to say it was the tail end of a bustling evening, despite the weather. The crowd was finally starting to thin. She was leaning against the hostess podium, listening to the pianist's evening-end Cole Porter medley when the door flew open and a gust of January snow thrust itself into the lobby.

"I was going to walk over and close the large wooden door when I was stopped dead in my tracks. It wasn't a gust of wind that had thrown the door open so forcefully. It was, in fact, this guy. This guy..."

She trailed off for a moment. Looking out her dining room window, Mimi left present day "Peppermint Land" and evanesced into 1996.

"This guy was six foot two inches tall with auburn hair down to the middle of his back. He walked in wearing sunglasses, apricot satin pants, and a beaver coat without a shirt! I nearly died! 'Uh, excuse me, sir,' I said to him. 'Are you the late-night entertainment? I didn't think they were doing that

377

again.' He said, 'No, babe, wrong dude. I'm just here for the brewski.'

"He laughed and promenaded to the bar, smiling back at me. Who was this diamond in the dust storm of Indianapolis, I wondered? I couldn't take my wide-eyed, eighteen-year-old gaze off him.

"Coincidentally, we left at the same time and struck up a lengthy conversation in the blustery snow. He told me his name was Mike and that he wasn't going to let me out of his sight without my phone number. When I gave it to him, he kissed me hard on the lips and walked down the road in the snow. I never saw him getting into a car—if he had one. He just kind of diffused into the wind, and then Dad drove up to take me home."

"Did he indeed call you, Mimi?"

"Oh, yes, at eight o'clock the next morning. And every day that week. He said he was a used car salesman, just back from a safari in Kenya, and living with his parents. He asked if I would meet him at a party the following week. How could I not? He said he was personal friends with Jon Bon Jovi."

RED FLAG
#8-1

"Looked like quite a cosmopolitan guy," I said. "Did you go to the party?"

"You bet. I walked in alone, nervous and extremely excited to see the long-haired

378

friend of Jon Bon Jovi's. When Mike saw me, he introduced me to the host of the party, stuck a beer can in my hand and whisked me upstairs. He led me to a couch in the master bedroom of this large house, and angled the couch so we could watch the snow fall outside. Some pretty driving rock-and-roll music was wafting its way from downstairs.

"'I need to turn out the light,' Mike announced, impulsively hitting the light switch.

"'Oh?'

"'I want to see the snowflakes falling outside the window better. I want to see the stars. Because you know that's all we are, darling—snowflakes, stars, and air. We are all one.'

"Ohhh, how deep and poetic it all sounded to me back then! It was a turn-on from that wide-eyed place. Then he moved closer to me on the couch and whispered, 'Tonight, you are the stars, too. Do you see it? Do you feel it?' And he removed my boots and socks.

"'What are you doing, Mike?'

"'Tonight I am Snowflake...let me dance between your toes.'

"Then he hunkered down on the floor and began to suck my toes, one by one. I loved it. I thought it was truly innovative—and affectionate. He really got into it. Then he said my toes were like sweet peaches, and he wanted to know if my lips were like berries that night...well, I fell right into that one.

"'Try them, Mike—I mean, Snowflake,' I said. 'You'll never know until you try them.'

"He popped back up on the couch and held my long hair in his hands, arching my head toward him. He just stared into my eyes...so *intensely*. Someone from the party walked in, but Mike never let go of my hair nor withdrew his gaze. Then, when the partygoer left, Mike stood up, placed his hands on the inside of his shirt and literally ripped—I mean, split his shirt in two—and threw it across the room.

RED FLAG #8-2

"'We are air. We don't need to be covered,' he said.

"Then he pulled me down to the floor and oh, so slowly, unbuttoned my vest and blouse—at least he had the courtesy not to rip them—and he planted this long deep kiss on me.

"I needed to slip into the unbridled passion of this figure. Actually, I needed to slip into *any* passion. This source just happened to come in the form of a bare-chested twenty-six-year-old man willing to guide.

380

He sniffed out that I was hungry to follow. I don't recall everything...but I do remember us making it over to the bed and being covered by the famous, voluminous beaver coat. And of course, making love. But something really strange happened during the lovemaking."

"Yes?"

"This has never happened to me since then, in any circumstance. My hands and arms went numb—completely. And my mind kind of...separated from my body and left—just went away. I felt him on my body, and through my numb extremities, and through my mind...does that make any sense at all?"

"Well, he did say you were air." We laughed. "And regardless," I went on, "the whole experience was a quite engaging hook for an eighteen-year-old who wasn't terribly sophisticated. What occurred after that? Do you want to tell me anymore about that evening?"

"Yeah, there is more. I must have fallen asleep, because I remember fixating on the one o'clock face of the clock by the bed, even though I had to be home by twelve thirty on the dot. I knew I'd be punished. For the first time, I just didn't give a damn.

381

RED FLAG
#8-3

I slowly dressed, and Mike walked me to the car. I asked when he was going to call me, and he answered, 'With the next blue snowflake that lands upon my mind.'

"I didn't cherish the indirectness of his response, but again, allowed his poetic nature to pacify me. Also, at this point I was chalking up his behavior to just being really creative and different. Anyway, when I got home, Mom gave me one of her classic haul-off slaps and grounded me from the car for the next month."

"When did you see Mike next?"

"Luckily, I ended up only being grounded for a week, so I got to see him the next Saturday. It was the first time he was going to meet my parents. I didn't tell them he was the reason I was late the previous weekend because I didn't want to prejudice them. Ha! It was irrelevant, because the prejudice was created at first glance. See, he came to pick me up wearing a tuxedo *with tails*, a top hat, and white gloves, and driving a vintage Cadillac convertible from the used car lot."

"It doesn't sound like your conservative, overprotective parents would have appreciated his theatrics."

382

Mimi threw her head back and openly laughed for the first time. "Not in the *least* ! But afterward, I reassured them that he was upstanding, respectable, and entertaining. Little did they know what our date consisted of."

"Well?"

"First we went to a club—me in my jeans, Mike in his tails, right? Then we went to the main drag in town and drove up and down the street while Mike threw money out of the open car. He said money didn't matter. Bills were flying everywhere—he must've emptied his pockets! Wow—what a unique guy, I thought.

RED FLAG
#8-4

"Well, as time went on, my nineteenth birthday was fast approaching, and I found a cute one-bedroom apartment near my modeling agency. I didn't need the restaurant job anymore because I'd become the number-one runway model in Indianapolis, and I was getting more and more jobs in Chicago. Marshall Fields, all the Sears catalogs, nonstop stuff."

"So you were totally supporting yourself at nineteen?"

"Totally, yeah. And have been ever since. It wasn't that my parents didn't have the

383

money. They just never offered—and I just never requested."

"So, how was your relationship with Mike going?"

"Well, since he was living at home at the time, he kind of moved in with me. It was pretty opportune for him. I remember the first two months as rather ideal. He was so attentive, so adoring...and supportive of my burgeoning career. And so, so passionate. He was so passionate! I never knew this kind of expression at home. This was a whole new opening for me, for my life."

RED FLAG #8-5

"You didn't have any type of inkling that something wasn't terribly kosher with this guy?"

"I guess our instinct knows all. The only thing close to that type of inkling was the night before I moved out of my parents' house. I remember sitting on my white chenille bedspread—sitting on my bedspread, by the way, was strictly prohibited by Mom because 'white dirties too quickly.' It was late at night, and I was watching the snow-flakes fall out of the stars—like Mike and I had done earlier. I remember feeling this sense of yearning for him, and then suddenly I was overcome with tears, and such sadness."

384

She went on to say, "There was some indistinguishable, subtle pain about this relationship. Just a fleeting, undefined stab. I think it was my instinct warning me. I think my inner voice was sounding some sort of alarm...I don't know...well, maybe that's jumping too far ahead."

RED FLAG
#8-6

I was moved by Mimi's pensive account. There was sadness in her eyes as she reenacted the moment, yet I felt a green light to proceed.

"So, Mike moved in—lock, stock, and barrel?" I asked.

She went on, "With my parents disowning me, yes. Lock, stock, and barrel. And he was very unemployed."

"But the used car lot job?"

"There was no used car job after he moved in. I think he was fired shortly before that, but the story was never straight. But you see, it didn't matter. He was so attentive and romantic when he first moved in, I didn't need him to work. Plus, I was modeling so much that my income was sufficient for two people who just looked into each other's eyes and read poetry."

"Did you see other friends very much?"

"Oh, no. Besides Mike, frankly, it was a pretty lonely time. My parents basically

RED FLAG
#8-7

disowned me for months, and Mike effectively kept me from all my other friends. I thought that was an act of true love—at first."

"So, everything dysfunctional was an act of love? Did you continue to chalk it up to that?" I asked.

"Kind of. We were basically in our own little universe. When I wasn't working, it was great to relax with him to music or TV. He actually did a good deal of the cooking, and some of the cleaning and shopping. When the weather warmed up, we'd do outdoorsy things: a lotta swimming, badminton, and always went on picnics. And we'd spend hours at the mall, window shopping. So he didn't really drain me financially. None of this stuff required much outlay. Oh, yeah—we also did art projects, crafts and things. Everything from hand-painted T-shirts to origami and Valentine's cards. We had a pretty creative, and very walled-off, safe world there—at first."

"So, you didn't mind being alienated from your friends at that point?"

"Only once, and in a really big way. It was the morning of my nineteenth birthday. Mike couldn't afford to buy me a gift or take me anywhere. I think he was pretty

386

embarrassed, because he presented me with a handcrafted card when I woke up, then immediately made himself invisible for the rest of the day. He said he was going out to sell encyclopedias. In fact, he used that one a lot. Maybe he did try selling them for a while. I'll never know.

RED FLAG
#8-8

"At any rate, it was the morning of my birthday, and I was seated at the kitchen table with a cup of hot chocolate and three gifts from my parents in front of me. Even though they wouldn't receive my phone calls, they did send some really nice birthday gifts. Put that one together. Anyway, because of the totally non-festive atmosphere, I couldn't even open my parents' prettily wrapped gifts for three days. There were no 'Happy Birthday' phone calls because Mike kept me alienated from my friends, no cards in the mailbox, no being taken to lunch at my favorite restaurant, no surprise cake or candles to blow out. It was easily the worst birthday of my life. But I told myself it didn't matter because I had someone as significant as Mike."

Mimi then stood up and walked into the kitchen. Lost in thought, she started preparing something to eat.

"It's lunchtime, Carole. I have some great salmon patties and salad that I made last night. Please join me."

I appeased her, although I wasn't hungry, and graciously accepted her offer. I wondered if she was really hungry or just needed a break from her sullen thoughts.

"I'm not concerned with what I eat anymore," she said, pulling out the salmon patties and salad fixings. "I eat for health and not for camera thinness. I never had a weight problem. I just decided to stop pretending I did. Do you want to hear more? Because the story really starts to thicken about here."

"Carry on."

"OK, about a month or two later, I was in the bedroom with the radio blaring, unpacking my suitcase from an overnight to Chicago. I didn't hear him come in because of the radio. When he suddenly appeared in the doorway, he didn't say hello, or welcome back, or whatever. He just held up one of the pictures from the Chicago shoot that was on the dining room table.

"'What is the meaning of this?' he asked, waving the picture at me.

"'Hi honey. I missed you. What? What is the meaning of what?' I asked. I walked over to hug him, thinking nothing of whatever he was waving at me, when he hauled me to the bed, pushed me down and sat on top of me.

RED FLAG
#8-9

"'What is the meaning of this picture? This is not a picture of you, my sweet. Who is this goddamn guy with the belly? And he's in a bunch of these pictures. Who is he?!'

"I tried to pull out of his hold. I didn't know why he was gripping so tightly; presumably, he was only teasing. 'Mike, that's just one of the photographers. Now would you please let go of me?' But he didn't.

"'Why is he in so many of these pictures with you?' he asked.

"'Damn it, he's just one of the guys shooting. It was a huge shoot. They needed it done in one day, so they hired three photographers. Photographers always take pictures of every which thing waiting for light set-ups—including each other. Now, damn it, will you please get off me?'

"Mike slowly moved away from me and sat up silently. Then, I said the wrong thing: 'Jeez, Mike, he is a great photographer with a really funny personality.'

"I thought it was an innocuous remark. It was the truth. I had no designs on this older, corpulent gentleman. Mike suddenly leaped at me, pinned me down on the bed, and whispered in my ear, 'If you ever have anything to do with him again, I will break every bone in his fat body. Do you hear me? I've never told you this before, but I have contacts in Chicago, and they'll do whatever I request.'

"Then he got off me, stormed into the dining room and tore up every picture from the shoot into bits. He disappeared until about three a.m.

"The next day, he seemed to be over his bout of irrational jealousy, but refused to talk about the previous night. When my agents asked to see the proofs from the shoot, I told them I'd left them on the plane by mistake."

"You covered for him?"

"I did."

"Were you frightened?"

"Not really. It was so out of character, from what I knew of him. I couldn't make sense of it. Or I didn't want to. I'm not sure. In any case, I finally had to pay attention to it because of what occurred the following weekend."

RED FLAG
#8-10

"That weekend...?"

"Yeah, we were invited to his parents' house for a Saturday barbecue. I'd only

390

spoken to his parents on the phone, and I was going to be meeting them for the first time. In retrospect, I think Mike kept me from them."

"Were they what you expected?"

"Not at all. I'm not sure what I expected back then, but somehow they didn't fit the bill. They were middle class, respectable, hardworking, but very compassionate people. His older sister, Judy, treated him with the utmost sensitivity and kindness, and consequently me too. I didn't understand this outpouring of tenderness, but I watched, and I listened.

"His dad and Mike were across the yard at the barbecue pit, while his mother and I watched them. His mom had this really worried expression on her face every time she looked at Mike. Then she turned to me, serious, and said, 'So, how is he?'

"'Excuse me, Mrs. Radcliffe?'

"'Has he been sleeping? At least he looks like he's eating again. Has he been sleeping?'

"She put her clenched hand to her cheek; concerned, resolute, and hurting somehow.

"'Ah, yes, ma'am. He sleeps fine as far as I know.'

"'He isn't working, is he dear? You can tell me.'

"'Uh, no. I mean, he can...he...ah...just doesn't want to. I'm doing so well modeling that there is enough money for both of us. I guess I bring home the bacon, and he kinda cooks it!'

"I tried to lighten the conversation, but was feeling a chill at the base of my spine. She continued to stare at him and follow his every move.

"'We're grateful for you, dear. You're doing a wonderful thing, you know, for his morale and the like. God bless you. *Blessed are the pure in heart, for they shall see God. Matthew.*'

"Well, I appreciated the Bible-based blessing, but was confused. Not until Judy joined us was some of the puzzle pieced together. Judy had the same look as her mom when she watched Mike.

"'It's really nice to meet you, Mimi. You're as sweet and as pretty as Mike said.'

"They were all so polite, but so strained. I wondered what these people weren't telling me. Then Judy broke some of the tension. She lowered her voice and asked, 'So, Mimi, how much of the institutionalizations did he tell you about?'

"I thought to myself—what? What institutionalizations—plural—were they talking about?

"'Er...not much, Just a bit,' I lied. 'You know, whenever the subject comes up...'

"'There was nothing we could do,' Judy continued. 'We did everything we could. Mom and Dad really went through the paces with him. I buried myself in my schoolwork at the time. It was all pretty horrific.' His mom bent her head down, as if praying.

"These people were so humble and lovely, I felt guilty pretending to understand whatever 'IT' was. Strange, but this thing also felt fairly recent—not as though it had occurred years and years ago. I didn't ask for any details. I just allowed Judy and Mrs. Radcliffe to fill in whatever they might.

"Judy continued, 'We used to play together so nicely when we were kids. It's just all so hard to swallow. When we were very young, we used to play this make-believe game where I'd be Princess So-and-So and he'd be the village knight. He'd come to my chamber–which was always the front porch–and would tell me about his knightly episodes, crusades and all, and I always rewarded him with gum or Oreos, plus a homemade crown.

"'Well, once, when I was ten and he was nine, he didn't want to be the knight anymore. Instead, he insisted on being...God. And he said since he was God, I had to stay in the closet until he let me out. I actually did for a while, but after that I refused to play make-believe again. Something about it—*him*, maybe—felt scary. Just felt wrong. After that, only Trivial Pursuit or Go to the Head of the Class with Michael.'

"I listened, but still couldn't put all this information together at the time.

"'And it lasted so long,' his mom added. She sighed and asked me, 'Of course, you know about the brunt of it?'

"Again, I lied, 'Oh, of course. Of course.'

"'And the medicines, the doctors, the attorneys, the attacks, court—'

"Then she stopped abruptly; she and Mike had locked eyes. She stood up, excused herself, and disappeared into the house.

"Judy went on, 'It's a horrible thing to say, but I'm not sure who I ever believed in the end; it was such a nightmare. But the illness...it's... Anyhow, Mom and Dad are living such a normal life now. They've even started traveling again. And bowling. Spent a whole month in Florida last winter. Never thought I'd see the day. I'd better go and help Mom. You just relax, honey. *Seek good and not evil, and that ye may live. Amos 5:14.*'

"And then she asked if I wanted pickles with my chicken! I declined. To this day I can't eat pickles."

RED FLAG
#8-11

"But what about the specifics, Mimi? What were they getting at? Did you ever go for them?"

"I couldn't...wouldn't. I just never did."

"What did you do with all that disjointed and upsetting information?" I asked. "You never brought it up to Mike?"

RED FLAG
#8-12

"I'm not sure what I did with it. All I know is it disturbed me—and I never brought it up to him."

"How did you feel toward him that night when you went home together? Weren't you frightened?"

"No...uh, I don't remember. How are the salmon patties, Carole?"

"What?" *Quite a segue,* I thought, but answered, "Best I've had in a while."

"Do you want to hear the next thing that happened in this bizarre series of events?" she asked.

"If you're in the market, go on."

395

"The next piece of the puzzle basically surrounded phone calls from a woman named Eva. She told me she was Mike's ex-girlfriend and had the total scoop on me. I asked Mike how she got my phone number and, from what I gathered, my address. But he seemed to slough me off. I remember him telling me I was one of God's flowers, and 'God protects all of his good flowers—as long as they are good.' I didn't know what he meant, but then again, I didn't question his line of reasoning. I was used to this kind of stuff by now.

RED FLAG
#8-13

"Then I started receiving threatening phone calls from women with different accents—until I realized that they were all Eva. Mike finally confessed that she was an old girlfriend, but when I asked why she'd never been brought up before, he dismissed it again.

"Not long after that, I received my first phone call from my mother in months. It was quite a surprise. She didn't open the conversation by apologizing for her distance, nor by telling me they missed me or anything. She got right to the point of her call. Her voice was all shaky and she said, 'Mimi, this is your mother. I need to tell you what's been happening here. We've been getting a series of disgusting phone calls from a woman named Eva. Do you know her?'

"I gasped. 'Uh, I think I know to whom you may be referring. Just hang up on her, Mom.'

"'No, there is a bit more to it than that. Frankly, I'm a little concerned for you. Remember the resort- and cruise-wear layout you did in the Marshall Field catalog last year?'

"'Yes...,' I said.

"'Well, this Eva sent the whole layout to us...each picture of you had a black dagger drawn across your heart, or a blotchy red ink stain over your face. And there were some foul and threatening letters that came with them. Mimi...'

"I had to conceal an audible choke. Thoughts were swimming inside my brain. I didn't hear some of what Mom went on to say because Mrs. Radcliffe's and Judy's voices were suddenly too prominent. And then I heard:

"'And you're not going to believe this one, Mimi. If this didn't give your father a heart attack—she actually showed up on our doorstep with three straggly girlfriends wanting to *meet* your father and me!'

"'Oh, Mom, no. That's not possible. How did she get your address? God, I'm so sorry. So sorry. What did you do?'

"'I don't know how you know this shady character, dear, but it's a good thing your older brother happened to be here that night. Why, of course we called the police and they came right over. I'm sorry to tell you this, but we're having our phone and your landline wiretapped for the next month.'

"'But Mom—'

"'I can order that, Mimi. Your phone is in our name. You are not twenty-one and you might be in possible danger. Starts tonight. And I want to encourage you to tape every message you get on your cellular. This little troublemaker is going to be found out.'

"I was numb. I could barely speak for the remainder of the conversation.

"Then she said, 'So, young lady, what is it going to take to get you back home? Are you still seeing that character, Mike?'

"She obviously hadn't put two and two together—that Eva was an offshoot of *that character, Mike*. After we hung up, I realized I was glad to have finally spoken to my mom, even though she was cold...and genuinely upset. I guess we reconciled, because after that call, we seemed to stay in contact."

"But what were you thinking of Mike at this point?" I inquired. "I mean, was everything still status quo, even after all of this?"

Mimi lowered her head and remained silent for a moment. There was some shame in her eyes when she looked up—as though she'd been found guilty somehow.

"I knew now that this man had problems—maybe even serious ones. But it didn't matter, because our love was so strong, it would ford any upcoming storm. You see, I thought that I held the key to fixing him."

RED FLAG
#8-14

"So love conquers all...and you are playing God to this man? That's an interesting reversal."

Mimi laughed and went on, "The next few months consisted of my getting longer and better-paying jobs in Chicago, and of his continued unemployment and increasing jealousy. He wouldn't even let me play my male vocalist CDs in his presence. Strange, though; his jealousy wasn't the thing that started to get to me the most. Something inside *me* was changing— regardless of his actions. I think, in hindsight, I was just growing...apart from him."

RED FLAG
#8-15

399

"Maybe," I began, "maybe you got what you needed. It seems as if you both started from a similar developmental space. Maybe you were mentally and emotionally growing up—and he wasn't able to. I'm not sure, but go ahead. What's next?"

"Thank you. You're going to love this. This is another 'returning home from Chicago' story. Just before I left for a week-long shoot, I told Mike that the prestigious Eileen Ford Agency in New York had called. With that information, he broke every one of my Bruce Springsteen CDs. Never did get what Bruce Springsteen had to do with my career expanding...but that was so Mike.

"Anyway, and needless to say, I was delighted to get away from his accelerating jealousy, even for a week. I ended up returning a day early from the long shoot in Chicago, and entered the apartment around midnight.

"'Mike? Mike, surprise, I'm back.'

"I heard music playing in the bathroom. I assumed he had the radio on and was taking a bath or something. But when I approached the bathroom door, I was abruptly halted.

"There stood my boyfriend in a darkened room, with ten or fifteen burning candles, gyrating in front of the mirror to loud music.

His long hair was curled up in my rollers, and he had on complete face makeup and false eyelashes. He was naked, except for underpants and one of my scarves knotted around his waist. He bumped his hips to the beat of 'Brown Sugar' and pranced before the mirror like some kind of hallucinated version of Mick Jagger.

RED FLAG
#8-16

"'Mimi, baby,' he said, looking in the mirror with his lips in a pout. 'Look at me, princess. Glad you're home so you can see how God looks when he's shining. Woo!'

"I ran into the bedroom and saw that my clothes, shoes, hats, and coats were strewn everywhere. He'd obviously been trying them on.

"'What do you think, babe? Pretty? Think I can get some high-fashion catalog gigs in Chicago? Maybe the Eileen Ford modeling agency will fall on their knees over my... mascara?'

"Then he pushed me aside and started putting away my clothes frantically. He said, 'This is all shit anyway. What God-fearing person would wear this unnecessary shit in public? At least I don't covet velvets and wools and...'

"Even though he made no sense, his voice accelerated, his eyes raged, and I felt a chilly tingle go up my spine. I slowly

401

inched for the door, knowing I couldn't sleep there that night. I finally felt frightened for my life.

"From the living room, I could see him rampaging in the bedroom. He just kept ranting about how unnecessary material things were. I quickly but quietly slipped out the door and went to a friend's apartment upstairs for the night.

"The next morning, I immediately called my parents and announced I was moving back home. I would make subsequent career plans after mellowing out at home for a while. They were delighted.

"I think Mom had a lump in her throat when she said, 'Your room hasn't been touched since you left, dear... It's been pretty lonely here...but the sitting-on-the-bedspread rule still holds.'

"And I earnestly replied, 'I wouldn't think of it, Mom.'

"I called some wonderful friends with a truck and they said they'd be over the next night to help me move. I felt pretty complete: I had a plan. I avoided the apartment for twenty-four hours, gathered cardboard boxes and stored them at my neighbor's until the move.

"The next morning, I went to the apartment alone to start packing. Mike wasn't there, thank God, so I ran around frantically throwing one and a half years' worth of stuff into boxes. Then he walked in. He had returned to his passive, withdrawn side.

"Looking down, he quietly said, 'What are you doing with all these boxes?'

"'Packing.'

"'Where to this time?'

"'Mike...I'm packing...I'm packing to move out.'

RED FLAG #8-17

"'Without me?'

"'Don't you think that's best?' I answered, stuffing towels into open boxes.

"'You still dating that fat photographer?'

"'Now, you know I never was...'

"Then he lowered himself to the floor in a sort of fetal position, and started to rock back and forth, repeating over and over, 'The kingdom will not separate. The kingdom will not separate. The kingdom will not separate.'

"I cautiously continued to pack.

"Later that evening, my friends and the truck arrived. Mike watched us from the window as we loaded boxes and furniture. And then, his temporary passivity turned around. My two male friends were downstairs loading the couch when Mike grabbed me, pulled my hair, and locked one of my arms behind my back.

"'You're moving to California without me, *aren't you?* You bitch. After all I've done for you to keep your life in order.'

"'I'm not moving to California, Mike, and you're hurting me.'

"'And you're moving in with those two scumbags helping you down there, aren't you? In the face of God, aren't you?'

"'Mike, you're really hurting me. Let go of my arm.'

"'Just let me tell you one thing, bitch. It's this—I have friends who really respect me on the coast, and they will do *anything* I ask. Just remember that!'

"His voice amplified and his eyes glared. Then he just threw me across the room—wham! I had to protect myself from falling headfirst on the hardwood floor. He stormed into the kitchen and slammed the door.

"I lay there panting. Thinking, thank God my two friends still had to come back up to get the chairs. How could I have had the naiveté to stay, even for an instant, alone with this maniac? What sick bravado. Sick bravado that could have killed me."

"Was that the last of the violence for the day?"

"Well, almost. I finally burst out crying and went into the kitchen to collect my box of houseplants that I really loved. I cradled it in my arms.

"'Get out of the kitchen,' Mike began. 'You don't live here anymore.'

"When I saw the venom in his eyes, I backed up, dropping the box of house-plants on the floor. My instincts directed me to get out, and get out fast.

"Just as my friends appeared in the doorway, I heard a crashing noise above my head. Mike had picked up the huge vacuum cleaner from the broom closet and hurled it at me. It missed me by three inches.

"I screamed to my friends at the door, 'Let's get out of here, now! That asshole is on fire!' And we tore out of the building, into the truck, and drove to my parents' house—with me tripping over my tears all the way."

Mimi fell back against her chair. She was out of breath from having relived the trauma. She placed her lunch napkin close to her clouded eyes. I almost wanted to hug her. Amazing how this man's presence had extended itself twelve years into the future and halfway across the country. I felt his madness today through the vulnerable woman in front of me.

Then I said, "It must have been a horror. I am so sorry you went through such an experience."

She regained her composure and replied, "I've never had another experience close to that, Carole. So I know I'm not 'addicted' to that type of craziness. But can I share a secret with you? I've never told anyone this."

Curious, I replied, "Of course."

"In all honesty, I missed him. I told everyone at the time I was glad to have him behind me, and that I'd made a poor choice, and all that contrite stuff. But truthfully, I continued to—metaphorically, of course—look for Mike.

"Two months after moving home, I landed my first modeling job in New York City. Shortly after that, I relocated there for three extremely lucrative years. The entire time I was in New York, would you believe I refused to date? I didn't go to parties, never went to a club. I just worked a lot, played my violin, perfected my Spanish...and looked for Mike."

"How?"

RED FLAG
#8-18

406

"Every night, before going to bed, I would listen to old tapes of our early phone calls. I would peruse our photographs and little art projects I had saved. I would put most of his poetry to violin music for hours on end. And...I would 'see' him all over the city. I'd see him hanging onto the leather straps on the subway. I'd see him milling through Bloomingdale's crowds at Christmas. I'd hear his voice in my Spanish class, and I would always, always feel his body at my side as we galloped past the Plaza Hotel in our horse-drawn carriage."

RED FLAG
#8-19

RED FLAG
#8-20

She settled back in her chair and smiled, "Like, wow. So that's what it's like to spill a secret. Wow."

"Of course, Mimi. You went from really caring for this guy to knowing you'd better have nothing to do with him, even though you still had residual feelings, to feeling guilty for having had any feelings. Maybe it's time to laugh at the guilt and let it float away."

She threw her head of waist-length hair far back and let out a deep and hearty belly laugh.

I liked it.

After I left her apartment and was in my car, I thought about the interview. I

407

knew. I knew. I knew there was even more to her secret than the shame and guilt she carried for maintaining feelings for Mike, a psychopath. However, there are some things to which we are never privy. Helping Mimi shake up the shame from such self-destructive dating down was good enough, I decided, as I leaned over and turned on the car heater.

It was getting dark out; a chilly, drizzly January, six p.m.

Stopping at a red light on Glendale Boulevard, I happened to notice the man on the curb next to my car.

He was wearing tattered pants, had long, mangy hair, and no shirt or jacket. "A little coincidental," I thought.

He was dancing and having a merry time under the street lamp.

As I drove by, he stopped his dance recital and winked at me. I courteously waved, but accelerated. I thought, *Isn't it just wonderful, once in a while, to hit the gas pedal and be able to simply move on?*

I laughed. I took a deep breath.

The man in my rearview mirror kept dancing.

DISCUSSION OF THE CHAPTER

Just to give you working definitions:

Psychosis is defined as impaired contact with reality in relation to time, place, and person. Extreme deviations of thought and emotion are commonly apparent.

A *Psychopath* is defined as one who violates explicit rules of property or personal space without remorse.

In psychological circles today, the terms psychopath and sociopath are no longer diagnostic categories. Instead, we use the term "antisocial personality disorder." This is a bit of a misnomer because these people, at least at first, are far from antisocial. In fact they can put up excellent fronts—displaying charm and likability at first. Antisocial personality disorder does not mean they are against socializing, as it sounds. If anything, their socialization process has been tainted.

The psychopath can be psychotic and vice versa. I believe, as illustrated by "Beware the Shirtless Man in January," Mike had his share of both.

409

RED FLAG #8-1

This is quite a mouthful in an initial phone conversation. This man was recently back from a safari in Kenya and was personal friends with Jon Bon Jovi.

Had it been the truth, however, why would anyone need to expose so much information at first blush? Knowing it was not the truth, nonetheless, we initially have a glaring red flag.

Basically, anyone offering so much information in a first phone conversation is rather suspect. It is as though he is screaming, "You must see me in this particular light." Generally, be careful when one gives you far too much information during early communication. He might be seeking a receptacle for his ventilation needs, or be seeking an audience member to applaud his ego. Both are possible.

If he doesn't ask questions about you in return, or listen to you, this could be a pretty bad sign of how the relationship might waltz. A good piece of early-on buyer beware.

Even if the information is true, the person a) probably requires enormous ego strokes, and/ or b) doesn't really live in the bubble of humility on a day-to-day basis. The receiver of this information should be conscious of such premature self-aggrandizement.

In truth, already Mike is exposing his psychosis (impaired contact with reality).

RED FLAG #8-2

If you are ever in this situation, would you please bolt? Do not give it a second thought. This should have scared Mimi silly. However, her deep-seated need to proceed toward intimacy with this man seemed to top all reasoning.

Here, it is obvious that Mike's impulsivity and compulsion to deviate from normalcy touches upon both the profiles of the psychotic and the psychopath.

If one is not hired to assist this man with good psychological aid, it is best to don a pair of well-made jogging shoes and RUN.

RED FLAG #8-3

"I asked when he was going to call...I didn't cherish the indirectness of his response."

Psychotics really haven't the capacity to track questioning. They will respond to everything in their personal language. Mimi considered this creative.

It is significant to bear in mind that if people have impaired contact to time and place, they cannot respond rationally to any time-bound questioning. It will be another language for them.

This is not to say that all men who are not sure when they are going to call are psychotic. We are merely observing behavioral clues to advance a greater insight into this personality type.

RED FLAG #8-4

Mike's total disregard for money (and, all his money was probably given to him by his parents, since he never really worked) was a blatant act of irresponsibility. He was a far cry from the "unique guy" Mimi implied.

In Mimi's family of origin, any type of creativity or passion was discounted. She was starved for it, yet at the same time had no baseline of understanding how it might look. Had she a baseline—some parental modeling of spontaneous joy, passion, or creativity from her family— she probably would have been less likely to title Mike's throwing money out of the car unique and creative.

RED FLAG #8-5

The antisocial personality disorder, as Mike might be referred to clinically, can be extremely attentive at first. It is confusing to the person on the receiving end because this initial adoration and attentiveness does not hold. All of a sudden it drops out when there is little cause.

Sometimes the drop-off can be gradual, sometimes not. Heads really spin with the latter. Because of the concept of intermittent reinforcement (refer to constant #3 in the introduction), the receiver keeps looking for the initial adoration. This can keep her hooked.

RED FLAG #8-6

Mimi was so lacking in and needful of spontaneity, coming from her rigid family of origin, she chose to bypass these warning signals. Other women would have seen the red flag long ago. She finally chose to allow a tiny glimpse of the situation to affect her. She was not ready to allow much more than a tiny glimpse, however.

RED FLAG #8-7

This is not necessarily strictly indicative of psychosis. I have seen this in my office too often. This is merely an unhealthy, unnecessary, and socially abusive behavior. There is no reason one should stop seeing old friends just because one is living with a partner. The red flag here is really the partner encouraging such avoidance.

413

I would advise one to never put up with such restrictions.

RED FLAG #8-8

How can a female living with a male not know what he does for a living?! This is not a pygmy-sized red flag, Mimi.

This red flag does not stem from his mental disorder. Rather, it is from her "starvation" behavior overlooking his irresponsibility. From this book's introduction's definition of dating down, she was fully exhibiting constant #1—taking full responsibility for his unhealthy, unproductive, and/or harmful behavior.

As adults, hopefully we begin to recognize our black holes of starvation and to figure out methods of filling them up with nurturance. Mimi's youth, sheltered-ness (except for the fact that she was modeling), restrictive parents, and cold family of origin kept her starvation, starving.

We can only hope that with time she would begin to recognize her self-destructive hunger.

RED FLAG #8-9

I was rather amazed that the physical abuse took this long to ignite. Mimi really should have boogied from the scene that evening. She obviously just

414

considered it an extension of Mike's "odd" behavior. Again, women who date down, deny.

I believe once a man cannot control his physically aggressive impulses toward the female, the female must sever all ties with him. I offer little advice in terms of leeway where physical abuse is present. For me, there is no negotiation.

RED FLAG #8-10

When pushed, the psychotic breaks with reality and is not aware of this severing. Since Mike needed to regain composure from his jealousy, he reverted into his clinically unsound world where, this time, his Chicago "contacts" would protect him.

Having psychosis truly requires medical monitoring and medication. It can be very sad and difficult for the psychotic, his family, etc. But it can prove dangerous for the girlfriend. Of course, enormous empathy goes out to the afflicted. This book, however, is about the danger aspect. Unfortunately, all this sadness and danger are realistic components.

RED FLAG #8-11

The only element cementing this couple, here, was Mimi's elegant denial system. I think this entire incident was beyond a red flag.

In my office, I commonly go for two end results in terms of relationships: a) what people feel they need, and b) why they are looking in all the wrong places—continuously.

All we see Mimi doing is hitting her head against the wall in hot, counterproductive pursuit. Were she my patient early on, she would have been receiving my feedback of how flawed her search looked. However, it was as though the couple was so very walled off from everyone and everything, nobody could intervene to assist her out. Mimi had to do it herself—with few tools.

RED FLAG #8-12

The entire afternoon at the family barbecue was so shocking. There is nothing psychological here to elaborate upon. It is obvious that the afternoon was fraught with staggering information.

RED FLAG #8-13

In that Mimi was enduring so much frustration and blindly tolerating his unacceptable behavior, she was truly in the throes of constant #5. The concepts of that constant—frustration, tolerance, blame—were fast becoming the bulwark of Mimi's existence.

416

In your present relationships, how much are you frustrated, overly tolerant, or constantly feeling blamed? This is not a healthy acceptance of reality, readers. This is dating down.

RED FLAG #8-14

All downdaters are more invested in fixing what is going on than in accepting it. The snag here is, the more they try to fix it, the worse the situation becomes.

At least in this story, Mike, a diagnosable psychopath, will never move toward healthy closeness. Psychopaths are not able to. They are biochemically ill. They are to be helped, not dated.

Watch for your very own feelings of "I hold the key to changing him."

RED FLAG #8-15

The internal device that non-downdaters naturally possess was starting to operate in Mimi. The job of this internal mechanism is to detect a lack of authenticity, irresponsibility, lack of safety, and so on; it is an emotional burglar alarm.

417

RED FLAG #8-16

We need to talk hard-core science for a minute. Some studies reveal the psychopath as exhibiting a malfunction of inhibitory mechanisms of the central nervous system. What this means is that it is almost impossible for the psychopath to learn normal inhibitory behavior. Also, because of other constitutional deficiencies, psychopaths are less sensitive to stimuli, and because of this are constantly seeking stimulation. The deficient autonomic arousal system can be the sole contribution to their compulsive, manic, odd behavior.

(For my hard-core scientist reader—psychopaths have a high incidence of EEG abnormalities, particularly involving the slow wave activity in the temporal lobe.)

It goes without saying that family influences can be the sole reason for antisocial behavior. I am merely citing some of the biological contributors. In the case of red flag #8-16, for whatever reason—biochemical, family background, etc.—Mike has demonstrably broken with reality. He is in Mimi's rollers, makeup, false eyelashes, and scarf. He is cavorting in a darkened, candlelit room, oblivious to any functioning life around him. Most importantly, and aside from any biology, psychology or legal ramifications, this man is potentially dangerous.

RED FLAG #8-17

Because psychopaths (or antisocials) commonly come from much parental rejection, although Mike did not, one should never proclaim such clear-cut abandonment to them without a third party present. This can be extremely perilous.

RED FLAGS #8-18 and #8-19

In order for Mimi to have maintained her connection with Mike, she had to romanticize and idolize him beyond the realms of reality. She was so practiced at connecting with him this way that she was able to continue doing so even after they split up.

This is a clear demonstration of what downdaters do: carry on a relationship with someone in their own head.

RED FLAG #8-20

My choosing Mimi for this interview was a rather apt plan. First, I received the exact story I needed to illustrate this downdatee. Second, it appeared that Mimi sloughed off some leftover Mike dust by merely having related her story.

Truthfully, I was never really sure just how much leftover Mike dust she possessed. What I was sure

419

of, however, was the stuck globule of shame/guilt she still harbored over having had feelings for a dysfunctional, emotionally challenged male.

This shame-based globule was why she needed to maintain the secret, years later. It was my hope this interview assisted Mimi in ridding herself of both the Mike dust and the shame/guilt globule.

It is necessary to keep in mind that we all make mistakes, and that holding on to the guilt of the mistake just extends the mistake! Forgive yourself, dust off, and move on.

Again, and not to minimize the requisite energy involved in a relationship, sometimes dating with integrity merely boils down to simple good choices and conscientious self-care.

Sometimes, it is as basic, simple, exposed, and shirtless as that, my good and kind readers.

CHAPTER NINE

WHAT HAPPENED TO THE GALS?

CHAPTER ONE – MARISKA

Mariska contacted me about six weeks after her relationship with Neil terminated.

As of the writing of this book, approximately one year had passed since their breakup. These were some of Mariska's changes:

First of all, I encouraged her to revisit her "skating" side. Within a short period of time, she was judging youth competitions around Los Angeles and even flew to Calgary, Canada, to judge a teen championship event. And her preschool continued to flourish.

About a month prior to my writing this, Mariska informed me that she needed to visit the sporting goods store where she met Neil. She needed skate guards and other materials they stocked. She did not care if she ran into Neil at that point, as she had successfully worked out her feelings for him in therapy.

When at the store, she asked a male, punk-type cashier about Neil.

The sprightly cashier replied, "Yo, lady, Neil got fired. He's one lazy dude."

Mariska said she laughed and replied, "I might agree with you, young man."

She has not started dating, but just of late she exclaimed, "If someone respectable dropped into my lap, I think I'd be ready to take a new plunge—with a new mind-set."

CHAPTER TWO – CONNIE (MARIA CONSUELA)

Due to being bilingual, Connie experienced a meteoric rise at the TV station. Within a few months, she was traveling to Mexico and working in TV programming throughout Latin America.

During one of her Mexican trips, Tony called her cell phone. He started the conversation as if nothing criminal, or questionable, had ever occurred. Connie quickly terminated the call, subsequently learning that he had called both of her sisters the same day.

Annie spoke only briefly to him, but he and Leti had a long and informative conversation. He told Leti he'd been in prison for six months, but got out on bail and was back to working in the "straight" computer field. He was also dating someone quite a bit younger than he. Leti asked him to please stay away from Connie and the whole family.

Connie has not wanted to date as of yet. Happily, though, her emotional connection to Tony is nonexistent.

425

CHAPTER THREE – RACHEL

It was extremely difficult emotionally for Rachel to rid herself of Rob.

Two months after she broke up with him, she planned a trip to Israel with her twin boys. I jokingly instructed Rachel to go to the Wailing Wall in Jerusalem, and to pray for her obsession with Rob to be removed. Upon Rachel's return, she said she had followed my suggestion and that her obsession had totally lifted.

This was important information for me. It is good for all clinicians to be reminded that there exists a higher source than even their insightful counseling! *Wowsville.*

CHAPTER FOUR – LYNDA

Lynda had a rather challenging time in her attempt to detox from both the deadly methamphetamine and Jason. Her mother was extremely supportive in helping her through the crisis.

Then, Lynda turned a delightful "180" on everyone. She abandoned the drug, said a final good-bye to her downdatee, and enrolled in college with the goal of becoming a veterinarian. The first semester, she took algebra, biology, English, and general chemistry. With that hefty schedule, I knew she was serious. She continued to stay in therapy. She says, "All I want to do, Carole, is cure sick little birds one day."

She is still dancing topless. One day at a time.

CHAPTER FIVE – JENNIFER

Jennifer and her friends, Nancy and Dulsie, conjured up a wonderful plan to give used TV and movie wardrobe items to below-poverty-line citizens in Alabama. They got a television station and two movie studios behind the plan.

All they required to get started with the plan was one paid employee on the other end to catalog and organize the shipments. He/she would be the only paid employee, and one of the TV studios was happy to pay the person's salary, as well as paying the shipping costs and absorbing any other expenses necessary for the project to take flight. Jen really wanted Jonathan to be this employee.

Jennifer explained how the system might work and that Jon would simply have to traffic control. It really looked like a labor of love and a win-win for everyone.

Jonathan flatly refused to be part of the project. Although not employed, he rejected a position that was being handed to him. Jennifer refused to speak to him after his rejection of her wonderful offer.

As of the printing of this book, Jennifer is dating a highly responsible hotel chef (who works!). And happily, her wardrobe project is in the advanced planning stages.

CHAPTER SIX – REGINA

Regina started therapy with me shortly after she returned from Palm Springs. Mark pleaded with her not to break up with him, so they came in for couples counseling.

Although he was mild-mannered and soft-spoken with me, he was demonstrably critical and verbally rough on her, even in my presence. Within four sessions, she asked him never to call her again.

Interestingly, Regina's community college performing group danced at a local congress-man's inaugural dinner. She said the piece she choreographed was half Viennese waltz and half staccato hip-hop to a Radiohead song. I don't know quite how she spliced that one. But what she really wanted me to get was the name of the piece: "Supportive Love, or Nothing."

Very good work, Regina.

CHAPTER SEVEN – KRISTINA

Kristina really became shame-based, embarrassed, and saddened by believing and staying so close to Dario for a whole school year. She did not want to date and mistrusted any guy who showed interest in her.

Her parents were insightful for insisting that Peter keep an eye on her—they even flew out to meet me. She went on Lexepro (an antidepressant) to ramp up the internal separation process and lift her unending melancholy. In her case this was highly indicated.

Kristina, demonstrably feeling much better of late, recently moved back to Maine to go to graduate school and to be closer to her roots.

CHAPTER EIGHT – MIMI

Just before the printing of this book, I received a note and a photograph from Mimi. The note read,

Dear Carole,

I hope this note finds you well. I am living in Northern California, managing an Internet-based musical instrument/import business. I love it. No more modeling and that's really fine with me.

The darling man in the photo is my wonderful husband, Alexander (he owns a busy electrical supply store, and plays a mean acoustic guitar).

The two-month-old bundle of joy in our arms is Baby Alexander. Isn't he fabulous?

We are very happy and feel more than blessed.

The guys and I will be in LA soon and would love to see you.

I am so grateful for your and my work together and your messages.
We all thank you from the bottom of our hearts.
~ Mimi

I must admit I absolutely can't wait to meet the guys. It might be a girl thing—you know, absolutely can't wait to meet the guys? Although, I can't chalk all of it up to "merely a girl thing." We may not do that.

I think Mimi's growth is pretty inspirational. It's a great reminder; a great example of how living in integrity can actually prove to be exciting, fun, productive, fulfilling, and oh so very cool.

And congratulations, Mimi. You really "model" travelling up from down.

CHAPTER TEN

A CLOSING WORD, OR, DATING UP FROM DOWN

One of my problems with personal growth/ self-help books is that there commonly exists a concluding chapter proclaiming to magically transform your life. I cannot and will not proclaim any such radical assurances.

Also, when these proclamations are announced (for example: "So, if you follow these twenty specific rules, you will gleefully leap into the sunset forever and..."), within about seventy-two hours after closing the book, the reader says, "What? What were those twenty rules the author/ psychologist set forth?" Big head scratch.

Since the format of this book alone established a different sort of self-help book, you, the reader, must join me in writing the final chapter. For it is your mulling over the red flags, taking notes, thinking about how the stories apply to you, discussing the chapters with your pals, and maybe buying the workbook (which is entitled "Dating Down and Those of US Who Do It- A learning workbook with funstuff") that will actuate a tailor-made change in you. This is your journey. Why should I manipulate?

But I will offer a few closing points:
1. Always be influenced by his acts of love, not your feelings of love.
2. Remember, relationship rough patches, occasional arguments, and small character

flaws do not equal dating down (refer to the introduction's Five Constants as your gauge).

3. Stop any and all active passivity. Express what you will and will not allow and what you do or do not need.

4. And most importantly, remember that dating down, the affliction so pronounced in the book, can be relieved by two simple words: Move On. There is no perfect time to activate this powerful movement. Some times are more appropriate than others. Ironically, this behavior of moving on alone is ultimately perfect. When, besides never, is it not? And as stated, the more energy you pour into your red flags, the more moving on might seem possible.

Yet I must throw this in, too. Do not expect insights and clearances on this front immediately. Be gentle with yourselves. The Chinese philosopher Lao-Tzu said, "True growth occurs slowly." In my many years of practice and in seeing hundreds of women in this predicament, I still always tell them, "You cannot yell at any plant or tree to grow." It takes time, watering, and consistent attention.

For right now, ask yourself: in your dating and romantic world, do you want to stay as you are?

Might there possibly be some uncomfortable victimization into DOWN occurring? Or would you prefer a life that exists only in the UP zone? It is so do-able.

There exists a greater force that is here to protect us in our changes, as the mirror is here to reflect the need.

With great sincerity, I wish the women in the stories—Mariska, Maria, Rachel, Lynda, Jennifer, Regina, Kristina, Mimi—and you, my readers, a life of UP. How entirely fabulous it is that we all have the freedom to choose.

When one door of happiness closes, another opens; but often we look so long at the closed door that we do not see the one which has been opened for us.

—Helen Keller

AUTHOR'S BIO

Carole Field is a writer, international lecturer, and psychotherapist in private practice in Los Angeles. She has lectured throughout the U.S, at the London Institute of Psychiatry,the University of Greece-Athens, and is published in Amsterdam.

She is also a trained ballet dancer and has four vocal octaves.

She would also like to make dinner for all of her readers but thinks some things might be impossible....maybe.

In the meantime, visit her at datingdownbook.com.

21114587R00257